Also by Janice Wald Henderson

WHITE CHOCOLATE

THE NEW CUISINE OF HAWAII

THE NEW CUISINE OF HAWAII
RECIPES FROM THE
TWELVE CELEBRATED CHEFS
OF HAWAII REGIONAL CUISINE

JANICE WALD HENDERSON

VILLARD BOOKS
NEW YORK
1994

All photographs by Steven Minkowski, except for those on pages 3, 7, 9, 53, 57, 62, 111, 114, and 127, which were taken by John De Mello.

Grateful acknowledgement is made to *Bon Appétit* magazine for permission to reprint three recipes:
Island Chicken with Ginger-Lime Sauce by Roy Yamaguchi (April 1991);
Hoisin-glazed Pork Ribs by Alan Wong (October 1992); and Caramel Miranda from Avalon restaurant (September 1993).
Copyright © 1991, 1992, 1993 by Bon Appétit Publishing Corp. Reprinted with permission.

Library of Congress Cataloging-in-Publication Data

Henderson, Janice Wald.
The new cuisine of Hawaii: recipes from the twelve celebrated
chefs of Hawaii Regional Cuisine / Janice Wald Henderson.
p.   cm.
Includes index.
ISBN 0-679-42529-2
1. Cookery, Hawaiian.   I. Title.
TX724.5.H3H46 1994   641.59969–dc20   94-2453

Manufactured in the United States of America on acid-free paper

Book design by Bob Cato

9876543

This book is dedicated to
all the Hawaii Regional Cuisine chefs,
whose passion for delivering
the consummate culinary experiences
is just cause to celebrate.

Also, to my beloved parents,
David and Blossom Wald, who encouraged me
to discover a world west of Westchester.

ACKNOWLEDGMENTS

This book could never have been written without Jeanne Thiel Kelley and Sarah Tenaglia. Jeanne's ability to test chefs' recipes and make them work for the home cook is phenomenal. Sarah Tenaglia, the quintessential recipe stylist, patiently, methodically and cheerfully wrote these recipes so that even a novice cook can follow them—a skill many will attest that few possess.

I must thank all the HRC chefs; each made enormous contributions to this book by generously sharing their knowledge and talent.

Mark Ellman must be singled out for serving as liaison between the chefs and myself; he truly transformed the idea for the book into reality.

Peter Merriman also deserves kudos for realizing that these talented island chefs should band together to promote the ingredients of the state. He was also of great assistance in preparing the glossary of HRC ingredients.

The insight, intelligence and unflappable disposition of Diane Reverand, my editor/publisher at Villard Books, made writing this book a supreme pleasure. Her contributions cannot be undervalued.

Bob Cato, a man of great charm and wisdom, transformed what could have been just another book into a tome of beauty with his graceful designs and brilliant art direction.

Nina Pfaffenbach Schneider artfully styled the food for the photographs and always gave more than was ever asked. Also, many thanks to Mary Bush, who served as photographer's and stylist's assistant. And a big *mahalo* of gratitude to John DeMello, the talented photographer who expertly completed the photography for this book.

Without the assistance of Robert Schuster, the *wunderkind* agent who put the HRC chefs together with Villard Books, this book would not have been made.

Chuck Furuya, the acclaimed master sommelier, best knows how to pair Hawaii Regional Cuisine and wine. His invaluable introduction and wine notes will ensure that the readers of this book will experience a treasure trove of food and wine pairings.

Thanks also to Shep Gordon, who is a true friend and advisor to the HRC chefs, and to George Greif, for his great support of the HRC chefs and for his superb slaw.

Roger Vergé, Wolfgang Puck and Nobu Matsuhisa are three legendary chefs whose encouragement and championing of the HRC chefs appear to have no bounds. And thanks to star chef Dean Fearing, who is considered an honorary HRC member.

The HRC chefs also wish to thank their wives, husbands, children and their devoted patrons for their love and support.

Thanks to Hawaii's Bishop Museum, Howard E. Deese, marine programs specialist at the State of Hawaii Department of Business, Economic Development & Tourism and Tish Uyehara, communications director of the State of Hawaii Department of Agriculture.

A heartfelt thank-you to Charles Park and Sheila Donnelly, who have long advocated my frequent visits to Hawaii, and who have nourished my love for these magnificent islands.

And over at *Bon Appétit*, thanks to editor-in-chief Bill Garry and dearest friend/executive editor Barbara Fairchild, who have allowed me to write so much about this wondrous state.

With much love to my husband, Kary; my daughter, Kerith; my sister, Donna, and my brother, Jonathan; great pal Diane Worthington; assorted Walds, Bartmassers, Karlins, Silvermans and Silversteins—whew, that's about it.■

The biggest *mahalo* goes to Steven "Mink" Minkowski, the dynamic photographer who captured the quality and originality of HRC cuisine in brilliant pictures before his tragic passing. He is now, and will always be, greatly missed.

CONTENTS

SAM CHOY ❂ 2

ROGER DIKON ✺ 10

MARK ELLMAN ✹ 20

Shrimp and Green Papaya Salad ☐ 22

Seared Sashimi ☐ 22

Asian Pasta ☐ 23

Hawaiian Foccacia ☐ 23

Steamed Ono with Soy-Ginger Sauce ☐ 24

Chili-seared Salmon, Tiki-style ☐ 24

Fried Maui Nabeta ☐ 25

Wok-fried Opakapaka with Spicy Black Bean Sauce ☐ 26

Indonesian Grilled Lamb Chops ☐ 27

Caramel Miranda ☐ 29

BEVERLY GANNON ❁ 30

Big Island Goat Cheese and Maui Onion Tart with Red Pepper Coulis ☐ 32

Smoked Salmon Bundles Filled with Spicy Molokai Prawn Salad ☐ 33

Duck Salad with Warm Goat Cheese and Chive Crêpes ☐ 34

Italasian Pasta with Shrimp and Scallops ☐ 36

Opakapaka Baked in Parchment with Leeks, Herbs and Lobster ☐ 36

Marinated Seared Chicken with Tropical Salsa ☐ 37

Braised Lamb Shanks with Black Bean Tomato Sauce and Kula Corn Bread ☐ 38

Paniolo Ribs with Haliimaile Barbecue Sauce ☐ 40

Piña Colada Cheesecake ☐ 40

Chocolate–Macadamia Nut Tart ☐ 41

PETER MERRIMAN ✿ 64

Lilikoi Vinaigrette ☐ 66
Mango Muffins ☐ 66
Papaya Bisque ☐ 66
Bean Thread Salad ☐ 67
Papaya Salsa ☐ 67

Pineapple Stir-fried Rice ☐ 68
Pineapple-Curry Sauce ☐ 68
Stir-fried Steak and Lobster Teriyaki ☐ 70
Taro and Chili Cakes ☐ 70
Coconut Crème Brûlée ☐ 71

AMY FERGUSON OTA ✸ 72

Banana–Macadamia Nut Waffles with Rum-Raisin-Maple Syrup ☐ 74
Pohole Fern Salad with Waimea Tomatoes, Maui Onions and Sesame Dressing ☐ 75
Ahi Yellowfin Tuna and Ulu Breadfruit Cakes with Lime-Cilantro Mayonnaise ☐ 75
Nori Fettuccine with Opihi and Garlic-Chili-Butter Sauce ☐ 76
Fish with Black Bean and Ka'u Lime–Butter Sauce ☐ 78
Wok-seared Ono with Banana Curry and Ti Leaf–wrapped Bananas ☐ 78
Rack of Lamb with Thai Curry Sauce ☐ 79
Black Sesame-cured Wild Boar Loin with Guava Sauce ☐ 82
Warm Mango Custards ☐ 82
Mango Ice Cream Sandwiches with Tropical Fruit Compote ☐ 83

PHILIPPE PADOVANI ✦ 84

Seared Ahi with Spicy Crust, Green Papaya Salad and Sweet-and-Sour Vinaigrette ☐ 86
Salad of Peking Duck with Bean Sprouts and Kim Chee ☐ 86
Opakapaka Lau Lau ☐ 87
Poached Onaga with Cucumber, Tomatoes and Basil ☐ 87
Pan-fried Moano with Snow Peas and Bacon in Curry Sauce ☐ 88
Pan-fried Kahuku Prawns with Mixed Greens, Papaya and Chili Vinaigrette ☐ 90
Hawaiian Lobster with Vanilla-Mint-Curry Sauce ☐ 90
Chicken with Oysters and Straw Mushrooms in Spicy Szechwan Sauce ☐ 91
Coconut-Tapioca Pudding with Mango and Papaya ☐ 93
Strawberry Sunburst with Almond Cream and Fresh Mint ☐ 93

GARY STREHL ✦✦✦ 94

ALAN WONG ☀ 104

INTRODUCTION

Welcome to the last frontier in American cooking. Dubbed Hawaii Regional Cuisine, this new culinary style is generating a buzz across America, from coast to coast to coast. Its practitioners are young, enthusiastic chefs who are fortunate enough to be cooking with the outstanding quality and almost dizzying variety of ingredients most chefs can only dream about.

Hawaii's premier chefs banded together in August 1991, to form an organization with the sole purpose of heralding the quality and diversity of the Hawaiian Islands' ingredients. These ingredients—as well as strong influences of the Chinese, Filipino, Korean, Japanese, Portuguese, Southeast Asian and Hawaiian people who live in our fiftieth state—have propelled these chefs to develop a distinct cooking style found only in Hawaii.

Throw out the preconceived notions of poi and pig washed down with mai tais, because Hawaii Regional Cuisine possesses the savvy, style and sophistication of other American regional cuisines. Hawaii Regional Cuisine blends the Asian and Western culinary styles of the state's ethnicities with Hawaii's distinctive ingredients.

Under this broad umbrella blossoms a whirlwind of creativity, as each HRC chef puts his or her own spin on Hawaii Regional Cuisine. They had to; when most of the chefs came to Hawaii (between 1978 and 1988), they were following in the footsteps of European chefs who usually disregarded local ingredients; almost everything was flown in from the mainland, Australia, New Zealand or Europe.

Visitors had their choice of dining in pricey restaurants on frozen, shipped-in, picked-before-it's-ripe food, or in tourist establishments that distorted traditional Hawaiian cooking for Western tastes. Small wonder that Hawaii has long been regarded as a paradise for beaches but a wasteland for food.

"When I first came to Hawaii in 1978," says Gary Strehl, the executive chef of the Hawaii Prince Hotel in Waikiki, "a waiter told me that his best meal was on the airplane before he landed. That gave me the drive and determination to help change the state of dining in the islands."

It was Gary and the other eleven chefs—primarily trained on the mainland and well versed in the tenets of American regional cuisine—who ultimately decided not to follow in the footsteps of their European predecessors. They encouraged the local farmers to grow specialty vegetables and raise lamb and beef. They explored Chinatown. They pleaded with local fishermen to teach them about the bounty from Hawaii's blue sea. Some, like Peter Merriman, speared fish and climbed coconut trees in search of the best product. Others spent days wandering around the Honolulu fresh fish auction. Each of the HRC chefs pursued similar paths, often oblivious to the fact that other chefs were engrossed in the same exploratory processes.

In a group so adventurous, it is not surprising to discover that the different chefs wound up with different styles. Some Hawaii Regional Cuisine chefs, like Mark Ellman and Alan Wong, play up the Pacific Rim in their dishes, while others, such as Roger Dikon, blend Asian and Western culinary techniques and ingredients. Still others, like Peter Merriman, base their menus on what is grown, raised or caught on their own particular island. Chefs Sam Choy and Beverly Gannon both serve hearty, country-style fare; others, like Roy Yamaguchi, George Mavrothalassitis and Jean-Marie Josselin, dazzle with sophisticated presentations and complex sauces.

Despite the diversity of HRC styles, what unites these chefs is their strong emphasis on island products. Indeed, Hawaii's ingredients are reason enough to spur such a creative culinary movement.

For example, Hawaii's bounty of moist and flaky fish possesses delicate, almost indescribable flavors, and many are found only in these tropical waters. Who could resist the coveted red snapper called *onaga*, or the highly prized reef fish, *kumu*? *Ahi*, star of sushi bars, pops up in various guises—HRC chefs like Philippe Padovani often sear the fish with tantalizing spices and serve it with cross-cultural sauces such as a sweet and sour vinaigrette.

Hawaii's tropical fruit is in a league of its own. Some twenty types of banana grow wild, including the ice cream banana, which really does taste like vanilla ice cream. It's difficult to name the many varieties of papaya; the several types of guava include the strawberry guava, with its faint taste of the sweet berry. Intensely flavored *lilikoi* (passion fruit), including the banana *lilikoi*, and the world's sweetest, juiciest mangos are just some of the selections for Shangri-la-like picking.

The varieties of bright-hued vegetables which, if unchecked, grow giant-size in the rich, volcanic soil, are almost uncountable. White eggplant, orange tomatoes—chefs merely think up what they want and farmers comply. A few years ago there weren't any vine-ripened tomatoes in the Hawaiian Islands—the chefs had to literally order tomatoes from the mainland!

Lychee, macadamia nuts, estate-grown Kona coffee and coconuts only add to the bounty of the islands. Aquafarming is one of the state's hottest industries; chefs now have access to aquafarmed sea vegetables (seaweed), shrimp, lobster and other fish. Growers are currently working on introducing the first fresh hearts of palm crop.

Hawaii is home to America's first chocolate—Hawaiian Vintage Chocolate—made from cocoa beans grown on the Big Island. Smooth and rich with a pleasing depth of flavor, this chocolate holds great promise for a bright future. Goat cheese, also produced on the Big Island, rivals the best found in California. Its lush, mellow flavor harmonizes beautifully with the bold taste of Hawaii Regional Cuisine dishes.

Where once only luaus were the culinary entertainment of Hawaii, today, spirited food and wine events—like Cuisines of the Sun at Mauna Lani Bay Hotel and Bungalows, and Big Island Bounty at The Ritz-Carlton, Mauna Lani (both on the Big Island)—draw participants nationwide who wish to learn more about Hawaii Regional Cuisine and to watch HRC chefs work side by side with some of the world's most celebrated chefs.

Hawaii Regional Cuisine may have been born in the last decade, but its roots are undoubtedly the oldest of any American cooking style. To understand the influences on and the development of Hawaii Regional Cuisine, it's necessary to understand the history of these tropical islands.

Hawaii Regional Cuisine's genesis goes back to the days of migrating Polynesians, who were the first to land their canoes on Hawaii's pristine shores. No one knows the exact date of their arrival; it is believed to be between 300 and 400 A.D.

The early Polynesian diet was a healthy one. Ancient Hawaiians believed that all foods had a life force and that eating meant adding to the life force in the body. Their diet consisted primarily of taro, breadfruit, fruit and fish. Early Hawaiian writers listed some 130 varieties of seafood swimming in the ocean. Poi (cooked, pounded and kneaded taro) was their main dish, consumed with greens from the tops and stems of taro plants, and supplemented by steamed or grilled fish, fruit, sea vegetables and other foods such as sweet potatoes. Some records say that in ancient Hawaiian times, some 230 varieties of sweet potato existed.

Young fernshoots (*warabi, pohole*) were considered a delicacy and consumed as a side dish. The highly nutritious sea vegetables, with their natural high-salt content, were used mostly as condiments to flavor other, blander foods. Seventy varieties were identified, although forty were in primary use. (Just a few are consumed today.) Although chickens were brought to Hawaii and cooked like fish, they were eaten less frequently.

Bananas, also brought over by migrating Polynesians, were a natural for dessert, as were mountain apples (a member of the myrtle family with a perfumed, applelike taste). Occasionally the sweet potato was used in desserts.

The luau introduced by Hawaiians remains a viable way to celebrate special occasions today in the state. This celebratory outdoor event provides a cornucopia of traditional Hawaiian food, like *lomi lomi* salmon (shredded, salted salmon, soaked and mixed with tomatoes and onions), *lau lau* (salted butterfish and pork, wrapped in taro leaves and steamed, or cooked in the underground oven called the *imu*), poi and such delicacies as *opihi*, a small, black limpet gathered from rocks.

The Hawaiian diet began its metamorphosis in 1778, when contact with the Western world began. Captain Cook landed in Hawaii and revealed the islands to the rest of the world. British traders and explorers arrived next, followed by French and Russian. Whalers came from New England. In 1820, the first Christian missionaries arrived from New England, bringing their own way of cooking and eating. American traders sailed in to supply them with ingredients for their Yankee diet.

Around the time of the California Gold Rush, Hawaii's plantation owners decided they needed more laborers than the islands could provide. Starting in 1852, thousands of Chinese indentured laborers were brought to Hawaii, primarily from southern China. They introduced Cantonese cooking—and rice—to Hawaii. Stir-fries, sweet-and-sour dishes and dim sum had found a new home.

The Japanese arrived around 1868, bringing soybean products—such as soy sauce, miso and tofu—dried seaweed and pickled vegetables. Japanese homes had no ovens, so the cooks fried, steamed, broiled and simmered. Japanese cooks familiarized Hawaii with tempura, noodle soups and sashimi.

The Portuguese, who first came in 1878, were among the first Europeans to arrive in Hawaii. Their robust cooking style included spicy fare like hearty sausages. Portuguese bean soup became an island staple. They also introduced breads and egg-rich pastries. Portuguese sweet breads, traditionally baked in ovens, were cooked in improvised, large outdoor stone ovens made from lava rocks or brick. *Malasadas*, Portuguese-style doughnuts, remain one of Hawaii's most popular sweets.

Beginning in 1903, the Koreans declared their own culinary presence, when they too came to work on plantations. They shared their fiery *kim chee* (pickled cabbage), and perfumed the tropical air with their barbecued marinated beef.

Many Filipinos arrived around 1909, the majority from the Manila vicinity. They contributed many types of peas and beans and the *adobo* style (vinegar- and garlic-flavored dishes) of cooking. The Filipinos boiled, stewed, broiled and fried, rather than baking their foods. Sweet potatoes, rather than rice, was their staple.

Puerto Ricans and Samoans also added to the ethnic mix. The Puerto Ricans, who came around 1900 to work on sugar plantations, brought their hearty, slightly spicy food. Thick soups, casseroles and meat turnovers—all with Spanish seasonings—flourished in their kitchens.

The Samoans, who arrived around 1919, cooked much like the Hawaiians. Their ovens, however, were above the ground—unlike the Hawaiian *imu*. They favored pork, ate salted beef, and often made poi from fruit rather than taro.

In the mid-1970s, Southeast Asians flooded Hawaii's shores. Thai and Vietnamese restaurants flourished on the Hawaiian islands, introducing such distinctive Southeast Asian spices and flavoring agents as lemongrass, fish sauce and galanga, and their own rendition of curries and chili-flecked salads.

Blending the cuisines of various cultures in the kitchen did not begin in Hawaii Regional Cuisine restaurants; it began in the home. Picture this scenario: A Japanese man marries a Hawaiian woman. Her sister weds a Filipino. The mind boggles when you think of what celebratory family meals would be like. Then take it a step further: When the children of these multicultural families grew up, imagine what they might have served for dinner, borrowing the best of their favorite foods from each ethnicity.

The melting-pot kitchens in Hawaii's homes were a mystery to early visitors; hardly what they were privy to in restaurants. Tourists began visiting Hawaii in the 1920s, arriving on luxury liners. For the next two decades, their impact on the cuisine of Hawaii was minimal. But the birth of air travel led to greater numbers of tourists flocking to the islands, and in the 1950s and 1960s, the quantity of visitors skyrocketed. These tourists expected nothing less than the quality and type of cuisine they enjoyed on the mainland.

French and German chefs were sent to cook for these visitors, and although many were extremely talented, they naturally favored foods they were familiar with. Thus, many ingredients—even fish—were flown in. A few of these European chefs were more daring, and in the late 1970s and early 1980s, attempted to encourage local farmers to grow vegetables and raise shrimp. Since most of these chefs worked for luxury hotels, they had the budgets to support the farmers.

But when the young American chefs—products of educations that taught them to accent American cooking—arrived, a more rapid transformation began. Eager to work with island ingredients, they took over what the European chefs had started. Some Hawaii-born chefs, like Sam Choy, and Alan Wong, who had traveled to the mainland and experienced the development of American regional cooking, added to the energy building around local food.

Although the birth of California cuisine once heralded America's initial emphasis on regional cooking, the development of Hawaii Regional Cuisine some two decades later may well be the last—though by no means is it fully determined. Like any serious creative endeavor, this young cuisine is still in a state of evolution.

"Hawaii Regional Cuisine is constantly evolving, the way California cooking has over many years," says Mark Ellman.

"What is guaranteed to survive in the long run is the relationship between the chefs and the farmers and fishermen," notes Alan Wong.

But Alan Wong is being modest. This new cooking style will endure. An honest effort on the part of the chefs who have finally harnessed the possibilities such a variety offers, Hawaii Regional Cuisine bends the basic tenets of cooking. Unrestricted by national boundaries in their melting pot society, they have modernized and redefined the very nature of cooking.

Some may wonder what Hawaiians think about the explosion of mainland-born chefs and the twist they've given some Hawaiian foods. "They're happy with what we're doing," explains Amy Ferguson Ota. "The local people are teaching us. Most believe we're assisting in preserving the culinary aspects of their culture."

"A ninety-year-old Hawaiian woman came up to me one day and said, 'I'm so glad to see that you're cooking with *Waipio* (Big Island) snails,'" continues Amy. "'It's such a delicacy to us.' My generation is seeing that Hawaiian foods are back in the forefront. We're really doing this more for locals than mainlanders."

For mainland food-lovers who venture to the Hawaiian Islands, the discovery of Hawaii Regional Cuisine feels as important as discovering a deserted white-sand beach or a sparkling waterfall. I know, because I've been venturing to and dining in Hawaii for more than twenty years, and I've carefully observed the development of this new cuisine with fascination.

As a food writer who likes to think she knows a good story when she tastes one, I often returned to the mainland with tales of the new developments in the cooking of Hawaii. Understandably, memories of poorly prepared luaus and frozen sole dinners die hard. At first it was difficult to convince many people that good food and Hawaii could be synonymous.

Over the last several years, I've written numerous articles about the new cuisine of Hawaii. Today, each time I pick up a magazine and see another writer's story about Hawaii Regional Cuisine, I smile. The more who share the word about its development, the better.

These chefs deserve every kudo they get. Their honest approach to food, their joy in showcasing Hawaii's ingredients and their love of these enchanting islands and their cultural mix make them appealing chefs, indeed.

While some of the HRC recipes utilize many ingredients, few are difficult to prepare. All are adapted for the home cook and substitutes are provided for ingredients that might be difficult to obtain. However, Asian markets carry most of the ingredients called for in the recipes, and the mail order sources in the back of the book should also assist.

I encourage you to delve into the glossary of ingredients, for it contains much in-depth information on Hawaii's wondrous products. And if you travel to Hawaii, do try to visit the farms listed in the Farm Tours section to better understand the state's bounty. You'll be struck by the spirit and pride of these farmers.

I also encourage you to be an adventurer in your own kitchen, for what you will reap from these recipes is magical indeed.■

SPECIAL INTRODUCTION

I've traveled to the "Islands of Paradise" numerous times, but I'm always astonished that each visit brings exhilarating new culinary experiences.

As a chef who specializes in fresh seafood, I am in awe of the quality of Hawaii's fish; it is unparalleled anywhere else in the world. I am also in awe of the young chefs now working in Hawaii, who are fiercely and proudly dedicated to showcasing both the indigenous ingredients of the islands and the culinary influences of the multiethnic people living in this tropical state.

When chefs like Avalon's Mark Ellman, Roy's Restaurant's Roy Yamaguchi, Merriman's Peter Merriman and A Pacific Café's Jean-Marie Josselin invite me to cook with them in their kitchens, I marvel at the makings of Hawaii Regional Cuisine. Their generosity has only enhanced my own East-meets-West culinary style, which I have been fortunate enough to introduce to Los Angeles at Matsuhisa restaurant. Perhaps one day I will open a Matsuhisa in Hawaii, or my fellow chefs will come to the mainland to share their talents with all of America.

Hawaii will always be like a second home to me, for I consider myself a student of good food. And a good student will always learn from the great chefs of Hawaii. ■

NOBUYUKI MATSUHISA

Chef/Owner, Matsuhisa
Beverly Hills, California

ON WINE AND HAWAII REGIONAL CUISINE

Hawaii Regional Cuisine is a challenge to the wine maven, for it is comprised of a whirlwind of flavors. It is bold, assertive and highly creative. It is also a blend of multiethnic ingredients and cooking techniques. Hawaii Regional Cuisine is defined by a broad spectrum of flavors, textures and sensations, ranging from the salty, pungent taste of black beans and the sweetness of luscious tropical fruit to the fire of the Hawaiian chili pepper.

Yet under that broad umbrella are chefs who each possess their own, highly individualistic style. Some lean more toward classic European techniques and ingredients, while others solely embrace the Asian style. Still more blend these two distinct culinary worlds in the most equitable—and deceptively easy—fashion.

Since Hawaii Regional Cuisine is a new and developing cooking style, there are no standards for pairing it with wine. It is uncharted territory, which makes it wonderfully exciting and thoroughly enjoyable to explore. It's a dangling, provocative carrot to the wine and cuisine enthusiast, for when a perfect pairing is achieved, the feeling of supreme pleasure is almost indescribable.

Throughout this book you will find recommended wines to pair with dishes when appropriate. By no means are these the only wines that will go with the respective recipes. They are merely meant as suggestions for experimentation, not the last word. I encourage you to discover your own favorite and thought-provoking combinations.

Here are some pointers to guide you in wine selection as you sample the many wonderful recipes in this cookbook.

Always keep in mind that Hawaii Regional Cuisine is a unique style of cooking. Thus, the standards of what usually work and don't work vary greatly from the norm.

When you peruse the wine notes, you'll see that German Riesling and other wines with similar characteristics—such as French Vouvray and slightly sweet California Gewurztraminer and White Zinfandel—are recommended with a good number of dishes. On first glance, it's easy to assume that the wine recommendations were written by a sweet wine devotee. This is hardly the case, so let me explain why such wines are frequently suggested.

In dishes with distinct Asian influences, you'll often encounter salt (from soy, black bean or oyster sauces, for example), or heat and spice (from ingredients like ginger, chilies and wasabi). Tropical fruits, like the Hawaiian pineapple and passion fruit, occasionally lend sweet notes to balance some of the heat of a dish.

Thus, slightly sweet, white wines are simply better equipped to handle hot, sweet and salty flavors than drier wines. A wine's sweetness assists in off-setting the heat and saltiness of a dish, while simultaneously complementing the recipe's own sweetness. Furthermore, low to moderate alcohol levels ensure a smooth, even finish to the pairing.

Many of the recommended wines are often Mediterranean in nature. This category includes the dry whites and rosés and the rustic red wine blends of southern France, and the delicate, mineral-scented white wines and the dry, firmly structured rosés and reds of Italy. The California avant-garde "lookalikes"—such as those made from grapes like Tocai and Barbera—also belong in this grouping.

To understand why Mediterranean wines work, take a look at many of the HRC recipes. Mediterranean ingredients such as garlic, olive oil, tomatoes, basil and eggplant are frequently showcased in these dishes.

Specific vintners are named only when necessary, if their wines' style is so distinctive that it best demonstrates the wine-and-food pairing.

Several of the recommended wines may not be familiar household names. You may encounter wines like Chinon, a red wine from the Loire Valley in France, or Gavi, an Italian white wine from the Piedmont region. Many of these wines differ from the traditional gold medal winners; they are best expressed on the palate with food. I encourage you to talk to your trusted wine merchant and try them. After all, isn't experimentation a good deal of the fun?

In some situations, Chardonnay and Cabernet Sauvignon can work, but the window is much smaller. You will often find that the oakiness, lower acidity and higher alcohol levels become cumbersome in many cases.

Please keep an open mind. In your exploration of this book, you will encounter wine recommendations with tastes, textures and weights that may be different from what you're used to. But then again, Hawaii Regional Cuisine may be unknown to you, too. How wonderful and rare an opportunity it is to sample great wine and great food together for the first time. It is an unparalleled adventure, one of the precious few such experiences left for us to explore.

I must thank each of the Hawaii Regional Cuisine chefs, Randal Caparoso, managing partner of Roy's Restaurant in Honolulu, and master sommelier Nunzio Alioto, general manager of Alioto's restaurant in San Francisco, for their generous and creative sharing and exchanging of ideas. ∎

CHUCK FURUYA
Master Sommelier
Honolulu, Hawaii

THE NEW CUISINE OF HAWAII

SAM CHOY

Think of a Hawaiian Paul Prudhomme, and you've just visualized Sam Choy. It's more about his charisma, his talent and his allegiance to his rural roots than it is about his size. As Paul Prudhomme is synonymous with Cajun, Sam's identity is quintessentially Hawaiian.

Sam Choy grew up in a sleepy fishing village on the north shore of Oahu. While other children were kicking sand around the beach, Sam was washing *ti* leaves and picking bones from salted salmon for his father's famous luaus during the mid-1960s and early '70s.

Sam's dad, also named Sam, is renowned throughout the state for presenting the first big, authentic luaus to tourists. Sam, Jr., was often by his side, assisting some twenty women in the meal preparation. "I remember things like stirring *haupia* [coconut pudding] and being reminded to put a lot of ice in the fruit punch back when I was twelve years old," reminisces Sam.

"My dad also owned a restaurant and often entertained at home, so I was always around food," he continues. "In our family, food was, and is, a way of life. I decided to become a chef when I was fourteen years old; it seemed like a natural choice."

After graduating high school, Sam moved to the mainland to attend college, but grew too homesick for the islands to continue. He returned to Hawaii and graduated from the culinary arts program at Kapiolani Community College on Oahu in 1972.

After working in various Oahu hotels, Sam moved to the Big Island to become executive chef of the Kona Hilton in 1982. It was here that he first began to attract attention. Sam began conducting cooking classes, and once the word got out that he not only taught well but entertained his pupils, too, his classes became sold-out successes. Newspapers and magazines around the country began to write about the magnetic chef with the irrepressible smile who shared authentic Hawaiian and Pacific Rim recipes.

Tempura Hirame with Macadamia Honey
Sweet-and-Sour Sauce
(See recipe, page 8)

"I suppose what I cooked was Hawaii Regional Cuisine, but it didn't have a name then," says Sam. "My cooking style developed from a love for the land and an understanding of the Hawaiian culture and the other ethnic groups who live here."

In 1991, Sam opened two restaurants in Kailua-Kona on the Big Island: Sam Choy's Diner and Sam Choy's Restaurant and catering. The diner, located by a bowling alley, draws many local families for plump, juicy burgers and fresh island fish. Over at the restaurant, visitors and residents alike clamor for Sam's Hawaii Regional Cuisine dishes.

As much as Sam loves to cook, he is just as content working the dining room. He bounces back and forth between his two restaurants, and is often found shaking hands and talking story (the Hawaiian equivalent of schmoozing) with his devoted clientele.

"Most chefs are stuck behind a stove, but I like to be with my guests, watching their faces light up when they taste a favorite dish," remarks Sam. "They're like kids in a candy store and I want to enjoy every minute. When they leave, I often feel like I've made friends for life."

Sam calls himself Hawaiian Chinese (his dad is Chinese) and Chinese influences often appear in his Hawaii Regional Cuisine dishes. He also tends to favor the use of Italian overtones. But perhaps more than any other HRC chef, Sam also stays true to the many traditional Hawaiian ingredients of his upbringing.

Sam's culinary motto may best be represented by a comment once made by a restaurant patron. "This guest said that every bite of my food explodes in his mouth," says Sam. "I loved that statement because I love big flavors. That's the rule I live by."

One of his other basic tenets is to stay active. Sam often jets around the world as a guest chef, spreading the word about his style of Hawaii Regional Cuisine from Tokyo to Paris. He published a best-selling cookbook, *Sam Choy's Cuisine*, in 1990 and is immersed in plans to open a third, most impressive restaurant in Kailua-Kona.

Servers will be garbed in muumuus with tropical blossoms tucked into their hair, yet they'll be carrying plates in a state-of-the-art, '90s-style exhibition kitchen. And don't plan on poi and pig—unless they're Hawaii Regional Cuisine interpretations, of course. What you can count on is the one and only Sam Choy, shaking and stirring those pots and pans, pumping guests' hands and, always, smiling that irresistible smile. ■

 MAUNA LOA SUNSHINE SALAD (WITH PUNA PAPAYA DRESSING)

Puna papayas from the Big Island lend an elusive, sweet flavor and assist in balancing the slightly spicy overtones of marinated tofu. This salad is a great selection for vegetarians, who might consume it as an entrée rather than a first course.

4 servings
TOFU
1 cup soy sauce
½ cup firmly packed brown sugar
½ cup sliced green onion
1 garlic clove, minced
1 teaspoon peeled, grated fresh ginger
Pinch of dried crushed red pepper
14 ounces firm Chinese tofu, cut into 4 pieces
DRESSING
¼ cup sugar
2 tablespoons white wine vinegar
2 tablespoons vegetable oil
1 teaspoon peeled, minced fresh ginger
½ papaya, peeled, seeded and diced
SALAD
12 cups mixed baby greens
½ cup julienne of carrot
½ cup julienne of daikon radish
½ cup julienne of peeled, cooked beets
1 papaya, peeled, halved, seeded and sliced

For the tofu: Mix the first 6 ingredients in a large bowl. Add the tofu and refrigerate 1 hour.

For the dressing: Purée the first 4 ingredients in a blender. Pour the dressing into a bowl. Mix in the papaya. Cover and refrigerate 1 hour.

For the salad: Preheat the broiler. Arrange the greens on broilerproof plates. Top with the tofu. Broil until the tofu is heated through, about 3 minutes. Spoon the dressing over the salads. Garnish with carrot, daikon, beets and papaya and serve.

PAPA'S ISLAND PIG'S FEET SOUP
WITH WILD MOUNTAIN MUSHROOMS,
MUSTARD CABBAGE, PEANUTS AND
GINGER

Pig's feet is one of the most popular soups in
Hawaii. Sam used to make this Hawaiian recipe with
his father when his dad had a restaurant on Oahu's
north shore.

6 servings

3 pounds pig's feet, cut into 2-inch pieces
8 cups Chicken Stock (see recipe, page 128) or canned
    low-salt broth
2 onions, quartered
2 celery stalks, cut into 2-inch-long pieces
8 star anise
1/2 cup raw peanuts
1 cup sliced, stemmed, fresh shiitake mushrooms
1/2 cup chopped mustard cabbage
1 1/2 teaspoons peeled, minced fresh ginger

Bring the first 5 ingredients to a boil in a heavy, large
saucepan. Reduce the heat, cover and simmer 1 1/2 hours,
skimming the surface occasionally. Add the peanuts,
cover and simmer 30 minutes. Remove the star anise from
the soup. Season to taste with salt. Stir the mushrooms,
cabbage and ginger into the soup. Ladle the soup into
bowls and serve.

WINE NOTES
*The call here is for a youthful French Beaujolais. The wine
should have good acidity and medium tannins to wipe the
palate clean.*

*Another option is a slightly chilled Domaine de la Gautière
from Provence. Fresh and fruity with a peppery edge, this
delicious wine is wonderful with dishes like this one.*

 "HANGOVER" FISH SOUP
WITH MOLOKAI SWEET POTATO,
HAUULA BREADFRUIT AND HILO
GINGER

You don't need to suffer from a hangover to
appreciate this nourishing soup. When Sam was
growing up, pots of the fish soup would simmer on
neighborhood stoves every weekend.

Hauula breadfruit is from the north shore of Oahu,
and Hilo ginger from the Big Island is renowned
for its juicy, sweet flavor. Substitute any firm, large-
flaked fish for the *opah*, or moonfish, and potatoes or
jícama for the breadfruit.

6 servings

3 tablespoons vegetable oil
2 green onions, cut into 2-inch-long pieces
2 tablespoons peeled, minced fresh ginger
2 pounds opah fillets, cubed and patted dry
2 tablespoons cornstarch
6 cups Fish Stock (see recipe, page 128) or
    bottled clam juice
1 cup peeled, diced sweet potato
1 cup peeled, diced and cored breadfruit
1 tablespoon dry sherry
1 tablespoon white wine vinegar
1 teaspoon soy sauce
1/2 teaspoon oriental sesame oil
4 teaspoons minced fresh cilantro

Heat 1 tablespoon of the oil in a heavy, large Dutch oven
over medium-high heat. Add the green onions and the
ginger and brown lightly, about 2 minutes. Using a slotted
spoon, transfer the green onions and the ginger to a small
bowl. Heat the remaining 2 tablespoons of oil in the
same Dutch oven over high heat. Toss the fish with the
cornstarch in a large bowl. Add the fish to the Dutch oven
and brown on all sides, about 1 minute. Return the green
onions and the ginger to the Dutch oven. Add the stock,
sweet potato, breadfruit, sherry, vinegar, soy sauce and
sesame oil and bring to a boil. Reduce the heat, cover and
simmer 30 minutes. Sprinkle the soup with cilantro.
Ladle it into bowls and serve.

WINE NOTES
*If, in fact, you have a hangover, you won't want to hear any
wine recommendation. Otherwise, choose a cool, snappy beer,
preferably a lager style.*

SAM'S "ONO"-STYLE FISH POKE SEAFOOD SALAD WITH SESAME-VINAIGRETTE DRESSING

Ono means delicious in Hawaiian, and this exotic salad readily fits the description. *Poke* is Hawaiian-style marinated raw fish. *Limu kohu* is a reddish seaweed with a pronounced sea flavor that's highly prized in Hawaii. Substitute radish sprouts if necessary.

Inamona is roasted, pounded and salted kukui nuts, but you can easily substitute toasted, crushed macadamia nuts, walnuts or even almonds. This spicy *ahi* and seaweed salad, abundant with texture, is tossed with a sesame-soy dressing.

6 servings

DRESSING
3 tablespoons sesame seeds, toasted
3 tablespoons sugar
2 tablespoons soy sauce
2 teaspoons oriental sesame oil
SALAD
2 tablespoons inamona *or toasted crushed walnuts or macadamia nuts*
1 teaspoon Hawaiian or kosher salt
1 cup limu kohu *(seaweed), coarsely chopped*
2 red jalapeño chilies, seeded and minced
6 tablespoons minced Maui onion or other sweet onion
2 pounds sashimi-grade ahi *fillet, cut into bite-size pieces*
4 teaspoons oriental sesame oil

For the dressing: Mix all of the ingredients in a small bowl. Cover and refrigerate until ready to use. (**Can be prepared 1 day ahead.**)

For the salad: Mix the first 2 ingredients in a large bowl. Add the seaweed, chilies and onion. Add the *ahi* and oil and toss well. Cover and refrigerate at least 1 hour. Place the salad in a bowl. Spoon the dressing over and serve.

WINE NOTES
A beer sounds great; in Hawaii it's one of the best combinations with poke. *However, if you really want wine, consider one that's slightly sweet, easy drinking and not too serious, such as a California White Zinfandel.*

 SOBA NOODLES WITH TOOTSIE'S FRIED KAJIKI

Kajiki is Pacific blue marlin. Sam suggests substituting swordfish, mahimahi, halibut or any other firm-fleshed fish in this recipe. Tootsie is Sam's mom's nickname, and this homey recipe is a takeoff on one of her specialties.

4 servings

FISH
½ cup soy sauce
1½ tablespoons oriental sesame oil
2 teaspoons minced onion
¾ teaspoon peeled, minced fresh ginger
2 pounds kajiki, *cut into 1-inch cubes*
6 green onions, chopped
1 tablespoon dried crushed red pepper
SOBA NOODLES
1 package (8 ounces) soba noodles
3 tablespoons vegetable oil
½ cup julienne of red bell pepper
½ cup julienne of yellow bell pepper
½ cup julienne of sugar snap peas
½ cup julienne of snow peas, strings removed
½ cup julienne of shiitake mushrooms

For the fish: Mix the first 4 ingredients in a large bowl. Add the fish, green onions and dried red pepper and mix well. Cover and refrigerate at least 2 and up to 6 hours.

For the soba noodles: Cook the noodles in a large pot of boiling salted water until just tender but still firm to bite. Drain. Rinse the noodles under cold water and drain again. Transfer the noodles to a large bowl. Heat 1 tablespoon of oil in a heavy, large skillet over medium-high heat. Add the bell peppers, all peas and mushrooms and sauté 2 minutes. Combine the vegetables with the noodles. Cover and keep warm.

Heat the remaining 2 tablespoons of oil in a heavy, large skillet over high heat. Add the fish mixture and sauté until the fish is cooked through, about 5 minutes. Divide the noodle mixture among 4 plates. Spoon the fish mixture over and serve.

WINE NOTES
A slightly sweet German Riesling from the Saar or Mosel is recommended. The wine's hint of sweetness would counter the soy sauce, sesame oil and ginger, while its innate crispness would handle the fish.

Soba Noodles with Tootsie's Fried Kajiki

SOUTH PACIFIC SEAFOOD STEW
WITH TAHITIAN SPINACH-DILL CREAM

It's difficult to resist this rich stew; it's simply too delicious to stop eating until the pot is empty. Feel free to substitute snapper, sea bass or John Dory for some of the Hawaiian fish.

Sam created this recipe from childhood memories; he used to visit Tahiti every summer during his high school years.

6 to 8 servings

2 tablespoons (¼ stick) unsalted butter
½ cup olive oil
2 cups minced Maui onions or other sweet onions
1 tablespoon peeled, minced fresh ginger
15 fresh mussels, scrubbed and debearded
12 large sea scallops
½ cup cubed opah *(moonfish)*
½ cup cubed mahimahi
½ cup cubed opakapaka
½ cup cubed monchong *(bigscale or sickle pomfret)*
6 cups whipping cream
1 cup canned unsweetened coconut milk
1½ cups firmly packed, coarsely chopped fresh
    spinach leaves
1 tablespoon chopped fresh dill
½ cup chopped fresh cilantro

Melt the butter with the oil in a heavy, large saucepan over medium-high heat. Add the onions and ginger and sauté 5 minutes. Add all of the seafood, cream and coconut milk and bring to a boil. Add the spinach and dill and simmer until the fish is cooked through, about 5 minutes. Ladle into bowls. Sprinkle with cilantro and serve.

WINE NOTES
Dry, crisp white or rosé wines would go well. Keep in mind the wine should have a crisp, refreshing acidity and an even, clean and flowing finish. Consider Savennières (bone-dry Chenin Blanc from France) from a ripe year, Swiss Fendant, Il Pescatore from California's Ca'del Solo or Italian Verdicchio from a ripe vintage. Even a slightly sweet French Vouvray or well-made Montlouis would work.

Champagne or its California counterpart is also recommended. Choose a sleek, elegant style with a high proportion of white grapes in the cuvée.

 TEMPURA HIRAME WITH MACADAMIA
HONEY SWEET-AND-SOUR SAUCE

A Japanese flat flounder, *hirame* lends itself to tempura cooking. Whole sole, however, is a good substitute. Cut into the *hirame*'s crispy exterior to reach the moist meat and dip it in the sweet, sour and spicy sauce. It's a quick trip to Hawaiian heaven.

6 servings
SWEET-AND-SOUR SAUCE
1 cup pineapple juice
1 cup sugar
½ cup apple cider vinegar
½ cup macadamia nut honey or other honey
1 tablespoon ketchup
1½ teaspoons peeled, minced fresh ginger
1½ teaspoons minced green onion
¼ teaspoon dried crushed red pepper
1 tablespoon cornstarch dissolved in 1 tablespoon water
¼ cup chopped roasted macadamia nuts
TEMPURA
Vegetable oil (for deep frying)
2 tablespoons peeled, minced fresh ginger
6 whole hirames *(Japanese flat flounder) (14–16
    ounces each)*, top of fish scored
2 cups rice flour *(for dredging)*
1 cup cornstarch *(for dredging)*

For the sauce: Bring the first 8 ingredients to a boil in a heavy, large saucepan, stirring frequently. Reduce the heat and simmer 5 minutes. Add the cornstarch mixture and bring to a boil. Mix in the nuts. **(Can be prepared 1 day ahead. Cover and refrigerate. Bring to a simmer before using.)**

For the tempura: Heat the oil in a heavy, large, deep skillet to 350° F. Rub the ginger into the *hirame*. Season with salt and pepper. Mix the rice flour and cornstarch in a bowl. Dredge the fish in the flour mixture; shake off the excess. Add 1 fish to the oil and fry, turning once, until cooked through, about 6 minutes. Using a slotted spatula, transfer the fish to a paper towel and drain. Repeat with the remaining fish in 5 more batches. Spoon the sweet-and-sour sauce over fish and serve.

WINE NOTES
This dish is a natural for a slightly sweet, well-made German Riesling. The wine's faint sweetness would match up well with the sugar, honey and pineapple juice in the dish. The wine's acidity would also complement the hirame.

"Laie Bay" Limu Poke Salad with Broiled Yellowfin Tuna and Ka'u Orange Dressing

 ### "LAIE BAY" LIMU POKE SALAD WITH BROILED YELLOWFIN TUNA AND KA'U ORANGE DRESSING

Sam grew up in a small fishing village called Laie Bay, on Oahu, and this salad, prepared with crunchy *ogo* (Hawaiian seaweed), pays homage to favorite local tastes. Although *poke* is usually made with marinated raw fish, in this case, the *ahi* is briefly broiled. Ka'u oranges are grown on the Big Island, and are superior in flavor. Slightly sweet and a little spicy, this salad makes a fine first course for a poultry or meat entrée.

6 servings

DRESSING
1/2 cup fresh orange juice
2 tablespoons vegetable oil
2 1/4 teaspoons sugar
1 1/2 teaspoons sesame seeds
1 1/2 teaspoons white wine vinegar
1 1/2 teaspoons soy sauce
SALAD
*2 cups ogo (Hawaiian seaweed), cleaned and
  drained*
3/4 cup soy sauce
1/4 cup white wine vinegar
1/4 cup mirin (sweet rice wine)
1 cup sugar
1 tablespoon black sesame seeds
1/8 teaspoon minced jalapeño chili
TUNA
1 cup soy sauce
1/2 cup firmly packed brown sugar
3/4 teaspoon peeled, minced fresh ginger
1/2 teaspoon dried crushed red pepper
1/4 teaspoon Chinese 5-spice powder
6 3-ounce (3/4-inch-thick) sashimi-grade ahi steaks

For the dressing: Combine all of the ingredients in a small bowl. Cover and refrigerate until ready to use or up to 6 hours.

For the salad: Blanch the seaweed in a large saucepan of boiling salted water for 2 minutes. Drain. Transfer to a bowl. Bring the soy sauce, vinegar, mirin and sugar to a boil in a heavy, small saucepan, stirring to dissolve the sugar. Pour the mixture over the seaweed. Mix in the sesame seeds and jalapeño chili. Cool completely. Drain before using.

For the tuna: Mix the first 5 ingredients in a large bowl. Add the *ahi* and toss to coat. Let stand 1 hour at room temperature.

Preheat the broiler. Place the *ahi* on a foil-lined baking sheet. Broil until rare, about 1 minute per side.

Arrange the seaweed salad on plates. Top with the *ahi*. Ladle the dressing over and serve.

WINE NOTES
A cool, refreshing and crisp beer is the ideal match for this dish.

ROGER DIKON

It's a long road from ski bum to beach bum to executive chef, but Roger Dikon made the transition with relatively few bumps and just an occasional sunburn. Roger began his culinary career as a dishwasher in a Vermont ski resort restaurant—not because he wanted to work his way up to chef, but because he liked the hours. By washing dishes in the morning and evening he was free to ski from practically sunup to sundown.

"It didn't take long to realize that dishwashing was not exactly the highlight of my life," admits Roger. "And I also discovered that I liked learning in the kitchen almost as much as I liked skiing."

The chef at the Vermont restaurant where Roger was working had a short fuse, and thanks to his histrionics, Roger took the first step in his transition to chef. "One day during a tantrum, the chef actually threw a quail out the window," says Roger. "I jumped in to help, and before long, I was promoted to a cook."

Roger eventually became a chef at a nearby restaurant before he received an offer to work at the Jenny Lake Lodge in Jackson Hole, Wyoming. He spent the winter season there and then flew to Florida to cook at a Ft. Lauderdale pizzeria/Italian restaurant. "I progressed from ski bum to beach bum," says Roger with a chuckle. "I cooked in shorts and a T-shirt and spent a lot of time sunning in the Keys."

Roger briefly became a chef on a private windjammer, sailing through the British Virgin Islands. He jumped ship to become sous-chef at a Rockresort hotel in the American Virgin Islands.

Manila Clam Scampi on Fresh Kula Corn Cakes
(See recipe, page 15)

While working for a Southern California restaurant in 1978, Roger learned that Kapalua Bay Hotel was opening on Maui. Missing the tropical island sun, he applied as a cook/saucier and was accepted. Fellow HRC chef Gary Strehl arrived at Kapalua Bay Hotel about the same time and the two became friends.

However, Roger's creativity was stifled cooking at Kapalua Bay. "I worked under a German chef who forced me to serve the same two specials every night for one year," says Roger. "I was going crazy. I had all these ideas so I just wrote them down. When that executive chef left, I was given free reign. It was then that I started my exploration of island regional cuisine, which was my name for this cooking style."

Roger trekked regularly to the local swap meet, buying as much produce as he could carry. He saw what Hawaii had to offer, and he also saw what it was missing. According to Roger, only 25 percent of the available produce was local at that time. "We needed different greens and vine-ripened tomatoes," says Roger. "We could only get iceberg lettuce and mainland tomatoes."

In 1986, Roger left Kapalua Bay to become executive sous-chef at the Maui Prince. The Prince Court restaurant became his domain, and although he is now the hotel's executive chef, he still keeps a creative hand in his signature dining room. Today, specials change daily, perhaps in response to his early days at Kapalua Bay.

When he began working at the Maui Prince he was desperate for diversified produce, so Roger planted an 800-square-foot garden at his home. Candy cane beets, thirteen types of lettuce and Japanese cucumbers were just some of the sixty to seventy vegetables sharing the soil. Most of his crop wound up on the Prince Court menu.

Today, the hotel contracts farmers for select produce. But Roger still can't resist picking kaffir lime leaves from the 20-foot-tree in his front yard and using them in the Prince Court.

Although Asian ingredients play a role in his dishes, Roger places less emphasis on them than some of the other HRC chefs. "I still have strong California and French influences in my cooking," he explains.

He calls his cuisine country Hawaiian, but dishes like slipper lobster hushpuppies with Haiku lime mustard sauce and *ahi* beggar's purse with tamarind seed vinaigrette can hardly be pegged down-home.

"Hawaii Regional Cuisine fits what I do," says Roger. "I use the tools of Hawaii to create my own cooking style and I enjoy every minute of it." ∎

AHI BEGGAR'S PURSES WITH TAMARIND VINAIGRETTE

I'd gladly become a beggar if it meant being fed appetizers like this one. The assertive vinaigrette achieves a tart, refreshing flavor from the tamarind; it's used sparingly, just to accent the rich, meaty taste of the *ahi*. This starter's stunning presentation makes it ideal for entertaining. Roger created this recipe with his executive sous-chef, Corey Waite.

4 servings

VINAIGRETTE
1½ tablespoons tamarind paste
1 tablespoon cilantro leaves
1 tablespoon rice wine vinegar
1 slice (¼ inch thick) fresh ginger, peeled and grated
1 small garlic clove, minced
⅛ teaspoon Szechwan chili sauce
¼ cup plus 2 tablespoons olive oil
1½ tablespoons (about) water
2 tablespoons fresh lemon juice
1 tablespoon fresh mint leaves
¼ teaspoon oriental sesame oil

FISH
4 rice paper sheets (8 inches in diameter)
½ pound sashimi-grade ahi *tuna, thinly sliced*
¼ package (2-ounce size) radish sprouts, roots trimmed
4 chives
½ small carrot, peeled, julienned
¼ English hothouse cucumber, peeled and julienned
1 tablespoon black sesame seeds

For the vinaigrette: Blend the first 6 ingredients in a blender for 20 seconds. Gradually add the olive oil and blend until thick, thinning with the water if the mixture becomes too thick. Blend in the lemon juice, mint and sesame oil. Season to taste with salt. Cover and refrigerate until ready to use. **(Can be prepared 1 day ahead.)**

For the fish: Fill a heavy, large skillet with very hot water. Add the rice sheets and submerge. Let stand until the sheets soften and turn opaque, about 1 minute. Transfer the rice sheets to a kitchen towel and drain. Spread 1 tablespoon of the vinaigrette on 1 rice paper sheet. Place ¼ of the *ahi* in the center of the round. Top with a pinch of sprouts. Bring up the edges and tie at the center with a chive, forming a purse. Repeat with the remaining rice sheets, vinaigrette, *ahi*, sprouts and chives, forming a total of 4 purses. Spoon a little vinaigrette onto each of 4 plates. Place 1 purse on the center of each plate. Arrange the carrot, cucumber and remaining sprouts decoratively around the purses. Sprinkle with sesame seeds and serve.

WINE NOTES
Babcock Fathom Rosé from California is a well-suited partner to the dish. It's simultaneously dry and fruity with real firm acidity. German Riesling also works well.

Also, consider Sauvignon Blancs like Regis Minet Pouilly-Fumé (French, unoaked), which has the fruit but is leaner, with a distinct flavor of apple and pear, with citrusy acidity.

 SLIPPER LOBSTER HUSHPUPPIES WITH HAIKU LIME–MUSTARD SAUCE

These hushpuppies are reminiscent of Cajun popcorn; it's difficult to stop popping them in your mouth. Haiku limes, grown on Maui, are large and seedless. Their sweet/tart flavor helps balance this appetizer's expected richness. Haiku Lime–Mustard Sauce can be used as a dip for almost any deep-fried food.

4 servings
SAUCE
6 tablespoons mayonnaise
2 tablespoons Dijon mustard
1½ tablespoons fresh lime juice
1 tablespoon macadamia honey or other honey

HUSHPUPPIES
¾ cup yellow corn meal
½ small Maui onion or other sweet onion, finely chopped
4 ounces cooked slipper or other lobster tail meat, chopped
¼ green bell pepper, finely chopped
¼ red bell pepper, finely chopped
⅓ cup cake flour
⅓ cup buttermilk
1 small celery stalk, finely chopped
1½ teaspoons macadamia nut oil or vegetable oil
1½ teaspoons ground cumin
½ lightly beaten extra-large egg
¾ teaspoon baking powder
½ teaspoon salt
4 cups vegetable oil (for deep frying)

For the sauce: Mix all of the ingredients in a bowl. Cover and refrigerate until ready to use. (**Can be prepared 3 days ahead.**)

For the hushpuppies: Mix all of the ingredients except the vegetable oil in a large bowl. Heat the oil in a heavy, large saucepan to 375° F. Working in batches, gently drop the batter by rounded teaspoonfuls into the oil and cook until deep golden brown, turning occasionally, about 2 minutes. Using a slotted spoon, transfer hushpuppies to paper towels and drain.

Place the sauce in a bowl in the center of a platter. Surround with hushpuppies and serve.

WINE NOTES
With a dish this playful, it's best to base your beverage selection on what you enjoy drinking. Champagne or its California sparkling counterpart is a fitting example. Or consider a slightly sweet white wine like Demi-Sec Vouvray from the Loire Valley. Just make sure it's rich and crisp.

Glazed Shrimp with a Passion for Champagne Served with Sweet Lychee Salsa

 GLAZED SHRIMP WITH A PASSION FOR
CHAMPAGNE SERVED WITH
SWEET LYCHEE SALSA

During Hawaii's lychee season (usually June and
September), the fresh-picked fruit often pops up on
Roger's menus in various guises. Roger created this
fanciful recipe for a popular television cooking show
in Hawaii and suggests serving it with pasta, rice or
sautéed julienned vegetables. Sweet Lychee Salsa
can also accompany almost any grilled or broiled fish
or meat.

4 appetizer servings

SALSA
*1 cup peeled, quartered and seeded fresh lychees or
    drained canned lychees*
1 large green onion, chopped
¼ cup peeled, diced papaya
*¼ cup peeled, diced fresh water chestnuts or drained
    canned water chestnuts*
2 generous tablespoons diced fresh pineapple
2 generous tablespoons diced red bell pepper
2 tablespoons seeded and diced tomatoes
2 tablespoons chopped fresh cilantro

14

½ red jalapeño or serrano chili, minced
1 teaspoon raw Hawaiian sugar
½ teaspoon Hawaiian or kosher salt
SHRIMP
⅓ cup passion fruit jelly or orange marmalade
⅓ cup dry Champagne or sparkling wine
3 tablespoons olive oil
1 teaspoon salt
½ teaspoon oriental sesame oil
20 large raw shrimp, peeled, tails intact

For the salsa: Mix all of the ingredients in a bowl. Cover and refrigerate until ready to use. **(Can be prepared up to 4 hours ahead.)**

For the shrimp: Mix all of the ingredients except the shrimp in a large bowl. Using a small, sharp knife, cut just below the tails of the shrimp on the underside, almost cutting in half to open lengthwise but not severing in two. Add shrimp to marinade and toss gently. Let stand 30 minutes at room temperature.

Prepare the barbecue (medium heat). Remove the shrimp from the marinade. Grill the shrimp until cooked through, about 2 minutes per side. Divide the shrimp between 4 plates. Spoon the salsa on the sides of the plates and serve.

WINE NOTES
If, as the recipe suggests, you are considering champagne, look to Demi-Sec versions. This dish has a lot of fruity sweetness, which the corresponding wine should be able to carry.

A Demi-Sec Vouvray from a ripe year, a slightly sweet Gaillac from southwestern France and even, despite the pineapple, a German Riesling, are other good options.

✹ MANILA CLAM SCAMPI ON FRESH KULA CORN CAKES

Manila clams possess a heavenly affinity with garlic, butter and white wine, and when combined with crispy sweet corn cakes, we're talking pure palatal triumph. Kula, an up-country Maui farming community, is hailed for the sweet quality of its corn.

4 servings
CORN CAKES
2 large ears fresh corn
½ cup whole milk
3 tablespoons yellow corn meal
3 tablespoons all-purpose flour
1 tablespoon unsalted butter, melted
1 tablespoon macadamia honey or other honey
½ teaspoon baking powder
⅛ teaspoon minced fresh thyme

CLAMS
½ cup macadamia nut oil or olive oil
3 tablespoons chopped garlic
6 pounds manila clams, scrubbed
2 cups unsalted Fish Stock (see recipe, page 128)
¾ cup dry vermouth
2 cups finely diced tomatoes
¼ cup chopped fresh basil
½ cup (1 stick) chilled unsalted butter, cut into pieces
¼ cup fresh lime juice

For the corn cakes: Preheat the oven to 200° F. Cut the corn from the cobs (you will need 1½ cups of corn). Transfer ¾ cup of corn to the blender. Add the remaining ingredients to the blender and purée until smooth. Pour the batter into a bowl. Stir in the remaining ¾ cup corn.

Lightly grease a heavy, large, nonstick skillet and place it over medium-high heat. Working in batches, drop the batter by 2 tablespoonfuls into the skillet and cook until the cakes are cooked through, about 2 minutes per side. Transfer the cakes to a baking sheet. Keep warm in the oven. Repeat with the remaining batter.

For the clams: Heat the oil in a heavy, large pot over high heat. Add the garlic and sauté 30 seconds. Add the clams, stock, vermouth, tomatoes and basil. Cover and cook until the clams open, about 10 minutes. Discard any clams that do not open. Using tongs, transfer the clams to a bowl. Boil the liquid in a pot until reduced by half, about 8 minutes. Add the butter and whisk until melted. Whisk in the lime juice.

Arrange 3 corn cakes on each of 4 plates. Top with clams. Spoon the sauce over the clams and serve.

WINE NOTES
Fresh, unoaked and fruit-laden styles of modern Italian Friulian whites made from Tocai, Pinot Grigio and Ribolla Gialla are interesting partners. There are also some stunning whites from other parts of Italy that work, such as the Biancos, made from low-yielding, indigenous vines from Campania, Sicily, Umbria and Latium. Select ones with balanced alcohol levels.

Or, experiment with southern French wines such as the St. Chinian Rosé from Mas Champart or Clos Nicrosi from Corsica. These wines possess a mineral character, a surprising richness and the needed structure to complement this dish.

For the nuts: Grease a small cookie sheet. Stir the sugar in a heavy, medium skillet over medium-high heat until melted and golden brown, about 2 minutes. Add the nuts, then water, and cook until the nuts are coated with sugar and almost all of the liquid evaporates, stirring frequently, about 3 minutes. Transfer the nuts to a greased cookie sheet and cool. (**Can be prepared 1 day ahead. Store the nuts in an airtight container at room temperature.**)

For the salad: Toss the greens in a large bowl with enough dressing to taste. Divide the greens among plates. Garnish with the smoked fish and dried fruit. Sprinkle with the caramelized nuts and serve.

WINE NOTES
Since this salad is smoky, somewhat spicy and slightly sweet, the corresponding wine should possess a little sweetness, too. Look to German wines made in the fruity style, French Vouvray Demi-Sec or light, forward and refreshing styles of California Gewurztraminer or Riesling.

KULA GREENS WITH SMOKED MARLIN, CARAMELIZED MACADAMIA NUTS AND GINGER-CHILI DRESSING

Few salads possess the pizzazz of this one; the smoky/sweet flavor combination is positively addictive. Roger gets his baby greens from nearby Kula, an up-country Maui farming community. When planning a menu, think of serving this salad before a spicy entrée; its sweetness will evocatively contrast the following course.

4 servings
DRESSING
¼ cup macadamia nut honey or orange clover honey
2 tablespoons peeled, minced fresh ginger
1 extra-large egg yolk (optional)
1 small jalapeño chili, seeded and minced
2 tablespoons rice wine vinegar
1 tablespoon Dijon mustard
2 teaspoons soy sauce
½ teaspoon oriental sesame oil
½ teaspoon salt
½ cup macadamia nut oil or vegetable oil
2 tablespoons fresh lemon juice
CARAMELIZED NUTS
2 tablespoons Hawaiian raw sugar
¾ cup diced raw macadamia nuts
2 tablespoons water
SALAD
8 cups mixed baby greens
12 ounces smoked marlin or tuna
½ cup chopped dried papaya, mango, cherries or raisins

For the dressing: Blend the first 3 ingredients in a processor or blender for 10 seconds. Add the chili, vinegar, mustard, soy sauce, sesame oil and salt and blend well. Gradually blend in the macadamia oil. Blend in the lemon juice. Cover and refrigerate until cold. (**Can be prepared 1 day ahead. If necessary, thin the dressing with water before using.**)

SEARED SHUTOME WITH TOMATO SALAD AND AVOCADO BUTTER

This preparation of *shutome*, or Hawaiian swordfish, may be easy, but the end result is a showpiece. The fragrant fresh herbs in the vinaigrette create an unusually aromatic bouquet.

4 servings
TOMATO SALAD
2 large ripe tomatoes, diced
⅓ cup chopped fresh basil
¼ cup minced Maui onion or other sweet onion
3 tablespoons balsamic vinegar
2 tablespoons extra-virgin olive oil
2 tablespoons minced fresh herbs (such as thyme, cilantro and parsley)
½ teaspoon minced garlic
AVOCADO BUTTER
1 large avocado, peeled and pitted
¼ cup extra-virgin olive oil
3 tablespoons fresh lime juice
FISH
4 shutome (swordfish) steaks (6 to 8 ounces and ¾ inch thick each)
3 tablespoons olive oil

For the tomato salad: Mix all of the ingredients in a bowl. Season to taste with salt and pepper. (**Can be prepared 4 hours ahead. Cover and let stand at room temperature.**)

For the avocado butter: Blend all of the ingredients in a blender or food processor until smooth. Season to taste with salt.

For the fish: Season the fish with salt and pepper. Heat the oil in a heavy, large skillet over high heat. Add the fish and cook until cooked through, about 4 minutes per side. For serving, divide the tomato salad among plates. Top with the fish. Spoon ¼ of the avocado butter atop each fish steak and serve.

WINE NOTES

Look for dry white wines from southern France or Italy to pair with this dish. They have an earthy essence that intermingles with the tomatoes, basil and garlic, and have high enough acidity levels to handle the olive oil and the fish.

You can also try some of the dry rosés from southern France and Italy, too. Consider the Rosato from Dr. Cosimo Taurino of Italy or Tempier's Bandol Rosé from Provence, France.

KIAWE-GRILLED EWA CHICKEN WITH HOISIN SAUCE

This Hawaii Regional Cuisine take on barbecued chicken is intriguing—it guarantees a burnished, crispy skin and slightly sweet, slightly pungent meat. *Kiawe* is the Hawaiian version of mesquite, and Ewa chicken is fresh, raised locally on Oahu. Even if you don't grill your chicken over wood, this recipe will come out great.

4 servings

SAUCE
1 cup hoisin sauce
½ cup finely chopped fresh cilantro
¼ cup macadamia nut oil or vegetable oil
¼ cup oriental sesame oil
12 kaffir lime leaves, julienned
3 tablespoons minced fresh lemongrass
2 tablespoons peeled, grated fresh ginger
CHICKEN
2 whole chickens, cut lengthwise in half (backbone removed)
4 tablespoons fresh lime juice
2 tablespoons soy sauce
4 garlic cloves, minced
4 teaspoons peeled, minced fresh ginger

For the sauce: Mix all of the ingredients in a large bowl. **(Can be prepared 2 days ahead. Cover and refrigerate.)**

For the chicken: Place the chickens on a large baking sheet. Brush the chickens with the lime juice and soy sauce. Rub the garlic and ginger over the chicken. Cover and refrigerate overnight.

Prepare the barbecue (medium heat). Grill the chicken until cooked through, turning occasionally, about 45 minutes. Brush the sauce over the chicken, grill 5 minutes more and serve.

WINE NOTES

This chicken is a real treat when served with more elegant Grenache-based wines that have a good deal of ripe, fresh fruit and low to medium tannin levels. Look for California versions like Bonny Doon's Clos de Gilroy or well-made Côtes-du-Rhône from France.

Another option is a soft, supple-style California Merlot with an abundance of rich, ripe fruit.

MEDALLIONS OF VEAL ON WARM MAUI ONION MARMALADE

Caramelizing Maui onions accentuates their inherent sweetness. This mild-flavored marmalade enhances the traditional cream sauce so often served with veal. The marmalade's flavor is so versatile, it can easily accompany sautéed or grilled fish.

4 servings

ONION MARMALADE
2 tablespoons olive oil
1½ large Maui onions or other sweet onion, julienned
¼ teaspoon minced fresh thyme
¼ teaspoon Hawaiian or kosher salt
1 cup whipping cream
VEAL
2 tablespoons (¼ stick) unsalted butter
8 veal medallions, 3 ounces and 1¼ inches thick each

For the onion marmalade: Heat the oil in a heavy, large skillet over medium heat. Add the onions and sauté 10 minutes. Add the thyme and salt. Reduce the heat to low and cook until the onions are a deep golden brown, stirring occasionally, about 1 hour. Add the cream and simmer until reduced to a sauce consistency, about 5 minutes. **(Can be prepared 1 day ahead. Cover and refrigerate. Bring to a simmer before using.)**

For the veal: Melt the butter in a heavy, large skillet over high heat. Season the veal with salt and pepper. Add the veal to the skillet and cook to desired doneness, about 4 minutes per side for medium.

Divide the onion mixture among 4 plates. Top each with 2 veal medallions and serve.

WINE NOTES

Try this dish with a well-made Pinot Noir—one with lots of ripe fruit and a good, firm structure that's not too heavy.

Other wines to keep in mind are red Grenache-based wines that are not too rustic, and friendly Italian reds such as Dolcetto D'Alba, Refosco or Rosso di Montepulciano.

MASHED POTATOES WITH CARAMELIZED MAUI ONIONS

French chef Roger Vergé taught Roger Dikon how to make perfect mashed potatoes when Roger assisted Vergé for a Beverly Hills celebrity dinner. When Roger returned to Hawaii, he decided to add one of his favorite local ingredients—Maui onion—slowly sautéed to a sweet richness and a tantalizing golden hue.

Roger often serves these potatoes with *kiawe*-grilled sirloin steak. Sometimes he mixes them with foie gras and roasted garlic or fresh pears for the ultimate indulgence.

6 servings

2 tablespoons olive oil
1½ Maui onions or other sweet onions, julienned
1 garlic clove, minced
6 medium potatoes, peeled and quartered
1¼ cups milk
½ cup (1 stick) unsalted butter, cut into pieces
Freshly ground white pepper

Heat the oil in a heavy, large skillet over low heat. Add the onions and garlic and cook until the onions caramelize, stirring occasionally, about 1 hour. Drain off any oil from the skillet. (**Can be prepared 1 day ahead. Cover and refrigerate.**)

Cook the potatoes in a large pot of boiling salted water until tender, about 20 minutes. Drain. Return the potatoes to the pot and mash. Mix the milk and butter into the potatoes and stir until the butter melts. Season with salt and white pepper. Mix in the onions. Stir over medium-low heat until heated through. Transfer to a bowl and serve.

MACADAMIA NUT TACOS WITH TROPICAL FRUITS AND LILIKOI CUSTARD

Roger devised this recipe—showcasing the Hawaiian Islands' premier produce—for one of his "chef's table" cooking classes. One bite of the buttery, crunchy "tacos" (similar to French *tuiles*) and you'll know why Roger's classes are always filled to capacity.

If passion fruit purée is unavailable in your area, boil 1½ cups passion fruit–mango juice until reduced to ¼ cup.

6 servings

MACADAMIA NUT TACOS
⅓ cup raw macadamia nuts
⅓ cup sugar
¼ cup all-purpose flour
¼ cup (½ stick) unsalted butter, melted
1 extra-large egg
1 tablespoon water
1 teaspoon vanilla extract
LILIKOI CUSTARD
8 extra-large egg yolks
6 tablespoons dark rum
¼ cup Hawaiian raw sugar
¼ cup frozen passion fruit purée, thawed
Assorted fresh fruits (such as sliced papaya, mango, bananas)
Fresh strawberries
Fresh mint sprigs

For the tacos: Preheat the oven to 350° F. Place the nuts in a food processor. Add the sugar and flour and blend to a powder. Add the melted butter, egg, water and vanilla and blend 20 seconds.

Butter a large cookie sheet. Spoon 1 tablespoon of batter onto the sheet. Spread with the back of a spoon to a 5-inch round. Repeat, forming a total of 6 cookies, spaced evenly apart. Bake until golden brown on the edges, about 8 minutes. Working quickly, lift 1 cookie from the sheet and drape it over the handle of a broom or wooden dowel, forming a taco shape. Repeat with the remaining cookies, returning the cookie sheet to the oven briefly if the cookies harden. Butter the same cookie sheet and form 6 more cookies. Bake, mold and cook as described above. (**Can be prepared 1 day ahead. Store between layers of waxed paper in airtight container at room temperature.**)

For the custard: Whisk the first 4 ingredients in a large metal bowl. Set the bowl over a saucepan of simmering water (do not allow the bowl to touch the water) and whisk constantly until a candy thermometer registers 160° F, about 5 minutes.

Spoon some of the custard into the center of each of 6 plates. Gently fill the tacos with sliced fruit. Place 2 tacos atop the custard on each plate. Spoon more custard into the tacos. Garnish with strawberries and mint and serve.

Macadamia Nut Tacos with Tropical Fruits and Lilikoi Custard

MARK ELLMAN

"Each musician had different tastes," recalls Mark. "One day I was preparing curries, another day soul food. I developed a passion for learning. All I wanted to do was keep refining my craft."

Mark also cooked at a Malibu recording studio for other eminent musicians, and at some of Los Angeles's and Denver's most noted restaurants. In Denver, he began to experience burn-out, and he and Judy decided to move to Hawaii. "I always dreamed of owning a restaurant on a tropical island," says Mark. "Growing up in Los Angeles, I went to the beach every weekend. I decided I wanted to be able to go every day."

By 1985, Mark was working at Longhi's, one of Maui's most popular dining establishments. Three years later, he entered into a partnership to open Avalon and soon bought his partner out. Dishes like his towering salmon tiki, wok-fried *opakapaka* with spicy black bean sauce and sweet Caramel Miranda brought throngs of diners in. They might not have known what they were eating, but they seemed to love every bite.

"My definition of Hawaii Regional Cuisine is to utilize as many products grown and raised here as possible, and to present them in the simplest, purest manner," says Mark. "I'd like to get back to what early Hawaiians were eating, and utilize those foods in mine."

Mark may talk about simplicity, but that doesn't mean that he is forsaking the exotic. "I love exotica, from baby coconuts to lotus root," he says. "I get so much pleasure out of putting foods on people's plates that they've never eaten before."

From the looks on the faces of Avalon diners, it's readily apparent that they're pleased, too. The one problem is that Mark is so busy keeping up with reservations, he's only been able to fulfill half of his lifelong dream. He's acquired the restaurant on the tropical island, but now that he's got it, there's no time for those daily trips to the beach. ■

Chicken-coconut may be the soup du jour, but ponytails are definitely the fashion statement du jour at Mark Ellman's Avalon restaurant in Maui. At this open-air, across-the-street-from-the-ocean Lahaina eaterie, it seems as if everyone sports the long-haired look, from Mark down the ranks to the wait help.

The ambience at Avalon may be casual, with its bright, tropical colors and courtyard locale, but there's much too much complexity to Mark's cooking to call it nonchalant. His Pacific Rim menu, which primarily showcases Hawaiian ingredients with a Southeast Asian spin, fearlessly and successfully explores flavors the way Captain Cook once explored the Pacific.

"I like preparing dishes that still leave an impression on the palate the following day," explains Mark. Since he uses flavoring agents like ginger, garlic, fermented black beans and chilies as freely as most of us use salt and pepper, his goal is easily achieved.

Avalon is a long way from Texas Tommy's, where Mark flipped burgers as a teenager in the San Fernando Valley, a Los Angeles suburb. Mark didn't begin his culinary career for the creative satisfaction; he was into earning pocket change.

The motivation of money propelled him to work his way up the kitchen ladder in local French cafés, but what may have got him hooked on cooking were the clients he worked for beginning in 1977, when, at the age of twenty-two, he opened the Can't Rock N Roll, But Sure Can Cook catering company with his wife, Judy. Many of his clients were leading musical artists, running the gamut from Neil Diamond and the Beach Boys to Earth, Wind and Fire and the Moody Blues.

Chili-seared Salmon, Tiki-style (See recipe, page 24)

SEARED SASHIMI

Mark was inspired to create one of Avalon's most celebrated dishes when he spotted an Oahu sushi chef cleaning *ahi* over an open flame.

By searing the *ahi* in a very hot pan, Mark fuses the flavor of the fresh herb coating to the fish. The ginger and garlic powerfully perfume the unconventional wine-butter sauce. Be sure to purchase sashimi-grade tuna for optimum quality.

4 servings
SAUCE
½ cup Chenin Blanc
¼ cup (½ stick) unsalted butter
¼ Maui onion or other sweet onion, finely chopped
1 small shiitake mushroom, stemmed and thinly sliced
1 tablespoon peeled, finely chopped fresh ginger
1 tablespoon soy sauce
2 garlic cloves, minced
1 tablespoon minced green onion
FISH
1 tablespoon chopped fresh basil
1 tablespoon chopped fresh mint
1 tablespoon chopped fresh cilantro
1 tablespoon oriental sesame oil
4 pieces sashimi-grade ahi *tuna, 2 ounces and ¾ inch thick each*

For the sauce: Boil all of the ingredients except the green onion in a heavy, medium saucepan over high heat until liquid is reduced by half, stirring occasionally, about 5 minutes. Mix in the green onion.

Meanwhile, prepare the fish: Mix the herbs together on a plate. Brush sesame oil over the *ahi*. Roll the *ahi* in the herbs, coating it completely. Heat a heavy, large skillet over high heat until very hot. Add the *ahi* and sear 20 seconds per side. Cut the *ahi* into ⅛-inch-thick slices. Spoon the sauce onto plates. Fan the ahi over the sauce and serve.

WINE NOTES
Since it's used in the recipe and its flavor is pronounced in the finished dish, Chenin Blanc seems to be the definitive selection. White Zinfandel would also work.

But even with a Chenin Blanc in the recipe, a light, fruity red with high acid levels and minimal tannins or oak would also be possible. Consider a fresh red Beaujolais, a light, low-tannin Rhône varietal or even a light Italian red such as Dolcetto or Refosco.

SHRIMP AND GREEN PAPAYA SALAD

In Bangkok, women vendors slice papayas on Thai mandolines (hand-powered slicing machines) and mix in peanuts, dried shrimp, chilies and fresh citrus juice for a salad designed to refresh passersby in the scorching Thai sun. To make Mark's version, which took one of the top honors in a national culinary contest, select unripe green papayas from the supermarket.

4 servings
5 tablespoons fresh lemon juice
*2 tablespoons fish sauce (*nam pla*)*
2 tablespoons sugar
2 small jalapeño chilies, minced
4 small garlic cloves, minced
3 cups peeled, grated green papaya
10 large peeled, cooked shrimp, sliced lengthwise in half
½ cup diced tomato
2 tablespoons chopped roasted peanuts
2 tablespoons finely chopped mixed fresh herbs (such as mint, basil and cilantro)

Mix the first 5 ingredients in a large bowl until the sugar dissolves. Add the remaining ingredients and toss well. Season generously with pepper and serve.

WINE NOTES
For the die-hard wine drinker, a Riesling Kabinett from the Rheingau region in Germany will work. The slight sweetness helps put out the fire and the wine will cleanse the palate between bites.

But the real vote goes to a light, ale-style beer—cool, crisp and thirst quenching.

ASIAN PASTA

One of Avalon's most popular dishes, this bold-flavored pasta blends such exotic Asian flavors as fermented black beans, sesame oil and mint with the more traditional basil, Parmesan cheese and tomatoes. Successfully prepared in a wok or skillet, this recipe is a splendid example of the virtues of fusing Asian and Western ingredients and techniques.

2 servings

¼ cup water
4 fresh clams, scrubbed
2 teaspoons olive oil
¼ teaspoon oriental sesame oil
2 teaspoons minced fresh cilantro
2 teaspoons minced fresh basil
2 teaspoons minced fresh mint
2 teaspoons minced green onions
1 teaspoon peeled, minced fresh ginger
1 teaspoon minced garlic
1 teaspoon minced Maui onion or other sweet onion
1 teaspoon minced jalapeño chili
1 teaspoon fermented black beans, rinsed and drained
2 ounces fresh ahi, cut into ½-inch pieces
2 ounces raw uncooked shrimp, peeled
2 ounces bay scallops
2 large shiitake mushrooms, stemmed and thinly sliced
1 large tomato, peeled, seeded and chopped
¼ cup (½ stick) unsalted butter, cut into pieces
⅓ cup freshly grated Parmesan cheese
6 large basil leaves, julienned
6 ounces linguine

Bring water to a boil in a heavy, medium saucepan. Add the clams, cover and cook over high heat until the clams open, about 5 minutes. Discard any clams that do not open. Set the clams aside.

Heat both of the oils in a wok or a heavy, large skillet over medium-high heat. Add the next 9 ingredients and stir-fry 1 minute. Add the *ahi*, shrimp, scallops and mushrooms and stir-fry 1 minute. Add the tomato and sauté 1 minute. Add the butter and stir-fry until the seafood is cooked through, about 2 minutes. Add the clams and stir to heat through. Sprinkle with Parmesan and basil.

Meanwhile, cook the pasta in a large pot of boiling, salted water until just tender but still firm to bite, stirring occasionally. Drain.

Divide the pasta between 2 plates. Spoon the seafood and sauce over pasta and serve.

WINE NOTES

The first thought might be to recommend a dry white or rosé wine, but the minced jalapeño chili makes its presence known. Try either a cool beer or a wine with a little sweetness, such as a simple, fruity American Gewurztraminer, which has a low alcohol level.

HAWAIIAN FOCCACIA

Ginger, oriental sesame oil and sesame seeds transform this Italian flat bread into a spectacular HRC dish.

6 servings

1 package dry yeast
¾ cup warm water (105° F to 115° F)
2 tablespoons olive oil
1 piece fresh ginger (2 inches long), peeled and sliced
2 large garlic cloves
2 cups bread flour
1 teaspoon sugar
¾ teaspoon salt
1 teaspoon oriental sesame oil
1 tablespoon white sesame seeds
1 tablespoon black sesame seeds
¼ teaspoon Hawaiian or kosher salt

Sprinkle the yeast over the warm water in a small bowl; stir to dissolve it. Whisk in 1 tablespoon of the oil. Mince the ginger and garlic in a food processor. Add the flour, sugar and ¾ teaspoon salt and blend in. Add the yeast mixture to the processor and blend in using on/off turns until combined. Turn the dough out onto a lightly floured surface and knead until smooth, about 2 minutes. Lightly oil a large bowl. Add the dough; turn to coat. Cover and let stand in a warm, draft-free area until doubled in volume, about 1 hour.

Preheat the oven to 375° F. Punch the dough down. Roll the dough out on a lightly floured work surface to a ½-inch-thick rectangle. Transfer to a baking sheet. Press your fingertips into the dough to create dimples. Brush the dough with the remaining 1 tablespoon of olive oil and 1 teaspoon of sesame oil. Sprinkle with all of the sesame seeds and Hawaiian salt. Bake until golden brown and cooked through, about 45 minutes.

STEAMED ONO WITH SOY-GINGER SAUCE

Ono, also known as *wahoo*, is a firm, lean fish of the mackerel family. Lobster, crab, rock cod, snapper or salmon can serve as substitutes in this redolent-with-ginger entrée. Mark likes to present this dish with steamed white or brown rice.

4 servings

> 4 ono *fillets, 6 to 8 ounces and 1½ inches thick each*
> 2 *ounces peeled, fresh ginger, sliced*
> 1 *piece peeled, fresh ginger (2 inches long), julienned*
> ¼ *cup chopped Maui onion or other sweet onion*
> ¼ *cup chopped fresh cilantro*
> 8 *small kaffir lime leaves*
> ¼ *cup chopped green onion*
> ¼ *cup soy sauce*
> ¼ *cup peanut oil*
> 4 *teaspoons olive oil*

Arrange the fish in a single layer in a bamboo steamer. Cover with the 2 ounces of ginger slices. Cover and steam just until cooked through, about 8 minutes. Arrange the fish on a platter; discard the ginger slices. Sprinkle ginger julienne, Maui onion, cilantro, kaffir leaves, green onion and soy sauce down center of fish.

Meanwhile, heat both oils in a heavy, small saucepan over high heat until smoking.

Pour the smoking oil over the fish immediately before serving.

WINE NOTES

This dish is another surprise for the wine purist; the soy-ginger sauce is the stumper. Try a lighter, slightly sweet, simpler style of California Gewurztraminer. If Gewurztraminer is what you have in mind, choose one that is not overly dramatized and has a lower alcohol level. Another consideration is to assist the palate with a refreshing California bubbly—round, ripe fruit, crisp acid and a lot of bubbles.

 ## CHILI-SEARED SALMON, TIKI-STYLE

Layers of salmon, mashed potatoes, sautéed eggplant, mixed greens and salsa make up this whimsical salad/appetizer that serves as one of Avalon's signature dishes. Mark admits this recipe sounds unusual, but advises you to withhold judgment until you taste it!

At Avalon, Mark assembles the components in a PVC tube to create the tiki shape. At home, simply use a 14½-ounce can of chicken broth with both ends removed for a mold.

4 servings

PLUM VINAIGRETTE
> ¼ *cup plum sauce*
> ⅓ *cup peeled, chopped mango*
> 1 *tablespoon fresh lemon juice*
> 1 *tablespoon red wine vinegar*
> 1 *teaspoon peeled, chopped fresh ginger*
> 1 *teaspoon minced garlic*

MANGO SALSA
> 1 *mango, peeled, pitted and finely diced*
> ¼ *Maui onion or other sweet onion, finely diced*
> 3 *tablespoons chopped fresh mint*
> 1 *tablespoon fresh lime juice*

TOMATO SALSA
> 1 *tomato, halved and finely diced*
> ¼ *Maui onion or other sweet onion, finely diced*
> 3 *tablespoons chopped fresh cilantro*
> 2 *tablespoons drained capers*
> 1 *tablespoon fresh lime juice*
> 1 *tablespoon olive oil*

EGGPLANT
> ¼ *cup olive oil*
> ¾ *pound Japanese eggplant (about 4 small), diced*

SALMON
> 1 *tablespoon Szechwan chili sauce*
> 1 *pound salmon fillets, cut into ¼-inch-thick slices*
> 1 *tablespoon olive oil*
> 1 *cup mashed potatoes, room temperature*
> 2 *cups (packed) mixed baby greens*
> ¼ *cup hoisin sauce, stirred until smooth*

For the plum vinaigrette: Purée all of the ingredients in a blender. Cover and refrigerate until ready to use.

For the mango salsa: Mix all of the ingredients in a small bowl. Cover and refrigerate until ready to use.

For the tomato salsa: Mix all of the ingredients in a medium bowl. Cover and let stand 2 hours at room temperature.

For the eggplant: Heat the oil in a heavy, large, nonstick skillet over medium-high heat. Add the eggplant and sauté until tender, about 6 minutes. Season with salt and pepper. Set the eggplant aside.

For the salmon: Brush the chili sauce over the salmon. Heat the oil in a heavy, large skillet over high heat. Add the salmon and sear until cooked through, about 30 seconds per side. Divide the salmon into 12 portions.

Place the chicken broth can (with both ends removed) in the center of a large plate. Spoon 1/4 cup of the mashed potatoes in the bottom. Top with 1 portion of salmon, 1/4 of eggplant, 1½ tablespoons of tomato salsa, 1/4 cup mixed greens and 1 teaspoon vinaigrette. Cover with 1 portion of salmon, 1½ tablespoons of the mango salsa, 1/4 cup of mixed greens, 1 teaspoon of vinaigrette and 1 portion of salmon. Carefully lift the can up. Repeat the layering process 3 more times on 3 plates, forming a total of 4 tikis. Drizzle remaining vinaigrette and hoisin sauce around each tiki and serve.

WINE NOTES
Not only is the dish tall, but it's also a tall order to find an appropriate wine when there are so many flavors coming together. Try a dry, lighter-bodied Grenache-based rosé from southern France.

This dish is also an interesting match with some red wines. Consider a Chinon from the Loire Valley, a California Pinot Noir, Domaine de la Gautière Rouge from Provence or Qupe's 1991 Syrah. Each offers fresh, lively fruit, good acidity and a slightly spicy quality.

FRIED MAUI NABETA

Nabeta (pronounced "nah-*be*-tah") is a small, gray reef fish with moist, white flesh and a mild flavor. A local Japanese delicacy, *nabeta* is often the subject of tournaments on Maui. It's also known as sheepshead fish in mainland Asian markets.

Feel free to substitute whole rock cod or pompano. Note that the sauce is wildly aromatic yet doesn't overpower the taste of the fish. The coconut milk smooths the sauce out and the lemongrass adds a citrusy sparkle.

4 servings
SAUCE
1 tablespoon olive oil
½ teaspoon oriental sesame oil
1 Maui onion or other sweet onion, chopped
1 lemongrass stalk, 12 inches long, sliced
4 kaffir lime leaves
1 teaspoon minced garlic
1 teaspoon peeled, minced fresh ginger
¾ cup Chardonnay or other dry white wine
¼ cup canned, unsweetened coconut milk
¼ cup (½ stick) unsalted butter
1 teaspoon fish sauce (nam pla)
1 teaspoon sugar
½ teaspoon minced fresh cilantro
½ teaspoon minced fresh basil
¼ teaspoon minced fresh mint
¼ teaspoon minced green onion
FISH
4 whole nabeta, rock fish or small pompano, 10 to 12 ounces each, scaled
2 cups vegetable oil
2 tablespoons oriental sesame oil

For the sauce: Heat both of the oils in a heavy, large skillet over high heat. Add the onion, lemongrass, lime leaves, garlic and ginger and sauté 2 minutes. Mix in the Chardonnay, coconut milk, butter, fish sauce and sugar and boil until reduced to 1⅓ cups, stirring occasionally, about 4 minutes. Mix in the herbs and green onion. Set the sauce aside while frying the fish.

For the fish: Using a small, sharp knife, score the fish diagonally, cutting to the bone and spacing the cuts 1 inch apart. Repeat, cutting diagonally in the opposite direction, creating a diamond pattern. Heat both oils in a heavy, large, deep skillet to 350° F. Add 2 fish and fry until cooked through, about 3 minutes per side. Using a slotted spatula, transfer the fish to paper towels and drain. Repeat frying with the remaining 2 fish. Divide the fish among 4 plates. Bring the sauce to a simmer, whisking constantly. Pour the sauce over the fish and serve.

WINE NOTES
For this preparation, the paired wine needs to have as little oak character as possible. Consider the well-made Italian Tocai Friuliano and Qupe's 1992 Marsanne and Ca'del Solo Malvasia Bianca from California.

Slightly sweet wines like Demi-Sec Vouvray, German white or even California and marginally sweet versions of Gewurztraminer also pair well with this delicate dish.

Wok-fried Opakapaka with Spicy Black Bean Sauce

 ## WOK-FRIED OPAKAPAKA WITH SPICY BLACK BEAN SAUCE

Red snapper, sea bass, trout, pompano or catfish would work equally well as a substitute for the Hawaiian pink snapper in this recipe, which is one of Avalon's signature dishes. For a milder meal, reduce the amount of jalapeño chilies.

The black bean sauce of a Hawaii Regional Cuisine chef is different from that of a Chinese cook in that it incorporates such Western elements as white wine (rather than rice wine or sherry) and butter, which both mellows and enriches its flavor.

2 servings

1 whole opakapaka, 1½ pounds, scaled and cleaned
All-purpose flour
4 cups soybean oil (for deep frying)
1 tablespoon olive oil
1 teaspoon oriental sesame oil
1 teaspoon minced garlic
1 teaspoon peeled, minced fresh ginger
1 teaspoon minced Maui onion or other sweet onion
1 teaspoon fermented black beans, rinsed and chopped
2 jalapeño chilies, seeded and minced
¾ cup dry white wine
½ cup (1 stick) unsalted butter
¼ cup chopped green onions

Using a small, sharp knife, make ½-inch-deep cuts all over the fish, spacing the cuts 1 inch apart. Dredge the fish in flour; shake off excess. Heat the soybean oil in a wok or deep fryer over medium-high heat to 350° F. Add the fish and cook until cooked through, about 3 minutes per side. Using a slotted spatula, transfer the fish to paper towels.

Meanwhile, heat the olive oil and sesame oil in a heavy, large skillet over high heat. Add the garlic, ginger, onion and beans and sauté 1 minute. Add the chilies and sauté 10 seconds. Add the wine and butter and boil until reduced to ¾ cup, whisking frequently, about 5 minutes. Mix in the green onions.

Transfer fish to plates. Spoon sauce over fish and serve.

WINE NOTES
Mark's black bean sauce is characteristically somewhat salty, spicy and pungent. Try a slightly sweet German Riesling or well-made California version like Babcock's 1992. The slight sweetness would cool and soothe the palate and counter the saltiness, yet not overpower the fish.

If you prefer drier wines, try a dry, nonoaked white wine like the Malvasia Bianca made under the Ca'del Solo label from California. Although it's light bodied, this wine has loads of fresh, lively fruit to neutralize the dish's spice and saltiness and enough crisp, snappy acidity to wipe the palate clean.

 ## INDONESIAN GRILLED LAMB CHOPS

Kecap manis is the secret ingredient in this simple-to-make dish. Pronounced "ket-chup mah-niece," this Indonesian condiment is a dark, thick, aromatic soy sauce sweetened with palm sugar and is sold in Asian markets. And yes, *kecap* is the root of our word *ketchup*.

In this recipe, the *kecap manis* permeates the lamb, imparting a seductive flavor. Be sure to take the time to marinate the lamb overnight for optimum taste.

4 servings

LAMB
½ cup kecap manis
½ cup peeled, chopped fresh ginger
¼ cup chopped fresh mint
2 tablespoons coarse-grained mustard
4 garlic cloves, finely chopped
1 tablespoon oriental sesame oil
8 lamb loin chops, about 2½ pounds total
SALAD
2 teaspoons olive oil
½ teaspoon oriental sesame oil
2 small garlic cloves, minced
2 teaspoons peeled, grated fresh ginger
6 ounces mixed baby greens

For the lamb: Mix all of the ingredients except the lamb in a small bowl. Place the lamb in a single layer in a large glass baking dish. Pour the marinade over; turn to coat. Cover and refrigerate overnight.

Prepare the barbecue (medium heat). Remove the lamb from the marinade. Grill to the desired doneness, about 3 minutes per side for rare. Transfer the lamb to a platter; tent with foil to keep warm.

For the salad: Heat both of the oils in a heavy, large skillet over high heat. Add the garlic and ginger and sauté 1 minute. Remove the skillet from heat. Add the greens and toss to coat. Divide the greens among 4 plates. Top each with 2 lamb chops and serve.

WINE NOTES
Red wines with ripe, flavored fruit, good, firm acidity and medium-plus tannins work well. Interesting pairings include: a wonderfully ripe and complex Côtes-du-Rhône; a Syrah-dominated Corbières Rouge; a majestic, classy Côte Rotie (with virtually no new oak); a ripe, fuller style of Italian Chianti.

California Cabernets, Merlots and even Zinfandels also are worth trying—as long as they're not too full-blown or oaky.

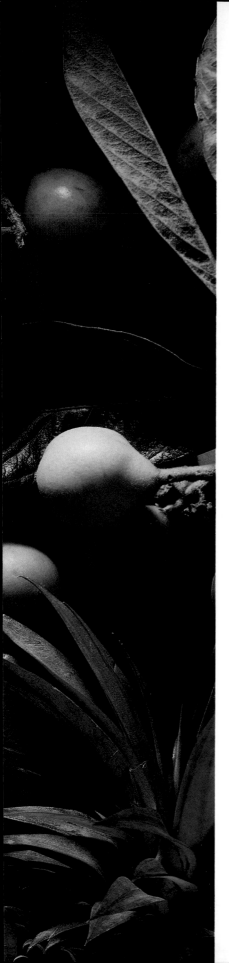

Caramel Miranda

 ## CARAMEL MIRANDA

Mark features only one dessert on Avalon's menu; when you taste Caramel Miranda, you'll know why it's the chosen one. Not only does it taste great, but the combination of caramel, fresh fruit and ice cream calms the palate down from a spicy meal. Mark says one reason he created this dessert when he first opened Avalon is that, like most chefs, he can't bake well, and when he opened, he couldn't afford a pastry chef. Avalon has become one of Hawaii's most successful restaurants and this dessert is a contributing factor.

Almost any variety of fruit will work. Mark often includes *durian*, a Southeast Asian fruit that possesses an unpleasant aroma yet creamy texture and sweet tropical fruit flavor.

6 servings

1²/₃ cups sugar
¹/₂ cup water
1 teaspoon cream of tartar
1 cup whipping cream
1 teaspoon butter
¹/₂ cup unsweetened shredded coconut, toasted
¹/₂ cup peeled, diced pineapple
¹/₂ cup sliced star fruit
¹/₂ cup fresh raspberries or blackberries
¹/₂ cup peeled, seeded and chopped cherimoya
¹/₂ cup peeled, diced bananas
4 fresh figs, diced
2 pints macadamia nut or vanilla ice cream

Stir the sugar, water and cream of tartar in a heavy, large saucepan over medium heat until the sugar dissolves. Increase the heat and boil without stirring until the caramel turns a deep amber color, swirling the pan occasionally. Add the cream (mixture will boil vigorously) and stir until smooth. Whisk in the butter. Cool to room temperature. **(Can be prepared 1 day ahead. Cover and refrigerate. Reheat over low heat before using.)**

Preheat the broiler. Spoon ¹/₄ cup of the caramel sauce onto each of 6 ovenproof plates. Sprinkle the fruit evenly over the caramel. Broil until the sauce bubbles, about 3 minutes. Spoon the ice cream in the center of the plates and serve immediately.

BEVERLY GANNON

Y ou can take the chef out of Texas, but it's difficult to take Texas out of the chef—even if she is happily ensconced in her Maui home. Just ask Beverly Gannon. This Dallas native will tell you that the Longhorn State's influence is reflected in dishes like *paniolo* (cowboy) ribs with Haliimaile barbecue sauce and chocolate macadamia nut tart, and she'll tell you proudly, with a Texan drawl.

Beverly's appealing cooking style emphasizes uncomplicated flavors, abundant portions and homey presentations. Her dishes are often heartier than most HRC chefs, in keeping with the cool, misty up-country locale of Haliimaile General Store, the restaurant she owns with her husband Joe. Beverly may rely less on Asian ingredients than some of her HRC counterparts, but she always emphasizes local produce and seafood.

"I don't get too creative, fancy or exotic," says Beverly. "My clientele is looking for familiar tastes more than culinary challenges. What they do get are the flavors of Hawaii, because that's what they want when they're here."

Located in a sea of pineapple fields, Haliimaile General Store is almost as much fun to drive to as it is to dine in. Turn off the highway onto a deserted road, climb a steep hill that unexpectedly shoots sharply downhill and then back uphill. Just when you break out in a sweat, convinced you took a wrong turn, you'll spot the blazing lights of Haliimaile General Store. Civilization never looked so good.

Or so sophisticated, considering the isolated setting. Contemporary art graces the walls and the partially open kitchen allows divine aromas to weave a tantalizing path through the dining room. Joe Gannon's thoughtful wine list would impress even the most urbane visitor.

Big Island Goat Cheese and Maui Onion Tart
with Red Pepper Coulis
(See recipe, page 32)

DUCK SALAD WITH WARM GOAT CHEESE AND CHIVE CRÊPES

This elegant starter combines an abundance of pleasing textures, from creamy goat cheese and tender duck to crunchy macadamia nuts. The slightly tart raspberry vinaigrette balances the dish's richness.

4 servings

CHIVE CRÊPES
1½ cups whole milk
1 cup plus 2 tablespoons unbleached all-purpose flour
4 extra-large eggs
½ teaspoon salt
3 tablespoons (approximately) unsalted butter, melted
2 tablespoons chopped chives

RASPBERRY VINAIGRETTE
½ cup olive oil
½ cup raspberry vinegar
1 tablespoon crème fraîche or whipping cream
1 tablespoon raspberries
½ teaspoon salt

DUCK SALAD
1 duck, 5 pounds
8 ounces soft, mild goat cheese, cut into 8 rounds
2 heads Belgian endive
6 cups mixed baby greens, torn into bite-size pieces
2 cups arugula, torn into bite-size pieces
1 cup sliced, drained canned hearts of palm
2 tablespoons chopped toasted macadamia nuts

For the crêpes: Whisk the first 4 ingredients in a large bowl. Pour the batter through a strainer into another bowl. Whisk 1 tablespoon melted butter into the batter; stir in the chives. Heat a 7-inch-diameter nonstick skillet over medium-high heat. Brush with some melted butter. Working quickly, pour ¼ cup of the batter into the skillet and swirl to coat the pan thinly; pour any excess batter back into bowl. Cook just until bottom is set (do not let brown), about 1 minute. Turn the crêpe over and cook the second side for 5 seconds. Turn the crêpe out onto a plate. Cover with a sheet of plastic wrap or waxed paper. Repeat with the remaining batter, stacking the crêpes and brushing the pan with more melted butter as necessary. **(Can be prepared 2 days ahead. Cover and refrigerate.)**

For the vinaigrette: Blend all of the ingredients in a food processor until smooth. Season to taste with salt and pepper. **(Can be prepared 2 days ahead. Cover and refrigerate. Bring to room temperature and rewhisk before using.)**

For the salad: Preheat the oven to 400° F. Prick the duck skin all over with a fork. Season with salt and pepper. Place the duck in a roasting pan. Roast the duck 30 minutes. Reduce the oven temperature to 350° F. Continue roasting until the skin is crisp and brown and the duck is cooked through, about 45 minutes more. Cool. Remove the skin from duck and place in a heavy, large skillet. Cook the skin over medium heat until fat is rendered, about 20 minutes. Transfer the cracklings to paper towels and drain. Cut the cracklings into strips. Cut the meat from duck, discarding bones. Cut the meat into strips. **(Can be prepared 1 day ahead. Cover and refrigerate duck and cracklings.)**

Preheat the oven to 350° F. Fold each crêpe in half. Place 1 cheese round in the center of one half of each folded crêpe. Fold each crêpe in half again, covering the cheese and forming a triangle. Place the crêpes on a baking sheet. Bake until the cheese melts and the crêpes are heated through, about 5 minutes.

Meanwhile, remove 8 endive spears and set aside. Chop the remaining endive. Place the chopped endive in a large bowl. Add the duck meat, greens, arugula and hearts of palm. Add enough vinaigrette to coat and toss well. Divide the salad among 4 plates. Garnish with endive spears. Top each salad with 2 crêpes. Sprinkle with the cracklings and nuts and serve.

WINE NOTES
This dish is somewhat of a challenge for a wine purist. There needs to be enough fruit to cope with the duck and goat cheese, enough acid to take care of the palate and just enough tannins to handle the duck's inherent fattiness. One idea is a lighter, more forward style of Pinot Noir.

An elegant and fruitier style of Loire Cabernet Franc is another consideration. Choose one from a riper vintage, so it has the fruit and mouth-feel to handle the duck and goat cheese, and at the same time has the needed tannin level. Consider a well-made Chinon from the 1990 vintage.

Duck Salad with Warm Goat Cheese and Chive Crêpes

BRAISED LAMB SHANKS
WITH BLACK BEAN TOMATO SAUCE
AND KULA CORN BREAD

4 servings

LAMB
4 large lamb shanks
2 tablespoons peanut oil
2 garlic cloves, smashed
All-purpose flour, for dredging
2 cups Chicken Stock (see recipe, page 128) or canned low-salt broth
2 cups Beef Stock (see recipe, page 128) or canned unsalted broth

SAUCE
1 tablespoon oriental sesame oil
½ small onion, chopped
1 large garlic clove, minced
1 tablespoon fermented black beans, rinsed and coarsely chopped
2 teaspoons Szechwan chili sauce
½ cup pale dry sherry
1 can (28 ounces) peeled Italian tomatoes
1 tablespoon oyster sauce

CORN BREAD
2 ears fresh corn
1 cup yellow cornmeal
½ cup all-purpose flour
1 tablespoon baking powder
½ teaspoon baking soda
½ teaspoon sugar
½ teaspoon salt
1 cup buttermilk
½ cup whole milk
¼ cup (½ stick) unsalted butter, melted
1 extra-large egg

For the lamb: Preheat the oven to 350° F. Season the lamb with salt and pepper. Heat the oil in a heavy, large Dutch oven over high heat. Add the garlic and cook until brown; discard the garlic. Dredge the lamb in the flour; shake off excess. Add the lamb to Dutch oven and brown well, turning occasionally. Drain off fat. Add both stocks to the lamb. Cover and transfer to oven. Bake the lamb until tender, about 1 hour and 45 minutes. Transfer the lamb shanks to a plate. Reserve the cooking liquid in the Dutch oven.

For the sauce: Heat the oil in a heavy, large skillet over medium heat. Add the onion and garlic and sauté until tender, about 5 minutes. Add the beans and chili sauce and stir 1 minute. Add the sherry and bring to a boil. Add the onion mixture to the cooking liquid in the Dutch oven. Add the tomatoes with their juices and oyster sauce and simmer until the sauce is reduced to 2½ cups, crushing the tomatoes with a spoon and stirring occasionally, about 2 hours. **(Can be prepared 2 days ahead.)**

For the corn bread: Preheat the oven to 400° F. Brush an 8-inch-diameter cast-iron skillet with vegetable oil. Place the skillet in the oven. Meanwhile, cut the corn from the cobs. Set aside enough corn to measure 1 cup. Mix the cornmeal, flour, baking powder, baking soda, sugar and salt in a large bowl. Whisk in buttermilk, whole milk, melted butter and egg. Mix in 1 cup corn. Using oven mitts, remove the skillet from oven. Pour the batter into the hot skillet. Bake until a tester inserted in the center comes out clean, about 30 minutes. Cool slightly.

Add the lamb to the sauce in the Dutch oven and simmer until the lamb is heated through. Cut corn bread into wedges. Place 1 corn bread wedge on each of 4 plates. Lean 1 lamb shank atop each corn bread wedge. Spoon sauce over lamb and serve.

WINE NOTES
Consider Grenache-based wines from California or France. Their ample ripe fruit seems to handle the salty, pungent, slight spice of Asian-influenced dishes and also possesses enough weight and finishing tannins to complement lamb.

It would also be fun to try a modern-style Italian wine with this dish, such as the Barberas from Moccagatta and Coppo, or simpler Sangioveses like Rosso di Montepulciano or Chianti. They have the ripe fruit and finishing tannins, but also possess the added dimension of higher acidity levels to wipe the palate clean.

Braised Lamb Shanks with Black Bean Tomato Sauce and Kula Corn Bread

PANIOLO RIBS
WITH HALIIMAILE BARBECUE SAUCE

I can unequivocally state that these are the best ribs I've ever tasted. When Beverly was growing up in Texas, Sunday night was rib night and her family would drive as much as forty-five minutes from their Dallas home in search of the tastiest ribs. Relying on memories of those Sunday suppers, Beverly spent weeks perfecting this recipe. Now Haliimaile patrons drive at least forty-five minutes to sample her *paniolo* (which means cowboy in Hawaiian) ribs.

Although this recipe is simple to make, the taste is wonderfully complex, due in part to the addition of fresh citrus. Beverly serves these ribs with mounds of mashed potatoes and pineapple chutney.

4 servings

> 1 *tablespoon butter or margarine*
> 1 *medium onion, chopped*
> ¼ *orange, with peel*
> ¼ *lemon, with peel*
> ¼ *lime, with peel*
> 1½ *cups ketchup*
> ¾ *cup bottled chili sauce*
> ¼ *cup cider vinegar*
> ¼ *cup firmly packed brown sugar*
> 2½ *tablespoons Dijon mustard*
> 2½ *tablespoons unsulphured molasses*
> 2½ *tablespoons Worcestershire sauce*
> ½ *teaspoon cayenne pepper*
> ½ *teaspoon liquid smoke*
> 4 *baby back rib racks (about 4 pounds total)*

Melt the butter in a heavy, 3-quart saucepan over medium heat. Add the onion and cook until tender, about 5 minutes. Squeeze the juice from the orange, lemon and lime into the onion mixture; add the peels. Add all of the remaining ingredients except the ribs and bring to a boil. Reduce the heat and simmer until thick, stirring occasionally, about 1 hour. Season to taste with salt and pepper. (**Sauce can be prepared 1 week ahead. Cover and refrigerate.**)

Preheat the oven to 400° F. Divide the ribs between 2 heavy, large roasting pans. Add enough water to the pans to cover the ribs. Cover the pans tightly with foil. Bake until ribs are tender, about 1 hour. Remove the ribs from water. Brush the ribs with sauce and let stand 1 hour at room temperature.

Prepare the barbecue (medium-high heat). Grill the ribs until brown and heated through, turning occasionally, about 7 minutes per side. Transfer the ribs to a cutting board. Cut between each rib to separate. Divide the ribs among 4 plates and serve.

WINE NOTES
This dish seems to ask for a big, strapping California Zinfandel, peppery and spicy with loads of concentrated fruit and good tannins to cleanse the palate. A peppery, mouth-filling Syrah from California, Australia or France's Rhône Valley would also be a hit.

PIÑA COLADA CHEESECAKE

Think of the tropical flavors of a piña colada blended with the creamy texture of cheesecake, and you've just imagined this soul-satisfying dessert. Since Haliimaile is located in the middle of pineapple fields, Beverly is lucky enough to be able to use fruit grown across the street.

If time is a problem, you can substitute 16 ounces of canned, unsweetened, crushed and drained pineapple for the fresh. Just omit the brown sugar and the pineapple cooking instructions. However, the flavor of fresh pineapple cannot be underestimated.

For a fancier presentation, spoon the whipped cream topping into a pastry bag fitted with a star tip and pipe decoratively over the cheesecake.

12 servings

CRUST
> 20 *whole graham crackers*
> ¾ *cup shredded unsweetened coconut*
> ¼ *cup sugar*
> ¾ *cup (1½ sticks) unsalted butter, melted*

FILLING
> 2 *cups peeled, coarsely chopped, fresh pineapple*
> 3 *tablespoons light brown sugar*
> 2½ *pounds cream cheese, at room temperature*
> 2 *cups sugar*
> 5 *extra-large eggs, room temperature*
> ½ *cup canned unsweetened coconut milk*

TOPPING
> 1 *cup chilled whipping cream*
> 2 *tablespoons canned cream of coconut (such as Coco Lopez)*
> 1 *teaspoon vanilla extract*
> ¼ *cup shredded unsweetened coconut, toasted*

For the crust: Finely grind the graham crackers in a food processor (you should have 3 cups of crumbs). Transfer to a bowl. Mix in the coconut and sugar. Add the melted butter and stir until combined. Press the crumb mixture on the bottom and up sides of 10-inch-diameter springform pan with 3-inch-high sides. Refrigerate for 15 minutes.

For the filling: Preheat the oven to 350° F. Cook the pineapple and the brown sugar in a heavy, medium, nonaluminum saucepan over medium heat until soft and syrupy, stirring occasionally, for about 10 minutes. Drain off any excess liquid and cool the pineapple.

Using an electric mixer, beat the cream cheese and sugar in a large bowl until well combined, stopping occasionally to scrape down the sides of the bowl. Add the eggs 1 at a time, beating just until combined. Beat in the coconut milk. Pour 2 cups of filling into the prepared crust. Carefully spoon pineapple over. Carefully spoon the remaining filling over the pineapple. Bake until the cheesecake no longer moves in center when the pan is shaken, about 1 hour and 15 minutes. Transfer the cheesecake to a rack and cool. Cover and refrigerate the cheesecake overnight.

For the topping: Beat whipping cream, cream of coconut and vanilla in a medium bowl until it forms stiff peaks.

Release the pan sides from the cheesecake. Transfer the cheesecake to a platter. Spread the topping over the cheese-cake. Sprinkle with toasted coconut. Slice the cheesecake and serve.

CHOCOLATE-MACADAMIA NUT TART

This tart tastes like a scrumptious candy bar in a flaky pastry crust. When creating this sweet treat, Beverly wanted to devise a dessert similar to her native Texas pecan pie but with a Hawaiian twist. If you can't find unsalted macadamia nuts, buy lightly salted ones and rinse and pat them dry with paper towels.

8 to 10 servings

CRUST
2 cups all-purpose flour
¼ cup unsweetened cocoa powder
¾ cup (1½ sticks) unsalted butter, cut into pieces,
*   room temperature*
½ cup sugar
2 extra-large egg yolks
1 tablespoon whipping cream
1 teaspoon vanilla extract
½ teaspoon salt

FILLING
1½ cups raw unsalted macadamia nuts
6 ounces bittersweet (not unsweetened) or semisweet
*   chocolate, chopped*
⅔ cup dark corn syrup
⅔ cup sugar
2 extra-large eggs
1 extra-large egg white
2 tablespoons (¼ stick) unsalted butter, melted
1 teaspoon dark rum
Whipped cream

For the crust: Mix the flour and cocoa in a large bowl. Make a well in the center. Add all of the remaining ingredients to the well and slowly mix them together. Incorporate the flour and cocoa into the well and continue blending until a soft dough forms. Gather the dough into a ball; flatten into a disk. Wrap in plastic and refrigerate at least 2 hours or overnight.

Preheat the oven to 425° F. Roll the dough out between sheets of waxed paper into a ¼-inch-thick round. Peel off the top sheet of waxed paper. Invert the dough and transfer it to an 11-inch-diameter tart pan with a removable bottom. Peel off the other sheet of waxed paper. Fit the dough into the pan; trim the edges (reserve remaining dough for another use). Freeze for 15 minutes. Line the dough with foil. Fill with dried beans or pie weights. Bake the crust 15 minutes. Remove the foil and weights. Continue baking until the crust is set, about 5 minutes more. Transfer the crust to a rack and cool. Using some of the remaining dough, carefully patch any cracks in the crust.

For the filling: Preheat the oven to 350° F. Spread the nuts out on a baking sheet. Bake until golden brown, about 15 minutes. Cool. Coarsely chop the nuts. Maintain the oven temperature.

Place the chocolate in a small metal bowl. Set the bowl over a saucepan of simmering water (or, place the chocolate in the top of a double boiler set over simmering water) and stir until the chocolate melts. Remove the bowl from over the water and cool slightly. Whisk the corn syrup, sugar, eggs and egg white in a large bowl to blend. Mix in the cooled chocolate, butter and rum. Mix in the toasted nuts. Pour the filling into the prepared tart shell. Bake until the filling is set and center no longer moves when the pan is shaken, about 35 minutes. Transfer tart to a rack and cool. Remove the pan sides from the tart. (**Can be prepared 1 day ahead. Cover and refrigerate.**) Transfer the tart to a platter. Cut into wedges. Serve cold, or at room temperature with whipped cream.

JEAN-MARIE JOSSELIN

Jean-Marie is one Frenchman who took to Hawaii the way foie gras takes to a canapé. Unlike many foreigners—or even mainland Americans—who transplant themselves to these tropical, melting-pot islands, Jean-Marie didn't blink twice at the vast cultural differences, the laid-back lifestyle or local dialect. Instead, he eased into his new home the way a hand fits into a soft kid glove. He embraced a cross-cultural cooking style, opened a couple of now packed restaurants and married a beautiful and talented Hawaiian. Small wonder that this chef is often spotted with a smile on his face.

It was natural that Jean-Marie become a chef. His family was crowded with good cooks, and those who didn't cook knew how to appreciate food and wine. "My grandfather was a farmer," Jean-Marie reminisces. "He was always bringing us chickens and vegetables. I used to go into the mountains to gather mushrooms. I remember those fresh flavors and use them as a guideline today."

At the age of fifteen, Jean-Marie attended culinary school in Paris, before cooking at Moët and Chandon winery for one and a half years. Jean-Marie then went to work at a hotel in Runjis, a town near Paris, before working at the Windsor Frantel hotel on Paris's famed Champs-Elysée. He then moved to Belgium to work at the Hilton International before deciding that there was more to the world than French cooking in Europe.

His life changed radically upon moving to the United States. He wound up in a hotel in New Orleans in 1982, cooking at a small French restaurant. "The food of New Orleans influenced me greatly," says Jean-Marie.

Grilled Lobster Salad with Spicy Greens and Cilantro Vinaigrette (See recipe, page 47)

Jean-Marie next took an executive chef position in a New Jersey hotel, where he was encouraged to create his own style of food. After one year, he received an offer to cook at Rosewood's new Crescent Court hotel. However, when he arrived in Dallas in 1984, the hotel wasn't ready to open, so he was sent to the Hotel Hana-Maui, a luxury resort in sleepy Hana, Maui, run by Rosewood at that time.

"Initially, I was in shock," he admits. "It was so isolated. I was given frozen and canned food to cook with; it was like being in a professional kitchen twenty-five years ago."

But after a brief period of adjustment, Jean-Marie threw himself into his work. He contacted and encouraged local farmers, eventually throwing out the freezers and cans. He developed stylish menus, blending his classic French techniques with Chinese, Thai and Japanese influences with a fluidity that belied his recent transplant status.

But Jean-Marie's sojourn in Hawaii was interrupted in eight months, as the Crescent Court hotel was ready to open. Jean-Marie flew to Dallas.

"I adapt to where I am," he says simply. "So I cooked with game, Southwestern spices and Texan fruit. But I missed Hawaii."

He was still missing Hawaii when he took an offer to cook at The Registry Hotel in Universal City, California. "Pacific Rim cooking snuck right back into my food," he admits. "The entire time I was in California, I wanted Hawaii. The colors, the smells—it's like nowhere else."

Finally he was able to return to Hawaii when he was offered a position in Kauai to cook at the historic Coco Palms resort. In 1990, he opened his own restaurant, A Pacific Café.

In the new wave of the developing Hawaii regional cooking, A Pacific Café hit like a tsunami, making a giant splash on the burgeoning dining scene. Jean-Marie's cuisine combines the bold, intense flavors that are the trademark of Pacific Rim cooking together with the smoothness and flair of superior French food.

Such savvy doesn't go unnoticed. Jean-Marie has won many awards, such as the Hawaii Seafood Championship in 1988 and 1989. He was also the grand prize winner of the National Seafood Challenge in 1989.

"I try to improve the quality of my cooking all the time," he says. "I'm never really satisfied with what I do. So I push it a little more each day, to try to stay at the edge."

One way he pushed himself was to write a cookbook; he is the author of the brisk-selling *Taste of Hawaii*. He has also just opened a new restaurant in Kihei, Maui, called Pacific Bar and Grill. At this new establishment, Jean-Marie takes his explorations an ocean further; he's added exotic Indian overtones to his food and often cooks with a tandoor.

"I like to think I was one of the first chefs who helped improve the quality of Hawaii's products," he says. "That's what Hawaii Regional Cuisine means to me." ∎

 SPICED HAWAIIAN FISH AND PRAWN SOUP

A soup this aromatic is a true treasure. The balance of flavors is idyllic; you can literally taste each ingredient—especially the chilies and cilantro—with each sip.

4 servings

1 teaspoon minced garlic
4 whole pink peppercorns, crushed
3 cups Crab Stock (see recipe, page 129)
1 piece lemongrass stalk, 6 inches long
6 kaffir lime leaves
2 teaspoons peeled, minced fresh ginger
8 large mussels, scrubbed and debearded
8 large raw prawns or 16 large shrimp
8 large sea scallops
6 ounces cleaned squid, cut into rings
4 ounces red snapper, cut into chunks
2 tablespoons fish sauce (nam pla)
2 tablespoons fresh lime juice
6 fresh cilantro sprigs
½ teaspoon (or more) minced red jalapeño or
  serrano chili

Using the back of a spoon, mash the garlic and peppercorns in a bowl. Bring 1½ cups of the stock to a boil in a heavy, large saucepan. Add the peppercorn-garlic mixture and simmer 3 minutes. Add the remaining 1½ cups stock, lemongrass, kaffir leaves and ginger. Add the mussels; cover and cook until the mussels open, about 5 minutes. Discard any mussels that do not open. Add the prawns, scallops, squid and snapper and simmer until the fish and shellfish are just cooked through, about 3 minutes. Mix the fish sauce, lime juice, cilantro and ½ teaspoon chili into the soup. Taste, adding more chili for a spicier flavor. Ladle the soup into bowls and serve.

WINE NOTES

An appropriate wine should be thirst quenching and refreshing enough to put out the fire and wipe the palate clean. Consider a California White Zinfandel, a German fruity-style white or an Italian simple, refreshingly fruity white wine such as Antinori's Galestro. A very cool ale or even porter-style beer sounds great.

CRAB AND WILD MUSHROOM RISOTTO

Jean-Marie makes this risotto with sea urchins at A Pacific Café, but crab is easier to obtain and tastes just as good. Although rice is constantly consumed in Hawaii, it's usually steamed or stir-fried, so when Jean-Marie first opened his restaurant, some of the local residents were surprised—quite pleasantly—to taste rice prepared this way.

6 servings

1 tablespoon unsalted butter
2 tablespoons extra-virgin olive oil
½ cup chopped onion
1 tablespoon minced garlic
½ cup diced carrot
2 cups arborio rice, uncooked
½ cup dry white wine
2 ounces fresh chanterelle mushrooms, sliced
2 ounces fresh shiitake mushrooms, stemmed and
* sliced*
5 cups Crab Stock (see recipe, page 129)
Reserved crabmeat from Crab Stock
1½ cups cooked fresh fava beans (optional)

Melt the butter with the oil in a heavy, large saucepan over medium heat. Add the onion and sauté until tender, about 5 minutes. Add the garlic and sauté 30 seconds. Add the carrot and sauté 1 minute. Mix in the rice. Add the wine and bring to a simmer, stirring constantly. Stir in all of the mushrooms. Add ½ cup of the crab stock and simmer until the rice has absorbed almost all of the liquid, stirring frequently, about 3 minutes. Repeat, adding the remaining stock by ½ cupfuls until the rice is tender but still firm to the bite, about 35 minutes. Season with salt and pepper. Add the reserved crabmeat and fava beans, and stir to heat through. Spoon risotto into shallow soup bowls and serve.

WINE NOTES
Any wine for this dish should have high levels of fresh fruit, good crisp acidity and moderate levels of alcohol. Consider wines such as Italy's San Quirico Vernaccia di San Gimignano, Australia's Coldridge Semillon/Chardonnay, California Sauvignon Blanc or even a dry rosé from southern France.

Another option is to go with a light, fruity red such as a Carignan/Grenache-based red from southern France or a fresh, easy-drinking example of Valpolicella from Italy.

 ## STEAMED KAUAI CLAMS WITH RED CURRY-BASIL BROTH

Jean-Marie likes to use clams from Palama Farm, a tiny farm some thirty minutes from A Pacific Café, which produces some of the freshest, sweetest clams in Hawaii. Although the broth is simple to make, its depth of flavor belies the ease of preparation.

4 servings

32 fresh clams, scrubbed
1 cup dry white wine
½ medium onion, chopped
2 teaspoons peeled, minced fresh ginger
1 teaspoon minced garlic
1½ cups canned unsweetened coconut milk
4 teaspoons red Thai curry paste
10 fresh basil leaves, julienned

Combine the first 5 ingredients in a large pot. Cover and boil until the clams open, about 8 minutes. Discard any clams that do not open. Using tongs, transfer the clams to 4 shallow soup plates. Add the coconut milk, red curry paste and basil to the clam cooking liquid and bring to a simmer. Ladle the broth over the clams and serve.

WINE NOTES
A Riesling from the Rheingau region of Germany—in the Kabinett style—is preferred for the fresh, sweet clams. You could go with a drier wine, but the red curry paste requires lower alcohol levels.

Try this dish with a light, crisp and refreshing California sparkling wine. Make sure the wine has an even, clean finish. Or try Bonny Doon's Clos de Gilroy. The red should have tons of fresh fruit, good acidity and low tannin and alcohol levels.

DEEP-FRIED SHRIMP LUMPIA
WITH CUCUMBER-MINT DIP

Lumpia are the Philippine rendition of egg or spring rolls. In Jean-Marie's version, the straight-from-the-fryer crispy *lumpia* are plunged into a cool and creamy yogurt dip.

4 servings

CUCUMBER-MINT DIP
½ small cucumber, peeled, seeded and diced
⅓ cup plain low-fat yogurt
6 fresh mint leaves
1 tablespoon fresh lemon juice
½ teaspoon minced garlic
½ teaspoon peeled, minced fresh ginger
Pinch of sugar

LUMPIA
2 tablespoons peanut oil
2 tablespoons minced garlic
2 tablespoons peeled, minced fresh ginger
1 cup mung bean sprouts
1 medium carrot, thinly sliced
½ onion, thinly sliced
½ zucchini, grated
½ medium yellow squash, grated
10 snow peas, strings removed, julienned
16 large peeled cooked shrimp, coarsely chopped
2 tablespoons soy sauce
2 tablespoons oyster sauce
½ teaspoon minced red jalapeño or serrano chili
8 lumpia *wrappers*
1 extra-large egg, lightly beaten (for glazing)
Peanut oil (for deep frying)

For the dip: Purée all of the ingredients in a blender. Pour the mixture into a bowl. **(Can be prepared 1 day ahead. Cover and refrigerate.)**

For the *lumpia*: Heat 2 tablespoons of oil in a wok over high heat. Add the garlic and ginger and stir-fry 15 seconds. Add all of the vegetables and stir-fry until crisp-tender, about 2 minutes. Add the shrimp, soy sauce, oyster sauce and minced chili and stir to combine. Transfer the mixture to a bowl and cool.

Place 1 *lumpia* wrapper on the work surface. Spoon ½ cup of the vegetable mixture on the bottom third of the *lumpia*. Roll 1 side of the wrapper over the filling. Tuck in the sides and continue rolling to enclose the filling completely. Brush the edges with an egg glaze to seal. Repeat with the remaining *lumpia* wrappers, filling and egg glaze.

Heat the oil in a deep fryer or heavy, large, deep saucepan to 375° F. Add the *lumpia* to the hot oil and cook until crisp and brown, about 3 minutes. Using tongs, transfer the *lumpia* to paper towels and drain. Divide the *lumpia* among plates. Serve with the dip.

WINE NOTES
I've tried this dish three separate times with three different wines that work well. Consider a fresh Sauvignon Blanc that has minimal, if any, oak aging, like Nautilus from New Zealand, Reverdy's Sancerre from the Loire Valley, France, or a fresh and fruity version from California.

German Riesling also works well. A well-made fruity style helps counter the ginger and chili peppers.

GRILLED LOBSTER SALAD WITH SPICY GREENS AND CILANTRO VINAIGRETTE

Spicy greens are balanced by the sweetness of the lobster in this sophisticated salad. The vinaigrette can be used in almost any recipe demanding an assertive dressing. For ease of preparation, ask your fishmonger to cut the lobsters in half for you.

4 servings

VINAIGRETTE
1/4 cup red wine vinegar
1 tablespoon peeled, minced fresh ginger
1 red jalapeño or serrano chili, seeded and chopped
1/2 teaspoon minced garlic
1/2 cup extra-virgin olive oil
1/2 cup minced fresh cilantro

LOBSTER
2 live lobsters, 1 1/4 pounds each, cut lengthwise in half
   (be sure to cook lobsters the same day they are
   halved)
1/4 cup olive oil
4 cups mixed baby greens
6 fresh basil leaves

For the vinaigrette: Purée the first 4 ingredients in a blender. Add oil slowly and blend until smooth. Add the cilantro and blend 10 seconds. **(Can be prepared 2 hours ahead. Cover and let stand at room temperature.)**

For the lobster: Prepare the barbecue (high heat). Season the lobsters with salt and pepper. Brush the lobsters with olive oil. Place the lobsters cut side down on the grill and cook 4 minutes. Turn and cook until the lobsters are cooked through, about 4 minutes more.

Toss the greens and basil in a large bowl with enough dressing to taste. Divide the greens among 4 plates. Top each with 1/2 a lobster. Spoon more vinaigrette over the lobster and serve.

WINE NOTES
You've got greens, the richness of lobster, a pinch of heat and a fairly assertive dressing to work with. California's Ca' del Solo makes a wine called Malvasia Bianco, which offers fresh, lively fruit to help cool the palate, and crisp, snappy acidity to counter the lobster's richness and to cleanse the palate.

Another option would be to select a wine with a little sweetness that's light and refreshing with good acidity. This covers white wines from Germany, White Zinfandel from California and even a French Vouvray. If choosing the latter, select at least a Demi-Sec with a lot of fresh fruit and preferably a moderate alcohol level to avoid conflict with the jalapeño chili and ginger.

WOK-SEARED SCALLOPS WITH CUCUMBER-CARROT SALAD AND PLUM WINE VINAIGRETTE

Serve these scallops as either a first course or a light entrée. The plum wine dressing adds an emphatic note to a mild dish.

4 servings

SALAD
1/2 cup plum wine
1/4 cup soy sauce
3 tablespoons oriental sesame oil
2 tablespoons sake
2 tablespoons rice wine vinegar
2 tablespoons peeled, minced fresh ginger
1 tablespoon minced garlic
2 cups peeled, grated carrots
2 cups peeled, seeded and grated cucumber
1 cup chopped fresh spinach
1/2 cup radish sprouts

SCALLOPS
1/4 cup olive oil
24 large sea scallops

For the salad: Mix the first 7 ingredients in a small bowl to blend. Toss the carrots, cucumber, spinach and sprouts in a large bowl with enough dressing to taste. Let stand 5 minutes.

For the scallops: Heat the oil in a wok or a heavy, large skillet over high heat. Add the scallops and stir-fry until seared and golden brown, about 2 minutes. Spoon the salad onto the center of 4 plates. Arrange the scallops around the salad and serve.

WINE NOTES
Since this dish has a little sweetness, a wine with a slight residual sugar content works best. Consider Gunderloch's fruity Kabinett (Germany), Babcock's 1992 Riesling (California), De Loach's White Zinfandel (California) or Felice Bonardi's light and zippy Asti Spumante (Italy).

Spiced Hawaiian Fish and Prawn Soup (See recipe, page 44)

STEAMED WHOLE ONAGA WITH LEMONGRASS AND CILANTRO BROTH

A spalike dish, this recipe emphasizes the natural good taste of Hawaiian red snapper. The fish is steamed with kaffir lime leaves (the aromatic leaves of a Southeast Asian fruit) and cilantro, and served in a delicate broth infused with lemongrass. Sea bass also works well in this recipe.

4 servings

5 *kaffir lime leaves*
2 *lemons, sliced*
3 *cilantro stems*
4 *onaga (red snapper) fillets with skin (8 ounces and 1½-inches thick each)*
2 *tablespoons (¼ stick) unsalted butter*
8 *fresh shiitake mushrooms, thinly sliced*
2½ *teaspoons peeled, minced fresh ginger*
2 *teaspoons minced garlic*
2 *cups Fish Stock (see recipe, page 128)*
4 *teaspoons fish sauce* (nam pla)
1 *lemongrass stalk, 12 inches long, thinly sliced*
¼ *cup chopped fresh cilantro*
¼ *cup* tobiko *(flying fish roe) (optional)*

Place the kaffir leaves, lemons and cilantro in the base of a steamer. Add enough water to come within 1 inch of the top of the steamer and bring to a boil. Arrange the fish in a single layer in the steamer. Season the fish with salt and pepper. Cover and steam the fish until cooked through, about 8 minutes. Divide the fish among 4 shallow soup bowls.

Meanwhile, melt the butter in a heavy, large saucepan over medium heat. Add the mushrooms and sauté until tender, about 4 minutes. Mix in the ginger and garlic. Add the stock, fish sauce and lemongrass and bring to a simmer. Add the cilantro and *tobiko*.

Ladle the broth over the fish and serve.

WINE NOTES

The profile of the wine that goes with this dish offers an abundance of fresh fruit; it's pure, youthful and alive, with crisp, refreshing acidity and a moderate alcohol level. Try Alsatian Pinot Blanc, French Vouvray, Spanish Albarino, various German whites, well-made Oregon Pinot Gris and simpler, fruitier styles of Italian whites. From California, consider Qupe's Marsanne 1992, Ca'del Solo's Malvasia Bianca and Arioso (under the Il Podere dell'Olivos label) from Jim Clendenen of Au Bon Climat. More traditional suggestions include not-so-oaky versions of California Pinot Blanc and Sauvignon Blanc.

STIR-FRIED CHICKEN SATAY WITH RICE NOODLES

I don't know what I like most about this dish—the garlicky-ginger chicken, the colorful, crunchy vegetables or the spicy peanut butter sauce. The latter is so good, you might want to also serve it with grilled chicken or fish, or lick it happily off a spoon.

4 servings

SAUCE
1½ *cups canned unsweetened coconut milk*
3 *tablespoons red Thai curry paste*
1 *teaspoon turmeric*
¼ *teaspoon curry powder*
½ *cup natural-style peanut butter*
⅓ *cup chopped roasted peanuts*
¼ *cup (or more) water*
12 *basil leaves, julienned*
NOODLES AND CHICKEN
1 *package (6 ounces) rice noodles* (mai fun)
4 *tablespoons peanut oil*
1 *tablespoon peeled, minced fresh ginger*
2 *teaspoons minced garlic*
1 *pound boneless skinless chicken breasts, diced*
1 *small carrot, julienned*
½ *cup snow peas, strings removed*
½ *cup sliced bok choy*

For the sauce: Bring the coconut milk to a simmer in a heavy, medium saucepan. Add the red curry paste, turmeric and curry powder and mix well. Whisk in the peanut butter, roasted peanuts, ¼ cup of water and the basil. Season to taste with salt. **(Can be prepared 1 day ahead. Cover and refrigerate. Bring to room temperature before using, thinning with more water if necessary.)**

For the noodles and chicken: Bring a large pot of water to a boil. Add the noodles and cook until just tender, about 1 minute. Drain; return the noodles to the pot. Add 1 tablespoon of oil and toss well. Heat the remaining 3 tablespoons of oil in a wok over high heat. Add the ginger and garlic and stir-fry 15 seconds. Add the chicken and stir-fry until almost cooked through, about 3 minutes. Add the carrot and stir-fry 1 minute. Add the snow peas and the bok choy and stir-fry 1 minute. Add 2 cups of sauce and cook to heat through. Mound the rice noodles on plates. Top with the chicken and sauce and serve.

WINE NOTES

With an abundance of Asian flavors, some spice and an array of textures, there's a lot going on in this dish. You need something a little sweet to soothe the palate and since chicken is the main ingredient, you'll want a wine with a little more richness. A German Riesling, preferably from one of the Rhine regions, is recommended.

Another option would be a simpler, slightly sweet style of American Gewurztraminer—something fruity and refreshing, with a lower alcohol level.

GRILLED MARINATED RACK OF LAMB WITH CABERNET-HOISIN SAUCE

The artful balance of East-West cooking may be most masterfully demonstrated by this dish. You can definitely taste the cabernet in the sauce, but the Asian ingredients get equal, harmonious time. Jean-Marie likes to cook the lamb over a wood-burning grill, but if it's winter and you crave these flavors, then roasting the lamb in the oven will more than do.

4 servings

SAUCE
2 cups cabernet wine
1/4 cup peeled, minced fresh ginger
1/4 cup chopped garlic
2 cups Chicken Stock (see recipe, page 128) or canned
    low-salt broth
2/3 cup hoisin sauce

LAMB
1/4 cup hoisin sauce
1/4 cup oyster sauce
2 tablespoons soy sauce
2 tablespoons dry white wine
1 1/2 teaspoons peeled, minced fresh ginger
1/2 teaspoon dried crushed red pepper
1/2 teaspoon minced garlic
2 racks of lamb, 1 1/4 pounds each, fat trimmed

For the sauce: Boil the wine, ginger and garlic in a heavy, medium saucepan until reduced to 1/2 cup, about 10 minutes. Add the stock and hoisin; boil until reduced to a sauce consistency, stirring occasionally, about 10 minutes. **(Can be prepared 1 day ahead. Cover and refrigerate. Bring to a simmer before using.)**

For the lamb: Mix all of the ingredients except the lamb in a glass baking dish. Add the lamb and turn to coat. Cover and refrigerate at least 4 hours and up to 12 hours.

Prepare the barbecue (medium heat). Remove the lamb from the marinade and grill to desired doneness, turning occasionally, about 12 minutes for medium-rare. Transfer the lamb to a cutting board. Cut between the bones to separate chops. Arrange the lamb chops on plates. Spoon the sauce over the chops and serve.

WINE NOTES
Grenache-based wines work well with this signature dish of Jean-Marie's; the ripe, almost sweet fruit marries well with the hoisin, despite cabernet being one of the ingredients. Bonny Doon's Le Cigare Volant from California is highly recommended.

For traditionalists, try a richer, riper California cabernet. More than one person has sworn that Silver Oak's Alexander Cabernet Sauvignon is this dish's definitive partner.

 ## ROASTED BANANA-RUM SOUFFLÉ WITH VANILLA CREAM SAUCE

This dessert really packs an intense banana flavor. Be sure to use very ripe fruit for optimum taste. These soufflés can be entirely prepared ahead and frozen, which makes them a great choice for entertaining. Bake directly from the freezer at 375° F, about 30 minutes.

6 servings

SAUCE
1 cup milk
1/2 vanilla bean, split lengthwise
4 extra-large egg yolks
1/4 cup sugar

SOUFFLÉ
1 large, very ripe banana (unpeeled)
2 1/4 cups whole milk
3 tablespoons dark rum
6 extra-large eggs, separated, at room temperature
1/3 cup sugar
3/4 cup unbleached all-purpose flour

For the sauce: Bring the milk and vanilla bean to a boil in a heavy, medium saucepan. Whisk the yolks and sugar in a medium bowl. Gradually whisk in the hot milk. Return the mixture to the saucepan and stir over medium-low heat until the custard thickens and coats the back of the spoon, about 5 minutes; do not boil. Strain into a bowl. Refrigerate until cold. **(Can be prepared 2 days ahead. Cover and keep refrigerated.)**

For the soufflés: Preheat the oven to 350° F. Place the banana on a cookie sheet and bake until the skin blackens, about 20 minutes. Cool the banana and peel (banana will be very soft). Bring the milk to a boil in a heavy, medium saucepan. Remove from heat. Add the banana and rum and whisk until combined. Using an electric mixer, beat the yolks and sugar in a medium bowl for 3 minutes. Beat in the flour. Whisk the milk mixture into the yolk mixture. Return the mixture to the saucepan and bring to a boil, whisking constantly. Pour the soufflé base into a bowl and cool completely.

Preheat the oven to 375° F. Butter and sugar the bottoms and sides of six 3/4-cup soufflé cups. Using an electric mixer, beat the whites in a large bowl to form stiff peaks. Fold the whites into the soufflé base (mixture will deflate). Divide the soufflé mixture among the prepared soufflé cups. Bake until the soufflés puff and are softly set, about 20 minutes. Transfer the soufflés to plates. Poke holes in the soufflés and ladle approximately 4 tablespoons of sauce into each soufflé. Serve immediately.

GEORGE MAVROTHALASSITIS

I n a "house befitting heaven," small wonder that George Mavrothalassitis creates a taste of heaven at each Le Mer meal. This energetic Frenchman doubles as both executive chef of Halekulani Hotel and chef of its signature La Mer dining room.

Halekulani, which translates from Hawaiian to "house befitting heaven," is perched on the shore of famed Waikiki Beach and is acclaimed as one of Hawaii's most illustrious hotels. Few would dispute that an integral component of the hotel's justifiable success is what comes out of this chef's kitchen.

What's coming out is so good in part because of what George puts into it. This chef is so dedicated to cooking with premium-quality fish that he actually receives three fresh seafood shipments each day.

"At seven A.M., all the large fish comes in," explains George with his thick French accent. "We start butchering the tuna, marlin and *ono*. Around eleven A.M., the bottom fish such as *onaga* and *opakapaka* arrive. And by three P.M., we receive fish like *kumu* and *monchong* for La Mer."

When George talks about his fortuity to work with such high-quality ingredients, he can't help but think of his fellow chefs on the mainland. "Many can only purchase ingredients by telephone. I can go to the Honolulu fish auction and Chinatown and deal with the fishermen and farmers, not just the distributors," he says.

Supplemented by tomatoes, potatoes and onions from Maui, chicken and shrimp from Oahu and mushrooms and herbs from Molokai, George has devised his own distinguishing style of Hawaii Regional Cuisine.

"A chef must work from local markets," he explains. "In California, I did California cooking. In Colorado, I cooked Colorado food. But just because I now work in Hawaii, my food shouldn't be labeled Pacific Rim. I have too much respect for Asian cuisines like Thai and Chinese to play around with them."

"My definition of Hawaii Regional Cuisine is to cook the food of Hawaii from the foods in the Hawaiian markets in a contemporary fashion," continues George. "Of course I'm influenced by French cooking, because it's in my blood," he says, thumping his heart emphatically.

"I don't take a recipe like sole Véronique, substitute *opakapaka* for the sole and think it's a new cooking style," says George. "I just like to incorporate interesting flavors, like tamarind, star anise, lemongrass and ginger into my cuisine. I always did, even in France."

George's dishes are the epitome of elegance and restraint, possessing an enormous depth of flavor with minimum ingredients. Always beautifully composed but never overdone, his food tantalizes the eye yet still tastes clean on the palate.

Talk to George about cooking and his eyes begin to sparkle, his hands wave circles through the air and his speech grows animated. This is one chef who truly comes alive at the mere mention of food.

George, who was born and raised in Marseilles with a Greek father and an Austrian mother, decided to become a chef when he was sixteen years old. What hooked him was when he first prepared a meal from a cookbook for relatives in the Provençal countryside. "I discovered I could make people happy by cooking," exclaims George. "That was enough for me."

Unfortunately, it wasn't enough for his father, who insisted that George follow in his footsteps and become a mechanical engineer. George became a highly successful engineer, but he wasn't a happy man.

"I used to dream about cooking," says George. "I almost became obsessed."

Pistou Salad of Waimanalo Rabbit (See recipe, page 54)

At the age of twenty-eight, he decided to pursue his long-time dream. He attended a Marseilles culinary academy and then became an apprentice at Les Trois Marches, a three-star Michelin restaurant in Versailles. He went on to apprentice at two other equally acclaimed restaurants—L'Archestrate in Paris and Restaurant Troisgros in Roanne—before opening his own establishment, La Presqu'ile, in Cassis in 1977. In short order, George's restaurant received a slew of culinary kudos.

George opened one more dining establishment, the popular Restaurant Mavro, in 1983. But in 1985, he flew to Los Angeles for a vacation and never went back. He became a consultant for the tony Regency Club before cooking at the famed L'Orangerie restaurant and its charming sibling, Pastel. George moved to Denver to become executive chef for an exclusive French restaurant before he received the offer to head the kitchen of Halekulani in 1988.

"I'm so lucky to be here," admits George. "I don't know if Hawaii is a good place to vacation, but it sure is a wonderful place to live and an even better place to cook." ∎

53

PISTOU SALAD OF WAIMANALO RABBIT

The tender Waimanalo rabbit is farm-raised on Oahu. This earthy salad does the high-quality meat justice; the rabbit is sautéed and presented with greens, soldier beans, fava beans and zucchini. The robust vinaigrette holds its own, with bacon and cayenne to lend zest. If you like, you can substitute boneless chicken breasts for the rabbit loins, but cook the chicken until done, rather than medium-rare.

4 servings

VEGETABLES
½ pound dry soldier beans or cannelini beans
1 medium zucchini, diced
½ cup fresh fava beans
DRESSING
¼ cup extra-virgin olive oil
2 bacon slices, cooked and crumbled
3 tablespoons fresh lemon juice
2 tablespoons chopped fresh basil
2 large garlic cloves, minced
1 teaspoon cracked coriander seeds
1 teaspoon chopped shallot
Cayenne pepper
RABBIT
2 tablespoons olive oil
2 rabbit loins, 6 ounces each
2 fresh basil sprigs
4 garlic cloves
8 sprigs mâche lettuce leaves
1 tomato, peeled, seeded and chopped
½ Maui onion or other sweet onion, diced
2 tablespoons chopped green onion

For the vegetables: Place the soldier beans in a saucepan. Add enough cold water to cover by 3 inches and soak overnight. Drain. Return the beans to the saucepan. Add enough cold water to cover the beans. Season with salt and bring to a boil. Reduce heat and simmer until the beans are just tender, about 20 minutes. Drain.

Cook the zucchini in a large saucepan of boiling, salted water, about 1 minute. Using a slotted spoon, transfer the zucchini to a bowl of ice water and cool. Drain. Return the water in the saucepan to a boil. Add the fava beans and cook until tender, about 10 minutes. Drain and cool. Remove the skins. **(Can be prepared 1 day ahead. Cover and refrigerate. Bring to room temperature before using.)**

For the dressing: Mix the oil, bacon, lemon juice, basil, garlic, coriander and shallot in a bowl. Season to taste with cayenne. Set aside.

For the rabbit: Heat the oil in a heavy, large skillet over medium heat. Add the rabbit, basil and garlic and cook until the rabbit is medium-rare to medium, turning occasionally, about 12 minutes. Season the rabbit with salt and pepper. Transfer the rabbit to a plate; cool.

Toss the mâche with enough dressing to coat. Place all of the beans, zucchini, tomato and both onions in a large bowl. Add enough dressing to coat and toss well. Arrange the vegetable mixture in center of plates. Slice the rabbit and arrange atop the vegetables. Garnish with the mâche and serve.

WINE NOTES
Pinot Noir immediately comes to mind. Choose one with an abundance of ripe, berrylike fruit and with a good, firm backbone, whether from France or California. Since rabbit isn't a red meat, you don't need a powerful, full-throttled red. You do need firm acidity to counter the salad.

Other wines to consider include Sangiovese-based reds from Italy such as Chianti or Vino Nobile di Montepulciano, youthful Spanish Rioja or even tempered reds of Carignan, Mourvedre or Grenache from southern France.

 SALAD OF CHARBROILED MARINATED LANAI AXIS VENISON WITH POHA BERRIES, WATERCRESS AND WARABI

Possessing a delicate, subtle gamey taste, Lanai axis venison may well be the best quality in the country. The accompanying slightly sweet, slightly spicy salad includes *warabi*, the Japanese name commonly used in Hawaii for fern shoots, which are the coiled new fronds of ferns. You can substitute *haricots verts*.

Fresh mainland gooseberries can replace the Hawaiian *poha*, a tart golden berry. If fresh gooseberries are unavailable in your area, forego the poaching process in sugar syrup and simply use drained canned gooseberries.

4 appetizer servings or 2 main-course servings

POACHED BERRIES
¼ cup sugar
¼ cup water
2 tablespoons fresh husked poha *berries or gooseberries*

VENISON

2 tablespoons soy sauce
2 tablespoons peeled, chopped fresh ginger
1 tablespoon oriental sesame oil
1 tablespoon vegetable oil
3 large garlic cloves, smashed
2 bay leaves
1 teaspoon brown sugar
1 red jalapeño or serrano chili, finely chopped
6 ounces venison loin medallions

SALAD

2 tablespoons extra-virgin olive oil
1 tablespoon fresh lemon juice
1 garlic clove, minced
Cayenne pepper
2 cups watercress
2 cups fern shoots or haricots verts (green beans), blanched

For the berries: Bring the sugar and water to a simmer in a heavy, small saucepan, stirring until sugar dissolves. Add the berries and simmer about 30 seconds. Pour the mixture into a small bowl and cool. **(Can be prepared 1 day ahead. Cover and refrigerate.)**

For the venison: Mix all of the ingredients except the venison in a large bowl. Add the venison and turn to coat. Cover and refrigerate 3 hours. Preheat the broiler. Remove the venison from the marinade and pat it dry. Broil about 4 minutes per side for medium-rare. Transfer to a cutting board and let stand 5 minutes.

For the salad: Whisk the oil, lemon juice and garlic in a large bowl. Season to taste with cayenne pepper and salt. Add the watercress and fern shoots and toss to coat.

Slice the venison into 1/4-inch-thick rounds. Fan the venison in the center of the plates. Drain the *poha* berries and spoon into the center. Surround with the salad and serve.

WINE NOTES

Since this dish possesses sweet and salty notes with a little heat, youthful, light Grenache-based red wines, more elegant versions of California Merlots or even some Australian reds such as Cassegrain's Chambourcin are recommended. Whichever wine you choose, it should be ripe, almost sweet and have just enough depth to handle the greens and the warabi.

SHUTOME WITH WATERCRESS CRUST AND GINGER CARROTS

Shutome, or Hawaiian swordfish, is treated to a watercress crust and colorfully garnished with gingered carrots and sautéed leeks. George gets his watercress from a friend's farm, and he's enamored with how its peppery taste enhances a simple fish dish.

4 servings

CARROTS AND LEEKS

2 cups water
5 tablespoons unsalted butter
1 tablespoon sugar
2 teaspoons peeled, minced fresh ginger
8 small carrots, peeled and cut into 1/4-inch-thick slices
2 leeks (white and pale green parts only), julienned
2 teaspoons butter

SHUTOME

2 cups firmly packed watercress leaves (about 2 bunches)
2 extra-large egg whites
6 tablespoons olive oil
4 shutome or swordfish steaks, 7 ounces and 1 inch thick each

For the carrots and leeks: Bring the first 4 ingredients to a simmer in a heavy, large saucepan. Add the carrots and cover and simmer until the carrots are very tender, about 20 minutes. Season with salt and pepper. Set aside.

Cook the leeks in a saucepan of boiling water until tender, about 2 minutes. Drain. Return the leeks to the saucepan. Add the butter and stir over medium heat until melted. Season with salt and pepper. Set aside.

For the shutome: Preheat the oven to 350° F. Blanch the watercress in a saucepan of boiling water for 1 minute. Drain and cool. Squeeze dry. Transfer the watercress to a food processor. Add the egg whites and 4 tablespoons of oil and purée. Set the purée aside.

Heat the remaining 2 tablespoons of oil in a heavy, large skillet over medium-high heat. Add the *shutome* and cook 1 1/2 minutes per side. Transfer the fish to a baking sheet. Spoon the watercress purée over the fish. Bake until the fish is cooked through, about 5 minutes.

Rewarm the leeks and carrots. Divide the leeks among plates. Place the fish atop the leeks. Surround with carrots and serve.

WINE NOTES

Since shutome *is a juicy fish, the wine paired with this dish should have a lot of fruit and mouth-feel. Look to wines such as California Chardonnay (not too oaky), Australian Semillon (again, not too oaky), Viognier from California or France and Grand Cru Alsatian Riesling or Pinot Gris from a ripe year.*

Red wine with high fruit and acid levels and lower tannins also works well. Consider California Pinot Noir, Cabernet Franc from the Loire Valley, France, or even a not-too-oaky German Spatburgunder.

BOUILLABAISSE OF HAWAIIAN FISH

George was born in Marseilles, France, and his motto is if there's no *rascasse* (scorpion fish), there's no bouillabaisse. When he discovered *nohu*, or Hawaiian rock cod, at the Honolulu fish auction, he was ecstatic, as it is most similar to the prized French *rascasse*. Then he ran for his stockpot.

Ask your fishmonger to fillet the fish, leaving the skin on. Be sure to reserve all of the trimmings, bones, heads and tails as you will need these to make the fish broth. If concerned about the raw yolks used in the *aioli*, substitute ²/₃ cup purchased mayonnaise for the yolks and oil and blend it with the garlic and lemon juice listed below.

8 servings

AIOLI
2 garlic cloves
2 extra-large egg yolks
2 teaspoons fresh lemon juice
²/₃ cup olive oil
Salt
Cayenne pepper
BOUILLABAISSE
2 whole nohu *(Hawaiian rock cod) (about 7 pounds total), heads and tails removed, filleted and cut into 3-inch pieces*
1 small whole hapu'upu'u *(Hawaiian grouper) (about 3 pounds), head and tail removed, filleted and cut into 3-inch pieces*
7 tablespoons olive oil
³/₄ teaspoon powdered saffron
5 quarts water
8 tomatoes, peeled, seeded and chopped
2 leeks, sliced
2 onions, thinly sliced
¹/₂ cup fresh parsley sprigs
¹/₂ cup fresh thyme sprigs
12 garlic cloves
¹/₈ teaspoon cayenne pepper
4 russet potatoes, peeled, cut into ³/₄-inch pieces
4 raw slipper or other lobster tails with shell, each cut crosswise into 3 pieces
1 French bread baguette, sliced and toasted

For the *aioli*: Blend the garlic, yolks and lemon juice in a blender until smooth. Add the oil drop by drop until the mixture thickens. Season with salt and cayenne. (**Can be prepared 1 day ahead. Cover and keep refrigerated.**)

For the bouillabaisse: Place the fish fillets in a large bowl. Add 4 tablespoons of oil and ¹/₄ teaspoon saffron and toss to coat. Cover and refrigerate 4 hours.

Heat the remaining 3 tablespoons of oil in a heavy, large pot over high heat. Add the fish heads, tails, bones and any scraps and sauté 5 minutes. Add the water, tomatoes, leeks, onions, herbs, garlic, cayenne pepper and remaining ¹/₂ teaspoon of saffron and bring to a boil. Reduce the heat and simmer 1 hour.

Strain the broth into a heavy, large pot. Bring the broth to a boil. Add the potatoes and cook until almost tender, about 10 minutes. Add the fish and lobster and simmer until the fish is cooked through, about 5 minutes. Ladle the soup into shallow soup bowls. Top with toasted baguette slices and *aioli* and serve.

WINE NOTES
With this flavorful, complex dish, classic pairings such as Clos St. Magdeleine's Cassis or a Tempier Bandol rosé (both from Provence) work best. Both are magical with seafood and can handle the tomatoes and saffron.

Bouillabaisse of Hawaiian Fish

HAWAIIAN SEAFOOD RISOTTO
IN TARO CUPS

This unctuous risotto reflects the briny essence of the ocean with the addition of seaweed, *tako* (octopus) and mussels.

Tako can be purchased at a sushi bar. If you're running short on time, serve the risotto in shallow soup bowls and forgo making the taro cups—but they do create a dazzling presentation.

4 servings

TARO CUPS
4 cups vegetable oil (for deep frying)
1 large taro root or russet potato, peeled, cut into
  ⅛-inch-thick slices

RISOTTO
1 cup water
5 fresh mussels, scrubbed and debearded
3 cups Chicken Stock (see recipe, page 128) or canned
  low-salt broth
¼ teaspoon powdered saffron
1 tablespoon extra-virgin olive oil
1 small Maui onion or other sweet onion, finely
  chopped
1 cup arborio rice, uncooked
¼ cup (½ stick) unsalted butter
1 cup shelled fresh peas or frozen, thawed
5 uncooked prawns or large shrimp, peeled and
  deveined
¼ pound tako (blanched octopus), sliced
¼ pound ogo (Hawaiian seaweed), finely chopped
2 tomatoes, peeled, seeded and diced
2 tablespoons chopped fresh basil

For the taro cups: Heat the oil in a deep fryer or a heavy, medium saucepan to 350° F. Overlap 4 taro slices in a small metal basket. Press another small metal basket over the taro slices to secure. Lower the basket into the oil and cook until the taro cups are golden brown, about 3 minutes. Lift the baskets from the oil. Remove the top basket. Remove the taro cup. Repeat with the remaining taro slices, forming a total of 4 baskets. (**Can be prepared 1 hour ahead. Cover and let stand at room temperature.**)

For the risotto: Bring the water to a boil in a heavy, medium saucepan. Add the mussels and cover and cook until the mussels open, about 6 minutes; discard any mussels that do not open. Strain the mussel cooking liquid into a heavy, medium saucepan. Remove the mussels from their shells and set aside. Discard the shells. Add the stock and saffron to the mussel-cooking liquid in the pan and bring to a boil. Reduce the heat so the liquid barely simmers.

Heat the oil in a heavy, large saucepan over medium heat. Add the onion and sauté until golden brown, about 10 minutes. Add the rice and cook 1 minute. Mix in ½ cup of the stock mixture and stir until almost all of the liquid is absorbed, about 3 minutes. Continue adding all but ⅔ cup of the remaining stock ½ cup at a time, stirring frequently until the rice is creamy and tender, about 35 minutes. Mix in the butter.

Meanwhile, heat the remaining ⅔ cup of stock in a heavy, large skillet over medium-high heat. Add the peas and cook 1 minute. Add the prawns, *tako, ogo,* tomatoes and basil to the stock mixture in a skillet and cook until the shrimp turn pink and the peas are tender, turning the shrimp occasionally, about 4 minutes.

Mix the shrimp mixture and the mussels into the risotto. Spoon the risotto into the taro cups and serve.

WINE NOTES
Consider dry rosés from southern France, such as Fontsainte's Corbières Gris de Gris or Domaine Ott's rosé—they're firm, flavorful and delicious.

Italian options include a well-made Verdicchio and a Tocai from Friuli. These wines are commonly served with seafood risottos because of their crisp, complementary acidity and their innate, subtle presence, especially toward the finish.

BAKED ONAGA IN ROCK SALT CRUST

Onaga, Hawaiian red snapper, gets treated to a princely presentation that only a fish this prized deserves. Deboned and stuffed with sautéed spinach, the snapper is encased in dough in the shape of a fish and then baked until golden. When the crust is cut open, the fish is so moist, the pleasure of eating it is almost indescribable. Substitute mainland red snapper, if necessary.

2 servings
ROCK SALT CRUST
3½ cups all-purpose flour
⅔ cup rock salt
5 tablespoons egg white
¾ cup plus 2 tablespoons (about) water
ONAGA
3 tablespoons butter
1 package (10 ounces) fresh spinach leaves
3 garlic cloves, finely chopped
1 whole onaga (about 2 pounds)
SAUCE
6 tablespoons olive oil
2 shallots, finely chopped
3 garlic cloves, finely chopped
½ cup dry white wine
1 tomato, peeled, seeded and diced
2 tablespoons finely chopped green onion
1 teaspoon chopped fresh tarragon
1 teaspoon chopped fresh chervil
1 teaspoon chopped fresh chives

For the rock salt crust: Mix the first 3 ingredients in a large bowl. Gradually mix in enough water to form a stiff dough. Wrap in plastic and let it stand at room temperature until ready to use.

For the *onaga*: Preheat the oven to 375° F. Melt the butter in a heavy, large skillet over medium-high heat. Add the spinach and garlic and sauté until the spinach wilts, about 3 minutes. Season with salt and pepper. Cool.

Debone the *onaga*, leaving the head and tail intact; do not remove the skin. Spoon the spinach mixture inside the fish. Roll out the rock salt dough on a work surface until it is large enough to wrap around the fish. Wrap the dough around the fish, shaping it to resemble the fish. Place the fish on a baking sheet. Bake until the fish is cooked through, about 40 minutes.

Meanwhile, prepare the sauce while the fish cooks: Heat 3 tablespoons of oil in a heavy, medium saucepan over medium heat. Add the shallots and sauté 2 minutes; do not allow the shallots to brown. Add the garlic, then the wine and simmer until reduced by half, about 3 minutes. Mix in the tomato, green onion and herbs. Mix in the remaining 3 tablespoons of oil. Season with salt and pepper.

Transfer the fish to a platter. Cut the top of the crust lengthwise and remove (do not allow the salt crust to fall into the fish). Remove the fish skin. Cut the fish and divide between plates. Spoon the spinach atop the fish. Spoon the sauce around the fish and serve.

WINE NOTES
This dish would go with hearty styles of southern French or Italian rosés. The rosé selected should have ample fruit and staunch, firm structure.

Red wine could also work. Consider well-made Cabernet Franc like Chinon from the Loire Valley, France, lighter-style Italian Sangiovese, such as Rosso di Montepulciano or even ripe, juicy California Pinot Noir. If selecting a red wine, choose one with a lower tannin level.

PAPILLOTE OF KUMU WITH BASIL, SEAWEED AND SHIITAKE MUSHROOMS

When George first began working at the Halekulani Hotel in 1988 as chef of the signature dining room La Mer, he encountered *kumu* and it was love at first sight. This reddish-skinned member of the goatfish family provides moist, delicate white meat, although you can substitute any tender snapper.

George was determined to protect the *kumu* from the aggressive heat of the cooking process, so he decided to bake it in parchment paper. His first HRC dish, the Papillote of Kumu is wildly popular and remains on La Mer's menu.

4 servings

> 5 *tablespoons olive oil*
> 1 *cup very thinly sliced Maui onion or other sweet onion*
> 2 *ounces fresh shiitake mushrooms, stemmed and thinly sliced*
> 4 *large sheets parchment paper*
> 1½ *pounds kumu fillets or red snapper with skin (about ¾-inch thick), cut into 1-inch pieces*
> 1 *cup ogo (Hawaiian seaweed)*
> 12 *fresh basil leaves, julienned*
> ¼ *cup dry white wine*
> 4 *teaspoons fresh lemon juice*

Preheat the oven to 450° F.

Heat 1 tablespoon of oil in a heavy, large skillet over medium heat. Add the onion and mushrooms and sauté until tender, about 10 minutes. Cool.

Fold 1 large square of parchment paper in half. Cut out a large half heart so that when the paper is opened, the paper resembles a whole heart. Repeat with the remaining parchment squares to form 4 hearts.

Open up all of the parchment hearts on the work surface. Place ¼ of the fish on one half of each parchment heart. Sprinkle the fish with the onion-mushroom mixture, *ogo* and basil, dividing evenly. Spoon the remaining 4 tablespoons of oil, wine and lemon juice over the fish, dividing evenly.

Fold the opposite side of the heart over to cover the fish. Fold the top and bottom edges of the parchment together, crimping to seal the fish completely. Arrange the packets on a baking sheet.

Bake the packets until the fish is cooked through, about 10 minutes. Transfer the packets to plates. Using scissors, cut an opening in the parchment and serve.

WINE NOTES

A wide range of dry whites and rosés from southern France and Italy work with this dish. The wine needs to have a lot of flavor and texture, yet minimal—if any—oak to avoid clashing with the seaweed and overpowering the fish. Clos Nicrosi, a dry white wine from Corsica, works well.

As this is a flavorful and richly textured dish, the most intriguing match-up may be Charles Joguet's Chinon Varennes du Grand Clos, as recommended by the Halekulani Hotel's cellarmaster, Randy Ching. This wine possesses ample, rich, juicy fruit with enough acidity to complement the fish and softer, moderate tannins in the finish.

HAWAIIAN SEAFOOD PLATE IN TAMARIND NAGE

It's rare to taste tamarind and tarragon in the same dish, yet once you sample their pairing in this recipe, you'll be tempted to experiment with the duo yourself. Although this entrée is almost spalike in its ingredients, its flavor is too rich to taste low-fat. The addition of fresh vegetables makes it a complete, memorable meal.

4 servings

> 1 *artichoke, leaves and choke removed, heart quartered*
> 8 *fresh asparagus stalks, trimmed and cut in half*
> ¼ *cup shelled fresh peas*
> 2 *cups fresh or bottled clam juice*
> 1 *cup dry white wine*
> 3 *tablespoons tamarind paste*
> 2 *moana fillets (red mullet) with skin, 2 ounces each*
> 4 *nohu (rock cod) medallions with skin, 1 ounce each*
> 4 *mahimahi medallions, skinned, 1 ounce each*
> 4 *raw Kahuku prawns (farm-raised, freshwater) or large shrimp, peeled and deveined*
> 2 *tablespoons chopped fresh tarragon leaves*
> 1 *tablespoon lime juice*
> ¼ *cup extra-virgin olive oil*

Bring a large saucepan of water to a boil. Add the artichoke heart and cook until almost tender, about 5 minutes. Add the asparagus and peas and cook until the vegetables are tender, about 2 minutes. Drain the vegetables and set aside.

Bring the clam juice, wine and tamarind to a boil in a heavy, small saucepan. Continue boiling 3 minutes. Remove the pan from the heat and let stand 5 minutes to allow the tamarind to settle to the bottom. Pour the liquid from the saucepan into a heavy, large skillet, leaving any tamarind pieces behind in the pan. Add all of the fish and prawns to the liquid in the skillet and simmer until the fish is cooked through, about 8 minutes. Add the vegetables and tarragon and stir to heat through. Mix in the lime juice. Season with salt and pepper.

Drain the shellfish and vegetables, reserving the cooking liquid. Divide the shellfish and vegetables among 4 shallow soup bowls. Return the cooking liquid to the skillet. Add the oil and stir until heated through. Spoon the cooking liquid over the fish and vegetables and serve.

WINE NOTES
Have fun with this dish with a bottle of Giacosa's Arneis or Carretta's Bianco del Poggio (both from Piedmont, Italy). Another option is to try Cauhape's Jurancon Sec "Vielles Vignes" from southwestern France or Ca'del Solo's Il Pescatore from California. These white wines possess fresh, distinctive fruit and are lean and lemony in structure. With seafood, they act as a squeezed lemon would—cutting through the fishy/oily properties and cleansing the palate between bites.

Or, choose a dry, well-made French rosé from Provence or Joguet's Chinon Rosé from the Loire Valley.

SAUTÉED ONO COATED WITH CUMIN AND ROSEMARY IN CURRY SAUCE

Ono, or *wahoo,* is a close relative of the king mackerel. Most abundant in Hawaii from summer to fall, *ono* is a dense, white-meat fish with a low fat content. Swordfish is a good substitute.

For this dish, the cumin adds crunch, the curry contributes flavor and the coconut milk provides richness. The Western flavors of rosemary and olive oil create a surprisingly harmonious marriage with an Indian-inspired curry.

6 servings
SAUCE
2 tablespoons olive oil
1 onion, chopped
3 tablespoons curry powder (preferably Madras)
3 garlic cloves, finely chopped
2 tart green apples, peeled, seeded and chopped
2 cups (or more) Chicken Stock (see recipe, page 128) or canned low-salt broth
1/2 cup canned unsweetened coconut milk
VEGETABLES AND FISH
6 small carrots, peeled and julienned
6 teaspoons cumin seed
6 small fresh rosemary sprigs
6 ono or swordfish steaks, 6 ounces and 1 1/2 inches thick each
7 tablespoons olive oil
6 small zucchini, julienned

For the sauce: Heat the oil in a heavy, large saucepan over medium heat. Add the onion and sauté until tender, about 8 minutes. Add the curry and garlic and sauté 1 minute. Add the apples and 2 cups of stock and simmer until the liquid is reduced by half, about 15 minutes. Add the coconut milk, cover and simmer 20 minutes. Strain the sauce into a bowl. Stir in more stock if it seems too thick. Season to taste with salt and pepper. (**Can be prepared 1 day ahead. Cover and refrigerate.**)

For the vegetables and fish: Blanch the carrots in a large pot of boiling salted water 1 minute. Drain. Transfer the carrots to a bowl of ice water and cool. Drain.

Sprinkle 1/2 teaspoon of cumin on each side of each fish fillet. Place rosemary sprigs on one side of each fish fillet; press into the fish. Heat 4 tablespoons of oil in a heavy, large skillet over medium-high heat. Add the fish and sauté until the fish is cooked through, about 3 minutes per side.

Meanwhile, heat the remaining 3 tablespoons of oil in another heavy, large skillet over high heat. Add the carrots and zucchini and sauté until crisp-tender, about 2 minutes.

Divide the vegetables among 6 plates. Top the vegetables with the fish; discard the rosemary. Bring the sauce to a simmer; spoon around the fish and serve.

WINE NOTES
Since George prefers Madras curry, this dish is significantly milder than most other Indian curries. A German Gewurztraminer Kabinett or a Rheingau Kabinett from a ripe vintage are two good options. Both possess a slight sweetness to cool the palate and a slight spiciness to make things interesting.

Or, look at rich, full-flavored Alsatian Pinot Blanc, which has moderate alcohol levels, or even a simple, slightly sweet version of Gaillac from southwest France.

WARM PINEAPPLE TART
WITH PINEAPPLE-COCONUT SAUCE

Despite the stylish sophistication of this dessert, it stays true to the purity of its simple island flavors. The pineapple is first browned in a skillet before it's broiled in the tart, resulting in a satisfying intensity of flavor.

4 servings

SAUCE
1/4 cup sugar
4 extra-large egg yolks
1/2 cup canned unsweetened coconut milk
1/2 cup peeled, cored and puréed pineapple
1 tablespoon dark rum

TART
1 package (17 1/4 ounces) frozen puff pastry (2 sheets),
*   thawed*
2 tablespoons powdered sugar
1 extra-large egg yolk
1 1/2 medium pineapples, peeled, quartered, cored and
*   cut into 1 1/2-inch-long, 1/4-inch-thick wedges*
4 tablespoons sugar
Fresh mint leaves (optional)

For the sauce: Whisk the sugar and yolks in a small bowl to blend. Gradually whisk in the coconut milk and pineapple purée. Pour the mixture into a heavy, medium saucepan and stir constantly over medium heat until the custard thickens and coats the back of a spoon, about 6 minutes; do not boil. Strain into a bowl. Mix in the rum. Cool. **(Can be prepared 1 day ahead. Cover and refrigerate. Bring to room temperature before using.)**

For the tart: Preheat the oven to 325° F. Unfold the pastry sheets on a work surface. Roll each sheet out to a 13x10-inch rectangle.

Cut out two 7-inch rounds from each sheet. Transfer the dough rounds to baking sheets. Pierce the dough all over with a fork. Whisk the powdered sugar and yolk in small bowl to blend. Brush the mixture over dough. Bake until golden brown, about 15 minutes. Cool.

Preheat the broiler. Heat a heavy, large, nonstick skillet over high heat. Add the pineapple and cook until golden brown, about 1 minute per side. Arrange the pineapple slices atop the pastry, covering completely. Sprinkle each tart with 1 tablespoon of sugar. Broil until the edges of the pineapple begin to color, watching carefully, about 5 minutes. Transfer the tarts to plates. Spoon the sauce around the tarts. Garnish with mint leaves and serve.

Warm Pineapple Tart with Pineapple-Coconut Sauce

PETER MERRIMAN

Dive for sea urchin for tonight's soup? Scale a tree to pluck the ripest coconut for sorbet? For Peter Merriman, it's all in a day's work as a chef.

Peter takes the word *fresh* and elevates its definition to extraordinary heights. His obsession with pristine, just-picked-or-caught ingredients is undoubtedly what led to his role in the development of Hawaii Regional Cuisine. Most members of this band of chefs are quick to point to Peter as one of the originators of the culinary style and the one who thought to form the HRC group.

Peter first came to Hawaii in 1983 as a cook in the kitchen of Mauna Lani Bay Hotel and Bungalows on the Big Island, one of the most prominent hotels in the state. "I was cooking in Washington, D.C., when the call from Mauna Lani Bay came, and it took me about five minutes to make up my mind," he says with a laugh.

Peter began at Mauna Lani Bay as saucier, moved up to banquet chef and then, at the age of twenty-eight, was named executive chef of the Gallery, a free-standing restaurant at Mauna Lani Resort, in 1985.

"When I was preparing to move to the islands, I visualized using exotic products from all over Asia and Polynesia," says Peter. "But when I got here, all I saw was sole almondine. I knew I wanted to try and express the greatness of Hawaii through cuisine."

Peter had one problem—he didn't know where or how to begin. He decided to ask island farmers to grow fresh herbs; at that time, all he had access to were mainland dried varieties. Then he requested produce like organic lettuces and vine-ripened tomatoes. "It took three years to develop a reliable source for those tomatoes," Peter says ruefully.

Fresh local fish was always available, but some chefs never took their value seriously. Many hoteliers and restaurant managers thought guests would prefer fillet of sole, even if it was frozen. "Up until 1990, many kitchens were actually flying in mahimahi from Ecuador and Fiji," says Peter. He immediately began to cook with local fish, experimenting with *onaga, opakapaka,* and yes, fresh Hawaiian mahi.

Peter dove for sea urchins, climbed coconut trees when he had to—to avoid using canned and packaged varieties—and planted his own garden at the Gallery's back door. "Mauna Lani Resort deserves kudos; they let me do exactly as I pleased," says Peter.

Not all of Peter's experimentation went smoothly. He recounts how he first saw taro and was awed at the sight of the big, purplish vegetable. He sliced off a piece and popped it into his mouth. "I thought I'd die," says Peter. "Raw taro tastes like needles in your throat."

Peter's culinary curiosity comes naturally; his mother is a food writer. By the time he was ten years old, he was testing recipes for her in their suburban Pittsburgh home.

Although Peter graduated from the University of Pennsylvania as a political science major, he never lost his yen for cooking. He enrolled in a three-year apprenticeship program through the American Culinary Federation before cooking at resorts throughout the mainland United States, Europe and eventually, Mauna Lani Bay in Hawaii.

In 1988, he left the Gallery to open his own restaurant with his wife Vicki in Kamuela, an upcountry town on the Big Island often dubbed "the Alps of Alohaland." Merriman's, with a Hawaiian art deco decor and California-style open kitchen, serves Hawaii Regional Cuisine prepared almost exclusively with Big Island foodstuffs.

Escargots from nearby Waipio Valley, sweet butter from Hilo, goat cheese from Puna, corn from Pahoa, humanely raised veal from Kahena, sun-dried organic Kona coffee—the list is lengthy and impressive.

"My food is straightforward country style, in part due to working so closely with local ranches," says Peter. "I have to buy whole lamb and veal, which means I also acquire less choice cuts. I'm forced to braise and roast, techniques often forgotten in many contemporary restaurants."

Peter is justifiably proud of his role in the development of Hawaii Regional Cuisine. "What really makes me feel good is when farmers call to say how much they appreciate what we're doing for the local economy," says Peter. "But really, I'm more appreciative of them and what they're doing for the quality of food now available on the Big Island." ∎

Stir-fried Steak and Lobster Teriyaki
(See recipe, page 70)

butter. Divide the batter among the prepared muffin cups. Bake until golden brown and springy to touch, about 15 minutes. Turn the muffins out. Serve warm or at room temperature.

 LILIKOI VINAIGRETTE

Made with the highly aromatic passion fruit, this delicate, slightly sweet dressing can be tossed with any salad, although it takes particularly well to equally mild-tasting ingredients, like butter lettuce, Maui onion and avocado.

If passion fruit purée is unavailable in your area, boil 1½ cups passion fruit–mango juice until reduced to ⅓ cup.

Makes about 1½ cups

3 tablespoons rice wine vinegar
½ small shallot
1 small garlic clove
1 tablespoon fresh lemon juice
1 teaspoon Worcestershire sauce
1 teaspoon Dijon mustard
½ teaspoon honey
Pinch of salt
¾ cup vegetable oil
⅓ cup passion fruit (lilikoi) *purée*
1 tablespoon chopped fresh parsley

Puree the first 8 ingredients in a blender. Gradually blend in the oil, then the passion fruit purée and parsley. (**Can be prepared 4 hours ahead. Cover and let stand at room temperature.**)

 MANGO MUFFINS

These moist, tropical muffins taste great for breakfast or a snack. They're not overly sweet, so they can even be presented with a homey meal instead of rolls. You can substitute papaya or *lilikoi* (passion fruit) for the mango.

Makes 12 muffins

2 cups all-purpose flour
½ cup sugar
1 tablespoon baking powder
½ teaspoon salt
1 small mango, peeled and pitted
½ cup milk
1 large egg
¼ cup (½ stick) unsalted butter, melted

Preheat the oven to 375° F. Line twelve ⅔-cup muffin tins with paper liners. Sift the first 4 ingredients into a bowl. Combine the mango, milk and egg in a blender and purée. Mix the purée into the dry ingredients. Stir in the melted

 PAPAYA BISQUE

This cool, refreshing summer soup has a kick of its own, thanks to *sambal olek*, an Indonesian and Malaysian chili paste. It's combined with lemongrass and banana, and sprinkled over the top of the soup. This garnish adds aromatic notes and a textural counterpoint to the creamy bisque.

6 servings

4 ripe papayas, peeled and seeded
1 pineapple, rind removed, halved, cored and cut into chunks
1 cup canned unsweetened coconut milk
¼ cup dark rum
¼ cup white crème de cacao
¼ cup fresh lime juice
2 tablespoons powdered sugar
½ teaspoon vanilla extract
2 teaspoons minced fresh lemongrass
½ teaspoon sambal olek
½ cup peeled, sliced banana

Purée the papayas and pineapple in a blender in batches. Blend in the coconut milk, rum, crème de cacao, lime juice, powdered sugar and vanilla. Cover and refrigerate just until slightly chilled, about 30 minutes.

Mix the lemongrass and *sambal olek* in a medium bowl. Add the banana and toss to coat. Divide the soup among bowls. Spoon the banana mixture into the center and serve.

BEAN THREAD SALAD

Also called cellophane noodles or bean thread vermicelli, these transparent noodles become slippery and soft when cooked. In Hawaii, they're called long rice, and residents cook them in a stewlike dish with chicken, or deep-fry them.

The almost haunting Southeast Asian flavors of Peter's lighter variation make it a welcome luncheon entrée or side dish on a sultry summer day. Peter uses *sriracha*, a Thai hot sauce with the color and texture of ketchup, to flavor this dish, but any other hot pepper sauce will do.

4 side-dish servings

2 packages (2 ounces each) bean thread vermicelli
3 tablespoons fresh lime juice
2 tablespoons fish sauce (nam pla)
1 tablespoon sugar
½ teaspoon sriracha or other hot pepper sauce (such as Tabasco)
1 tablespoon oriental sesame oil
½ cup raw macadamia nuts, toasted and chopped
¼ cup chopped green onion
2 tablespoons chopped fresh cilantro
1 tablespoon chopped fresh mint

Place the bean thread vermicelli in a large bowl. Add enough hot water to cover and let it soak until pliable, about 3 minutes. Drain the vermicelli. Bring a large pot of water to a boil. Add the vermicelli and cook 2 minutes. Drain. Rinse under cold water until cool. Drain. Whisk the lime juice, fish sauce, sugar and hot pepper sauce in a large bowl until the sugar dissolves. Whisk in the oil. Add the vermicelli and remaining ingredients and toss well. Divide among plates and serve.

 ## PAPAYA SALSA

The quintessential refreshing foil to accompany any dish with heat, this salsa can also be used to enliven plain grilled chicken or fish. To Peter, papaya salsa—which he also makes with pineapple—is meant to be as ubiquitous as ketchup.

4 servings

⅓ cup chopped tomato
1 tablespoon chopped Maui onion or other sweet onion
1 jalapeño chili, halved and seeded
1 small garlic clove
1 teaspoon ground coriander
½ teaspoon ground cumin
¼ teaspoon salt
½ cup diced tomato
½ cup peeled, diced papaya
2 tablespoons chopped Maui onion or other sweet onion
1 tablespoon coarsely chopped fresh cilantro
1 tablespoon fresh lime juice

Purée the first 7 ingredients in a processor. Transfer the mixture to a bowl. Mix in the remaining ingredients and serve.

PINEAPPLE STIR-FRIED RICE

Cut up the ingredients in advance and this dish is easy to assemble. It's sweet, spicy, crunchy and pungent; so many good flavors jump around in your mouth, you'll grow more intrigued with each bite. At Merriman's, Peter sometimes adds about 12 ounces of diced shrimp or scallops at the same time as the garlic to transform a side dish into a main course.

4 servings

1/4 cup oriental sesame oil
1/4 cup peeled, grated fresh ginger
1/4 cup finely chopped fresh lemongrass
2 jalapeño chilies, finely chopped
2 tablespoons minced garlic
3 cups cooked brown rice, chilled
1 1/2 cups peeled, finely diced pineapple
1 cup coarsely chopped fresh cilantro
2/3 cup coarsely chopped raw macadamia nuts
1/2 cup chopped fresh mint
2 tablespoons fish sauce (nam pla)

Heat a wok or heavy, large skillet over high heat. Add the first 4 ingredients and stir-fry 30 seconds. Add the garlic and stir-fry 30 seconds. Add the rice and cook until heated through. Add the remaining ingredients and toss until heated through. Divide rice among plates and serve.

 PINEAPPLE-CURRY SAUCE

There's only minimal coconut milk in this sauce, but you can leave it out if desired. Peter's Pineapple-Curry Sauce is not only delicious, it's exceptionally versatile and can be served with sautéed or grilled vegetables, chicken or fish. Peter often presents it with sautéed scallops and Papaya Salsa (see recipe, page 67).

Makes about 1 1/2 cups

1 tablespoon olive oil
1/4 cup finely chopped onion
2 tablespoons peeled, grated fresh ginger
2 tablespoons minced garlic
2 tablespoons curry powder
1 tablespoon chopped fresh lemongrass
1 can (6 ounces) frozen pineapple juice concentrate, thawed
3/4 cup Chicken Stock (see recipe, page 128) or canned low-salt broth
1/4 cup canned unsweetened coconut milk (optional)
2 teaspoons fish sauce (nam pla)
1/2 teaspoon pepper

Heat the oil in a heavy, large saucepan over medium heat. Add the onion and sauté 5 minutes. Add the ginger, garlic, curry powder and lemongrass and sauté 1 minute. Add all of the remaining ingredients and bring to a boil, stirring occasionally. Reduce the heat and simmer until reduced to 1 1/2 cups, about 5 minutes. Season with salt and pepper. Strain the sauce if desired. (**Can be prepared 1 day ahead. Cover and refrigerate. Bring to a simmer before using.**)

Pineapple Stir-fried Rice

STIR-FRIED STEAK AND LOBSTER TERIYAKI

Taro and Chili Cakes

Surf-and-turf entrées are big on traditional menus in Hawaii, but they're never offered stir-fried with teriyaki. In the islands, teriyaki is generally brushed on hamburgers, chicken or fish. Peter's take is a lighter, more modern way of enjoying steak and lobster in one meal.

2 servings

TERIYAKI SAUCE
¼ cup soy sauce
2 tablespoons water
2 tablespoons sugar
1 tablespoon minced green onion
1 garlic clove, minced
1 piece fresh ginger (¼ inch long), peeled and chopped
Pinch of dried crushed red pepper
STIR-FRY
1 tablespoon plus 2 teaspoons peanut oil
4 ounces raw lobster tail meat, sliced
4 ounces beef tenderloin, sliced
½ cup julienne of green bell pepper
½ cup julienne of red bell pepper
¼ cup julienne of onion
⅛ cup mung bean sprouts
⅛ cup julienne of carrot
¼ cup dry sherry
1 tablespoon unsalted butter

For the sauce: Mix all of the ingredients in a small bowl. Set aside.

For the stir-fry: Heat 1 tablespoon of oil in a wok over high heat. Add the lobster and stir-fry 1 minute. Using a slotted spoon, transfer the lobster to a bowl. Add 1 teaspoon of oil to the wok. Add the beef and stir-fry 1 minute. Using a slotted spoon, transfer the beef to the bowl. Add the remaining 1 teaspoon of oil to the wok. Add all of the vegetables and stir-fry 1 minute. Add the sherry to the wok, cover and cook 30 seconds. Return the lobster and beef to the wok. Add 3 tablespoons of teriyaki sauce and the butter and stir-fry 15 seconds. Using a slotted spoon, transfer the meat, lobster and vegetables to plates. Reduce the sauce in the wok until slightly thickened, about 2 minutes. Spoon the sauce over the stir-fry and serve.

WINE NOTES
With most teriyaki dishes, slightly sweet wines work well. For a recipe with this much flavor and character, I recommend a simple quaffing wine, such as a White Zinfandel. Beaujolais or Chinon, light red wine with loads of fresh fruit, could also work. Choose the wine wisely, or a little alcohol could show up in the finish.

TARO AND CHILI CAKES

Don't turn up your nose at taro if all you've sampled is Hawaiian poi (a grayish paste of pounded, water-thinned cooked taro that's often fermented), which is usually an acquired taste for tourists. Taro actually tastes like a cross between an artichoke heart and a chestnut, and possesses the texture of the latter. HRC chefs have delved into taro cooking with a passion, resulting in wonderful recipes like this one, which highlights the tuber's admirable flavor. Think of this side dish as the HRC version of jalapeño potato pancakes.

Two notes of caution: Don't be tempted to try taro raw as it will irritate the throat (see Peter's chapter introduction); taro sometimes releases an acrid juice which can also irritate the skin while handling, so you might want to wear gloves.

Makes 21 cakes

3 pounds taro root
1 tablespoon vegetable oil
2 onions, diced
2 jalapeño chilies, minced
½ cup (1 stick) unsalted butter, room temperature
All-purpose flour
3 tablespoons (about) butter

Place the taro in a heavy, large pot. Add enough cold water to cover and bring to a boil. Reduce the heat and simmer until a tester inserted in the center of the taro goes through easily, about 40 minutes. Drain and cool. Peel the taro and transfer to the bowl of a heavy-duty mixer fitted with a paddle attachment. Beat the taro until smooth.

Line 2 baking sheets with waxed paper. Heat the oil in a heavy, large skillet over medium heat. And the onions and chilies and sauté until very tender, about 10 minutes. Add the onion mixture and ½ cup butter to the taro and beat to blend. Season with salt and pepper. Form the taro mixture into 3-inch-round, ½-inch-thick patties. Dust the patties generously with flour. Place on waxed paper–lined baking sheets. Cover and refrigerate until cold and firm, about 4 hours. **(Can be prepared 1 day ahead.)**

Melt 1 tablespoon butter in a heavy, large skillet over medium-high heat. Add the cakes and cook in batches until golden brown and heated through, about 1 minute per side, adding more butter to the skillet for each batch. Transfer to plates and serve.

 COCONUT CRÈME BRÛLÉE

This tropical crème brûlée is everything you want to cool a palate down after a spicy meal. The pure, pronounced coconut flavor comes from unsweetened powdered coconut milk, which is often sold in Filipino or Southeast Asian markets.

6 servings

2 cups whipping cream
1/2 cup sugar
8 extra-large egg yolks
3/4 cup unsweetened powdered coconut milk
3 tablespoons sugar

Preheat the oven to 325° F. Scald the cream in a heavy, medium saucepan. Whisk 1/2 cup of sugar and the yolks in a medium bowl. Whisk the hot cream into the yolk mixture. Return the mixture to the saucepan and stir over medium-low heat until the custard thickens, stirring constantly, about 3 minutes; do not boil. Remove the pan from the heat. Add the powdered coconut milk; stir until dissolved. Divide the custard among six 2/3-cup soufflé dishes. Place the soufflé dishes in a large baking pan. Place the pan in the oven. Add enough hot water to the pan to come halfway up the sides of the cups. Bake until the custards are set around the edges, about 20 minutes. Remove the custards from the water and cool. Cover and refrigerate overnight.

Preheat the broiler. Sprinkle the remaining 3 tablespoons of sugar over the custards. Broil until the sugar caramelizes, watching carefully, about 5 minutes. Serve.

71

AMY FERGUSON OTA

I f there is one element of Amy Ferguson Ota's personality that strikes you, it's her intensity. This chef possesses a drive that extends beyond a typical artist's passion. Perhaps it may be described as a spirited determination to excel at her craft, and a desire to preserve and protect the foods of a culture she so greatly admires.

"There's an old saying that goes 'fresh eyes always see clearer,' " says Amy. "Well, I might be a *haole* [Caucasian], but maybe I do possess new eyes. I certainly have enormous admiration for the foods of this region."

Amy's respect for indigenous ingredients began long before she moved to Hawaii in 1985. Growing up in Houston, Texas, she acquired much of her interest in quality cooking from her grandmother. Amy spent hours in her Cajun grandmother's kitchen, watching and tasting her Cajun and Southern specialities.

It's difficult for Amy to remember when she didn't like to cook; she's been almost glued to the stove since she was eight years old. When young girls were reading Nancy Drew novels, Amy was engrossed in cookbooks. By the age of eleven, she had purchased her first set of Sabatier knives and a *Larousse Gastronomique*. "I didn't understand a darned thing in the book, but I kept rereading it until I did," reminisces Amy.

After high school, Amy headed to Europe. She decided if she was going to be a chef, she had better learn French. She moved to France for two and a half years, attending college with an art history major, but spending a lot of time working in neighborhood charcuteries and boulangeries.

When she was twenty, she returned to Houston and taught cooking while she attended the Hotel and Restaurant Management School at the University of Houston. Eager to jump into a professional kitchen, she quickly worked her way up to executive chef of Che, a small French restaurant. Then she was lured to Charley's 517, which promptly put Amy smack-dab on the culinary map.

*Wok-seared Ono with Banana Curry
and Ti Leaf–wrapped Bananas (See recipe, page 78)*

Her distinctive Southwestern dishes were hailed as wonderful, and restaurant writers from all corners of the country dubbed her one of America's finest chefs. In the flush of success, Amy appeared on television programs, taught cooking and consulted, but she felt something was missing. Like many talented chefs who feel compelled to keep learning, Amy decided to continue her culinary education.

In 1985, she moved to Hawaii to become food and beverage manager of the Kona Village Resort, an idyllic Big Island retreat. "I was like a sore thumb in the middle of paradise," recalls Amy. "I was headstrong, ambitious and intense. I just wanted to do a good job."

Amy was surprised at the style of cuisine in many Hawaiian hotels at that time. "Old World chefs were running the kitchens and preparing mostly continental cuisine," she says. "Sometimes they even cooked with frozen produce. MSG was a kitchen staple. And I kept wondering why they were serving Scandinavian buffets instead of foods of Hawaii."

Amy began experimenting with local products when she worked with Peter Merriman at Mauna Lani Resort's Gallery restaurant. "One of the cooks was complaining about algae in a pond by the Gallery," she recalls. "Someone suggested he put Waipio Valley snails in the water to purify it. The snails looked like ones I saw in France, so I cooked them. They tasted great."

Within the year, famed chef Stephan Pyles requested that Amy come to Texas to open Baby Routh in Dallas. Again, Amy won widespread recognition. She returned to Hawaii in 1988 to marry Frank Ota, a local fisherman.

Amy was offered the position of executive chef of Hotel Hana-Maui, a luxurious, isolated resort. "My goal was to go strictly Hawaiian," says Amy.

Her everyday agenda included picking banana and *ti* leaves, breadfruit and other tropical produce for her constantly evolving menu. Her classic French training coupled with her expertise with Southwestern cooking were infused into the dishes she formulated. "Many Hawaiian ingredients—like mangos, avocados, chili peppers and papayas—are also grown in Texas, so it felt like a natural progression to me," she explains. "I say with a giggle that my food is Pacific Southwestern. After all, I am cooking in the most southwestern region of the United States," she says with a smile.

Dishes she devised at Hotel Hana-Maui—like fiddlehead fern salad, and *nori* fettuccine with *opihi* and garlic-chili-butter sauce—are now part of her regular repertoire.

The Ritz-Carlton, Mauna Lani on the Big Island hired Amy in 1991 and she became their executive chef the following year. She still stays true to her exploration of Hawaiian foods. "When I think about HRC, I see it as preserving food's integrity," says Amy. "I am totally committed to the principle." ■

BANANA–MACADAMIA NUT WAFFLES WITH RUM-RAISIN-MAPLE SYRUP

Any breakfast menu starring this dish makes morning a joyous occasion. Who could possibly start the day grouchy when presented with crisp, buttery waffles topped with sweetened cream cheese, bananas, macadamia nuts and rum-raisin-maple syrup?

8 servings

CREAM CHEESE
1 package (8 ounces) cream cheese, room temperature
6 tablespoons golden brown sugar

RUM-RAISIN-MAPLE SYRUP
2 cups pure maple syrup
¾ cup golden raisins
¾ cup dark raisins
½ cup dark rum

WAFFLES
1½ cups all-purpose flour
¼ cup sugar
1 tablespoon baking powder
1¼ cups milk
2 extra-large eggs
3 tablespoons unsalted butter, melted
1 banana, peeled and coarsely chopped
2 bananas, peeled and sliced
Chopped macadamia nuts

For the cream cheese mixture: Beat the cream cheese and brown sugar in a small bowl to blend. Set aside.

For the syrup: Bring all of the ingredients to a boil in a heavy, medium saucepan; keep warm.

For the waffles: Preheat the oven to low. Preheat a round waffle iron. Mix the flour, sugar and baking powder in a large bowl. Whisk the milk, eggs and butter in a small bowl to blend. Whisk the egg mixture into the dry ingredients. Stir in 1 chopped banana. Add some of the batter to the hot waffle iron and cook according to the manufacturer's instructions. Remove the waffle from the iron. Keep warm in the oven. Repeat making waffles with the remaining batter. Cut the waffles into quarters. Fan the waffles on 8 plates. Top with a dollop of the cream cheese mixture, sliced bananas and macadamia nuts. Serve with syrup.

POHOLE FERN SALAD WITH WAIMEA TOMATOES, MAUI ONIONS AND SESAME DRESSING

Pohole is the word used in Maui for a type of fern shoot; the ones available on the mainland are called fiddlehead ferns. Waimea is a town on the Big Island where Amy gets her delicious tomatoes.

In this recipe, the pickled ginger adds an extra smidgen of exotica and also contributes a hint of sweetness to offset the fern shoots' slight bitterness. Amy sometimes adds cuttlefish or *opihi* to this texture-rich salad.

4 servings

DRESSING
1/2 cup rice vinegar
1/3 cup pickled ginger
1/4 cup oriental sesame oil
1 tablespoon soy sauce
1 garlic clove, minced
SALAD
1 pound fern shoots, cleaned*
2 tomatoes, seeded and julienned
1 Maui onion or other sweet onion, julienned
Toasted sesame seeds

For the dressing: Mix all of the ingredients in a bowl.

For the salad: Toss the fern shoots, tomatoes and onion in a large bowl with enough dressing to coat. Divide the salad among plates. Sprinkle with sesame seeds and serve.

*The fern shoots obtained on the mainland may be tougher or woodier in texture that those found on Maui or other Hawaiian islands. It may be necessary to blanch them before using in this salad.

AHI YELLOWFIN TUNA AND ULU BREADFRUIT CAKES WITH LIME-CILANTRO MAYONNAISE

This HRC recipe combines two of Hawaii's staples —*ahi* and breadfruit (*ulu*)—and transforms them into an exotic cousin of crabcakes. The Lime-Cilantro Mayonnaise balances the richness of the cakes while complementing their flavor. Cooked potato, yam or taro can be successfully substituted for the breadfruit.

4 servings

MAYONNAISE
1 1/2 cups mayonnaise (preferably homemade)
1/4 cup chopped fresh cilantro
3 tablespoons fresh lime juice

TUNA CAKES
2 tablespoons (1/4 stick) unsalted butter
12 ounces ahi tuna, cut into 1/3-inch cubes
1 cup finely diced onion
1 tablespoon chopped green onion
1 shallot, minced
1 garlic clove, minced
3/4 teaspoon salt
1/2 pound ulu (breadfruit), peeled, cored, steamed and grated
4 1/2 tablespoons whipping cream
2 tablespoons chopped cilantro
1 1/2 tablespoons beaten extra-large egg
2 tablespoons plus 3/4 teaspoon cornstarch
1 tablespoon fresh lemon juice
1 teaspoon baking powder
3 tablespoons (about) clarified butter
Lime slices
Fresh cilantro sprigs

For the mayonnaise: Mix all of the ingredients in a small bowl. Cover and refrigerate until ready to use. **(Can be prepared 1 day ahead.)**

For the tuna cakes: Melt 2 tablespoons of butter in a heavy, large skillet over medium heat. Add the *ahi*, both onions, shallot, garlic and half of the salt and cook until the *ahi* is no longer pink, about 3 minutes. Transfer the mixture to a bowl and cool. Mix the *ulu*, cream, cilantro, egg, cornstarch, lemon juice, baking powder and remaining salt into the *ahi* mixture.

Heat 1 tablespoon of the clarified butter in a heavy, large skillet over medium-high heat. Drop the *ahi* mixture by 1/4 cupfuls into the skillet; flatten slightly with a spatula and cook until cooked through, about 2 minutes per side. Transfer the cakes to plates. Repeat with the remaining butter and *ahi* mixture in batches. Garnish with lime slices and cilantro sprigs. Serve with mayonnaise.

WINE NOTES
You can have some real fun pairing wine with this dish. Just remember that the wine should have good, firm acidity to cut through the mayonnaise. Consider Champagne and its California counterpart; Sauvignon Blanc, American, French or a New Zealander; Riesling, dry or slightly sweet; and even lighter red wines such as Chinon or Bourgueil.

NORI FETTUCCINE WITH OPIHI AND GARLIC-CHILI-BUTTER SAUCE

Nori, which is dried seaweed, adds both dramatic color and a briny sea flavor to homemade fettuccine. It also complements the *opihi*, a Hawaiian shellfish or limpet with an oysterlike flavor and a snaillike texture. Cooked scallops or shrimp can be substituted.

6 servings
FETTUCCINE
3 cups all-purpose flour
2 ounces nori
1 teaspoon salt
3 extra-large eggs
2 tablespoons water
2 teaspoons vegetable oil
SAUCE
6 tablespoons dry white wine
1 large shallot, minced
2 large garlic cloves, minced
¾ teaspoon sambal olek *(Indonesian red chili paste)*
¼ cup whipping cream
½ cup (1 stick) chilled unsalted butter, cut into pieces
2 pounds opihi, *shelled*

For the fettuccine: Blend the flour, *nori* and salt in a food processor until the *nori* is cut into small pieces. Whisk the eggs, water and oil in a small bowl to blend. Add the egg mixture to the flour mixture and blend in using on/off turns until the dough begins to form moist clumps. Gather the dough into a ball. Wrap in plastic. Let rest 20 minutes.

Cut the dough into 4 pieces. Flatten 1 dough piece into a rectangle. Roll the dough through widest setting of the pasta machine. Repeat the process twice. Adjust the machine to a narrower setting and roll the pasta through. Continue rolling, adjusting the machine as necessary to form ¹/₁₆-inch-thick pasta sheets. Repeat rolling with the remaining dough pieces. Allow the pasta strips to stand 15 minutes to dry slightly. Hook the fettuccine attachment to the pasta machine. Roll the dough strips through, dusting lightly with flour if sticky. (**Can be prepared 6 hours ahead. Toss fettuccine with flour and arrange on baking sheet; refrigerate.**)

For the sauce: Boil the wine, shallot, garlic and *sambal olek* in a heavy, small saucepan until almost no liquid remains in the pan, about 3 minutes. Add the cream and boil until thickened, about 2 minutes. Add the butter and whisk until melted. Keep warm.

Meanwhile, cook the pasta in a large saucepan of boiling salted water until just tender but still firm to the bite, about 2 minutes. Drain; return the pasta to the pot.

Add the sauce and *opihi* to the pasta; toss until the *opihi* are heated through. Season to taste with salt and pepper. Divide the fettuccine among 6 plates and serve.

WINE NOTES
The wine that immediately comes to mind is Italian Gavi. The Gavi must have good, firm acidity to cut through the butter sauce and have enough fruit to weigh in against the pasta. Since opihi *has a distinctive, briny nuance reminiscent of ocean spray, La Rocca, a specific vineyard site of Gavi—and whose wines possess an innate saline quality—would provide an interesting match-up for the* opihi, *pasta and sauce.*

A well-made Sauvignon Blanc would also be a good selection. Like the Gavi, the Sauvignon Blanc should have lots of fresh fruit and good, crisp acidity. You can find many fine examples from California.

Nori Fettuccine with Opihi and Garlic-Chili-Butter Sauce

Rack of Lamb with Thai Curry Sauce
(See recipe, page 79)

BLACK SESAME-CURED WILD BOAR LOIN WITH GUAVA SAUCE

Wild boar roam most of the Hawaiian Islands, but can only be hunted for personal purposes. Pork loin is a good substitute. In this recipe, Amy expertly balances subtly sweet and spicy undertones. The guava sauce is a particularly fine accompaniment to the smoked meat.

8 servings

WILD BOAR
1/4 cup sugar
2 1/2 tablespoons minced shallots
2 tablespoons kosher salt
1 tablespoon minced garlic
1 tablespoon chopped fresh thyme
1 tablespoon chopped fresh cilantro
1 tablespoon chopped fresh lemongrass
1 tablespoon chopped fresh ginger
2 tablespoons oriental sesame oil
1 center cut wild boar loin, 3 pounds
1/2 cup black sesame seeds
GUAVA SAUCE
1 guava, peeled
1 tablespoon minced shallot
1 teaspoon minced fresh ginger
1/4 teaspoon minced garlic
1 tablespoon fresh lime juice
1 tablespoon rice vinegar
1 tablespoon sugar
1/4 cup vegetable oil
1 teaspoon minced fresh lemon thyme or regular thyme
*Mango or apple wood chips, soaked 30 minutes in
    water*
Sunflower sprouts

For the wild boar: Mix the first 8 ingredients in a small bowl. Rub the sesame oil over the boar. Rub the sugar mixture over the boar. Roll the boar in sesame seeds, coating it completely. Press the seeds into the boar to adhere. Wrap the boar in plastic wrap and refrigerate overnight.

For the guava sauce: Purée the first 4 ingredients in a blender. Pour into a bowl. Whisk in the lime juice, vinegar and sugar. Gradually whisk in the oil. Mix in the lemon thyme. Season to taste with salt and pepper.

Prepare the barbecue (medium heat). When the coals are white, spread evenly over the grill. Drain the soaked chips and sprinkle over the coals. Add the boar, cover and cook until medium doneness, turning occasionally, about 40 minutes. Slice the boar.

Spoon the sauce into the center of the plates. Fan the boar around the plates. Garnish with sprouts and serve.

WINE NOTES
If the boar didn't have the guava sauce, the right wine might be a very rustic, old-fashioned style red Rhône wine like Cornas or Hermitage. The boar's slightly gamey edge and smoky preparation would work nicely with the wine's earthy, peppery qualities. The sauce changes the perspective, so a slightly tamer wine from the southern Rhône, such as well-made Châteauneuf-du-Pape or Gigondas, should work nicely.

Or, here's the opportunity to open that Cabernet-based wine you've been aging, whether it's from California or from Bordeaux, France. However, don't select one too old, as this dish still needs fruit and especially the tannic finish to clean the palate.

 ### WARM MANGO CUSTARDS

Served warm in all its creamy rich glory, this dessert is tropical comfort food at its best. Caramel and fresh mango hide beneath a silken custard and a crunchy topping. In case any custard is left over, know that this dessert is also delicious served cold.

6 servings

CARAMEL
1/2 cup sugar
1 tablespoon water
TOPPING
3 tablespoons all-purpose flour
3 tablespoons brown sugar
1 tablespoon sugar
1 tablespoon unsalted butter, room temperature
2 tablespoons chopped macadamia nuts
CUSTARDS
1/2 cup whipping cream
2 extra-large eggs
6 tablespoons sugar
1/4 cup (1/2 stick) unsalted butter, room temperature
2 tablespoons brandy or Calvados
1/2 teaspoon vanilla extract
Pinch of salt
Pinch of ground cinnamon
Pinch of ground nutmeg
1 mango, peeled, pitted and thinly sliced

For the caramel: Stir the sugar and water in a heavy, small saucepan over low heat until the sugar dissolves. Increase the heat and boil without stirring until the syrup turns golden brown, brushing down sides of pan with pastry brush dipped in water, about 5 minutes. Carefully pour caramel into bottom of six ⅔-cup soufflé dishes. Set aside.

For the topping: Mix the first 4 ingredients in a small bowl until the mixture forms moist crumbs. Add the nuts and press with your fingers until the mixture forms small clumps.

For the custards: Preheat the oven to 325° F. Scald the cream in a heavy, medium saucepan. Whisk the eggs, sugar and butter in a medium bowl. Gradually whisk in the hot cream mixture. Add the brandy, vanilla, salt and spices and whisk to blend. Arrange the mango slices atop the caramel in soufflé dishes. Spoon the custard over. Sprinkle the topping over the custards. Place the soufflé dishes in a heavy, large baking pan. Place the pan in the oven. Add enough hot water to the pan to come halfway up the sides of the dishes. Bake until a knife inserted into the center of the custards comes out clean, about 45 minutes. Remove the custards from the water. Transfer to plates and serve.

 MANGO ICE CREAM SANDWICHES WITH TROPICAL FRUIT COMPOTE

Try these dashing ice cream sandwiches, and you'll never eat storebought again. They practically sing with the flavors of the tropics. To make the mango purée, peel and pit ripe mangoes and purée them in the processor. Enjoy any leftover cookies the next day.

Makes about 12 sandwiches

ICE CREAM
½ cup half-and-half
½ cup sugar
3 extra-large egg yolks
1¼ cups whipping cream
6 tablespoons mango purée

COOKIES
½ cup plus 2 tablespoons (1¼ sticks) unsalted butter, room temperature
½ cup sugar
2 tablespoons beaten egg
⅛ teaspoon vanilla extract
1 cup all-purpose flour
⅛ teaspoon salt
3 tablespoons chopped macadamia nuts

COMPOTE
1¼ cups peeled and chopped kiwi fruit
1¼ cups peeled and chopped pineapple
1¼ cups peeled and chopped mango
2¼ cups mango purée
Fresh mint leaves
Tropical flowers

For the ice cream: Bring the half-and-half and the sugar to a boil in a heavy, medium saucepan. Whisk the yolks in a medium bowl to blend. Whisk in the hot half-and-half mixture. Return the mixture to the same saucepan and stir over medium-low heat until the custard thickens and coats the back of a spoon, about 5 minutes; do not boil. Strain the custard into a bowl. Refrigerate until cold. Whisk the cream and the mango purée into the custard. Transfer the custard to an ice cream maker and process according to the manufacturer's instructions. (**Can be prepared 3 days ahead. Freeze in covered container.**)

For the cookies: Using an electric mixer, cream the butter and the sugar in a large bowl until light and fluffy. Beat in the beaten egg and the vanilla. Mix in the flour and the salt, then the nuts. Drop the cookie dough on a sheet of plastic wrap and form into a 2½-inch wide cylinder. Refrigerate the dough overnight.

Preheat the oven to 350° F. Line cookie sheets with parchment. Cut the dough into ⅛-inch-thick rounds. Arrange on the prepared cookie sheets, spacing evenly apart. Bake until golden brown on the edges, about 12 minutes. Transfer the cookies to racks and cool. Sandwich 2 rounded tablespoons of ice cream between 2 cookies; press gently to flatten. Place in the freezer. Repeat with the remaining ice cream and cookies.

For the compote: Mix the chopped fruit in a large bowl. Spoon the mango purée on the center of each plate. Cut the sandwiches in half and place, split open, atop the purée. Spoon the compote between the sandwiches. Garnish with mint and tropical flowers and serve.

PHILIPPE PADOVANI

As soon as Philippe Padovani stepped off the jet from Paris and onto the tarmac at Honolulu International Airport in 1986, foodies jumped on the "coconut wireless." The word was out that the famous French chef from Restaurant La Tour Rose, the tiny Michelin-starred dining establishment in Lyon, was taking over the kitchen at the Halekulani, Waikiki's premier luxury hotel.

Philippe had already spent two years flying back and forth from France as a consultant for the oceanfront hotel's La Mer dining room, but this was decidedly different. "I realized I had fallen in love with Hawaii," says Philippe. "I was ready to make a commitment."

Halekulani guests and Honolulu sophisticates alike awaited a classic French menu—after all, that was the route most Gallic chefs preferred. But unlike the masters who came to the islands before him, Philippe refused to rely on the security blanket of French and mainland ingredients. Instead, he flung off his apron and went exploring.

He wandered through Chinatown, fingering exotic roots and sniffing unusual herbs. He lingered at the fish market, poking yellowfin tuna, *moana*, *onaga* and *opakapaka*. And everywhere he went, he talked incessantly to merchants and fishmongers. Only then did Philippe return to his kitchen, determined to create dishes that utilized choice local products.

"When I arrived in Hawaii, most of the hotels were actually flying in seafood," says Philippe. "It made no sense to me. I wanted to cook with foods that the local population deemed valuable."

Although he showcases Hawaiian fish and meats, Philippe Padovani brings an elegant French twist to the Hawaii Regional Cuisine equation. Unlike many of the HRC chefs, who work strictly with Asian techniques, Philippe often adheres to modern French.

His sauces are primarily enhanced reductions of natural meat or fish juices. "I try not to make sauces that are overpowering," explains Philippe. "If you're lucky enough to cook with the best fish and meat, why overwhelm them?"

Philippe is no stranger to Asian flavors; he studied Thai cooking in Bangkok and has now lived on the islands for more than seven years. Ginger, seaweed, cilantro, lemongrass and coconut milk pop up as frequently as balsamic vinegar and olive oil in his recipes. Sometimes he works with classic Hawaiian dishes and refines them according to his French sensibilities.

Perhaps his ability to adapt so well to foreign foodstuffs relates back to his atypical childhood. Philippe may be the only French chef with a twangy Australian accent. When he was a baby, his family moved to a tiny outback town where his parents dished up fish and chips in a small snack shop to local farmers. When Philippe was fourteen years old, he reluctantly returned with his family to France.

Philippe soon began culinary training; he saw it as a route back to his beloved Australia. However, he had one major problem. He was a Frenchman who couldn't speak French. He actually had to learn his homeland's language in restaurant kitchens. Philippe trained and cooked in many of France's Michelin-starred dining establishments, often working side by side with such celebrated chefs as Michel Rostang and Georges Blanc. When he took over the kitchen at Restaurant La Tour Rose in 1983, he promptly achieved acclaim. Soon after he was tapped for the Halekulani consulting chef position.

After four years as executive and then corporate chef for the Halekulani hotel, Philippe moved to The Ritz-Carlton, Mauna Lani and then to The Manele Bay Hotel on sleepy Lanai.

As executive chef of Manele Bay, Philippe depends on local fishermen and farmers and likes it that way. From the signature Ihilani Dining Room at Manele Bay, guests watch dolphins splashing and playing in the Pacific waters. As these pampered visitors happily devour such specialties as pan-fried Kahuku prawns, *opakapaka lau lau* or Hawaiian lobster with vanilla-mint-curry sauce, they probably feel like the luckiest people in the world. But those who are passionate about cooking see Philippe as the fortunate one. ∎

Chicken with Oysters and Straw Mushrooms in Spicy Szechwan Sauce (See recipe, page 91)

SEARED AHI WITH SPICY CRUST, GREEN PAPAYA SALAD AND SWEET-AND-SOUR VINAIGRETTE

The quality of Hawaii's yellowfin and bigeye tuna is so superb, it's not surprising that tuna pops up frequently on Hawaii Regional Cuisine menus. HRC chefs often sear the fish and serve it with a bold-flavored sauce or salsa. In this recipe, spicy *ahi* is tempered by a cool, slightly sweet salad.

The best and freshest *ahi* possess very red, fatty meat that's tacky to the touch. For the salad, purchase an unripe green papaya from the supermarket.

4 servings

VINAIGRETTE

¼ cup white wine vinegar
¼ cup peanut oil
2 teaspoons minced onion
2 teaspoons sugar
½ teaspoon minced red jalapeño or serrano chili
¼ teaspoon chili powder
¼ teaspoon peeled, minced fresh ginger

FISH

1½ tablespoons paprika
1 teaspoon black pepper
1 teaspoon white pepper
1 teaspoon cayenne pepper
1 teaspoon garlic powder
1 teaspoon onion powder
1 teaspoon dried thyme
1 teaspoon dried rubbed sage
1 teaspoon cumin powder
1 teaspoon chili powder
1 teaspoon salt
4 sashimi-grade ahi steaks, 4 ounces and 1 inch thick each

SALAD

1 medium green papaya, peeled, halved, seeded and coarsely grated
1 tomato, peeled, seeded and julienned
½ cup fresh cilantro leaves
½ cup roasted macadamia nuts

For the vinaigrette: Purée all of the ingredients in a blender. **(Can be prepared 6 hours ahead. Cover and let stand at room temperature.)**

For the fish: Mix all of the ingredients except the *ahi* on a large plate. Add the *ahi* and turn to coat. Heat a heavy, large cast-iron skillet over high heat until very hot. Add the *ahi* and sear 30 seconds on each side for rare.

For the salad: Toss all of the ingredients in a medium bowl with enough vinaigrette to taste. Divide the salad among 4 plates. Top with the *ahi*.

WINE NOTES

A German Riesling is one answer for this dish, preferably something slightly sweet, crisp, appley and refreshing. Look to the Saar region for a fitting wine; choose one from a great producer.

Another recommendation is a slightly sweet, profusely fruity Chenin Blanc from the Loire Valley. Consider a fine Vouvray—it has lots of fresh, vibrant fruit and enough crisp, snappy acidity to keep things lively.

SALAD OF PEKING DUCK WITH BEAN SPROUTS AND KIM CHEE

Philippe believes Peking duck is the finest dish the Chinese have ever invented. When creating this summer salad, he added Korean *kim chee* (pickled cabbage), which imparts a spicy note to the rich duck meat. The red peppers and green onions add bursts of color to the salad.

4 servings

½ cooked Peking duck*, boned and cut into thin strips (about 2 cups)
1 pound mung bean sprouts
3 green onions, julienned
½ small red bell pepper, julienned
⅓ cup radish sprouts
¼ cup drained kim chee, chopped (2 tablespoons of juices, reserved)
1 tablespoon sesame seeds, toasted
1 tablespoon oriental sesame oil
1½ teaspoons soy sauce

Combine all of the ingredients including the reserved *kim chee* juices in a large bowl and toss well. Season to taste with salt and pepper. Divide the salad among 4 chilled plates and serve.

*Available at Chinese markets.

WINE NOTES

A dry, Grenache/Mourvedre-based rosé like the Vin Gris de Cigare from Bonny Doon or other versions found in southern France is highly recommended with this dish. This wine can handle the oiliness of the duck and has the crispness to cleanse the palate.

Another viable alternative would be to select a Pinot Noir, something light-bodied with a lot of fresh fruit, crisp acidity and lower tannin levels. Examples include a Sancerre Rouge 1990 from the Loire Valley or Aubert de Villaine's Bourgogne Rouge from the Chalonnais region in Burgundy, France.

OPAKAPAKA LAU LAU
(Baked Pink Snapper in Ti *Leaves)*

A Hawaiian staple, traditional *lau lau* is made with fresh belly pork or pork butt, and salted butterfish or salmon. It's wrapped in the smooth, green leaves of the *ti* plant and steamed in an *imu*, or underground oven. Philippe's healthful, oven-baked HRC rendition eliminates the pork but adds exotic seasoning; the play of flavors seem to unfold on the tongue one by one.

4 servings
FILLING
¼ cup peanut oil
1 cup sliced Maui onion or other sweet onion
6 garlic cloves, minced
1 teaspoon peeled, minced fresh ginger
6 ounces fresh shiitake mushrooms, stemmed and
*   thinly sliced*
1 teaspoon Szechwan chili sauce
1 green onion, julienned
⅓ cup finely chopped fresh cilantro
FISH
2 tablespoons fish sauce (nam pla)
2 tablespoons soy sauce
2 tablespoons peanut oil
1½ pounds opakapaka *fillets, cut into 2-inch pieces*
8 ti *leaves or banana leaves*
1 cup fresh ogo seaweed or 1 sheet nori, cut into strips

For the filling: Heat the oil in a heavy, large skillet over medium-high heat. Add the onion and sauté 3 minutes. Add the garlic and ginger, then the mushrooms and chili sauce and sauté 5 minutes. Mix in the green onion and cilantro. **(Can be prepared 1 day ahead. Cover and refrigerate.)**

For the fish: Mix the fish sauce, soy sauce and oil in a large bowl. Add the fish and toss well. Let stand 10 minutes at room temperature.

Bring a large pot of water to a boil. Add the *ti* leaves and boil until softened, about 2 minutes. Drain. Rinse under cold water and drain again. Arrange 2 *ti* leaves on a work surface to make a cross. Cut off the stem end of leaf closest to you. Spoon ¼ of the filling in the center of the *ti* leaves. Top with ¼ of the fish and sprinkle with ¼ of the *ogo*. Fold the leaf without the stem over filling. Then fold the opposite leaf over the filling. Tie 2 opposite *ti* leaves in a knot over the bundle. Repeat with the remaining leaves, filling, fish and seaweed for a total of 4 bundles. **(Can be prepared 3 hours ahead. Cover and refrigerate.)**

Preheat the oven to 400° F. Place the *ti* leaf packets on a baking sheet. Bake until the fish is cooked through, about 20 minutes, and serve.

WINE NOTES
This dish possesses some heat, yet it is delicate and flavorful. It's another natural match for German Rieslings that are slightly sweet and fruity with lower alcohol levels. Look for Kabinett-level wines from quality producers.

 POACHED ONAGA WITH CUCUMBER, TOMATOES AND BASIL

Onaga, a red snapper, inhabits the deep waters surrounding the Hawaiian Islands. This understated recipe ensures that the delicate flavor of the fish isn't overpowered by its preparation. This dish tastes best in the summer, when vine-ripened tomatoes and fresh basil are available. Salmon or sea bass can be successfully substituted for the *onaga*.

4 servings
STOCK
2 cups dry white wine
1 cup water
¼ cup finely chopped carrot
¼ cup finely chopped onion
¼ cup finely chopped shallots
¼ cup finely chopped celery with leaves
1 lemongrass stalk (12 inches long), finely chopped
2 garlic cloves
2 tablespoons fresh lemon juice
2 whole cloves
1 bay leaf
1 fresh parsley sprig
1 teaspoon Hawaiian or kosher salt
Pinch of white pepper
Pinch of cayenne pepper
TOMATO SALAD
3 medium tomatoes
¼ cup olive oil
½ cup fresh basil leaves, julienned
2 tablespoons fresh lemon juice
1 garlic clove, minced
FISH
1 large cucumber, peeled, julienned
4 onaga (red snapper) fillets, 6 ounces and 2 inches
*   thick each*
4 fresh basil sprigs

(continued on next page)

For the stock: Bring all of the ingredients except the salt and peppers to a boil in a heavy, large saucepan. Cover and continue boiling for 15 minutes. Add salt and both peppers. Cover and continue boiling 15 minutes. Strain the stock through a fine sieve. **(Can be prepared 1 day ahead. Cover and refrigerate.)**

For the tomato salad: Bring a large pot of water to a boil. Cut an X in the top of each tomato just deep enough to pierce the skin. Add the tomatoes to the water and blanch 15 seconds. Drain. Refresh under cold water. Peel off the skin. Cut the tomatoes crosswise in half. Squeeze out the seeds. Cut the tomatoes into julienne strips. Transfer the tomatoes to a bowl. Add olive oil, basil, lemon juice and garlic. Season with salt and pepper.

For the fish: Place half of the cucumber in the bottom of a heavy, large skillet. Add the fish in a single layer and cover with the remaining cucumber. Add the stock to the skillet and bring to a boil. Cover the skillet, reduce heat and simmer until the fish is cooked through, about 8 minutes. Divide the fish and cucumber among 4 warm dinner plates. Spoon the tomato salad around the fish. Garnish with basil sprigs and serve.

WINE NOTES
The wine needed for this dish should be delicate enough for the onaga, possess enough acidity to cut through the olive oil and have enough flavor to avoid being overpowered by the fresh tomatoes, basil and garlic. Recommendations include a dry Rosato (Italian rosé), a dry southern French rosé such as those from Bandol, or a dry, minerally white like Clos Nicrosi from the island of Corsica.

For more readily available selections, consider well-made Italian wines like Soave, Pinot Grigio or Gavi from high-quality producers or even some of the sturdier, better made examples of refreshing white wines from regions like Provence in southern France.

PAN-FRIED MOANO WITH SNOW PEAS AND BACON IN CURRY SAUCE

Philippe originally created the idea for this recipe in France, but he put it all together when he stumbled across tiny *moano* wedged next to gargantuan tuna during one of his first encounters with a Honolulu fish market. *Moano*, a goatfish, is an Indo-Pacific species of the red mullet. This red reef fish is similar to the prized Mediterranean "rouget."

In this dish, the vibrant curry powder and crunchy snow peas balance the richness of the creamy sauce. Snapper, sea scallops or lobster can be substituted for the *moano*.

4 servings
- ½ cup Chicken Stock (see recipe, page 128) or canned low-salt broth
- 2 cups whipping cream
- 2 teaspoons curry powder
- 1 tablespoon butter
- ¼ cup diced smoked bacon
- ½ pound snow peas, strings removed, julienned
- 4 moano fillets, 6 ounces and ¾ inch thick each
- 3 tablespoons olive oil

Boil the stock in a heavy, medium saucepan until reduced to a glaze, about 4 minutes. Add the cream and curry powder and simmer until reduced to 1 cup, about 15 minutes. **(Can be prepared 1 day ahead. Cover and refrigerate.)**

Melt the butter in a heavy, medium skillet over medium-high heat. Add the bacon and sauté until brown, about 5 minutes. Add the snow peas and sauté until crisp-tender, about 2 minutes. Season with salt.

Season both sides of the fish with salt and pepper. Heat the oil in a heavy, large skillet over high heat. Add the fish and cook until cooked through, about 3 minutes per side.

Bring the sauce to a simmer. Spoon the sauce onto plates. Top with the snow pea mixture and fish and serve.

WINE NOTES
Philippe's curry sauce is toned down; there's tang, but not a lot of heat. The wine that goes best with this dish is a German Gewurztraminer from a producer like Pfeffingen. It offsets the curry, handles the snow peas and does wonders for the fish.

Or, pair this dish with a very cold California sparkling wine. It should have an abundance of ripe fruit to match up with the cream sauce as well as moderate alcohol levels, and crisp, refreshing acidity to cleanse the palate.

Poached Onaga with Cucumber, Tomatoes and Basil (See recipe, page 87)

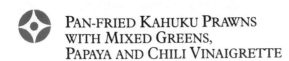

PAN-FRIED KAHUKU PRAWNS WITH MIXED GREENS, PAPAYA AND CHILI VINAIGRETTE

Kahuku prawns (freshwater, farm-raised prawns from Oahu) stand up well to the assertive flavors of a Southeast Asian–inspired vinaigrette. Juicy papaya soothes the palate, while roasted macadamia nuts contribute appealing crunch. This colorful starter can also serve as a luncheon entrée.

4 servings

VINAIGRETTE
2 green onions, minced
3 tablespoons fresh lime juice
2 tablespoons sugar
2 tablespoons fish sauce (nam pla)
1 tablespoon minced fresh cilantro
2 teaspoons peeled, minced fresh ginger
1/2 teaspoon Szechwan chili sauce

SALAD
2 tablespoons oriental sesame oil
1 pound raw prawns or shrimp, peeled and
  deveined
8 cups mixed baby greens
1 papaya, peeled, seeded and cubed
1 small red bell pepper, chopped
1 small Japanese cucumber, halved lengthwise and
  cubed
1/2 cup chopped toasted macadamia nuts
4 sprigs fresh cilantro

For the vinaigrette: Whisk all of the ingredients in a small bowl to blend. **(Can be prepared 6 hours ahead. Cover and let stand at room temperature.)**

For the salad: Heat the sesame oil in a heavy, large, nonstick skillet over medium heat. Add the prawns and sauté until cooked through, about 3 minutes. Remove from heat; tent with foil to keep warm.

Toss the greens with enough vinaigrette to taste. Divide the greens among 4 plates. Garnish with prawns, papaya, bell pepper, cucumber, macadamia nuts and cilantro sprigs and serve.

WINE NOTES
This is a dish seemingly tailor-made for a German Riesling; specifically one with ripe, tropical-like fruit. Try a Kabinett (fruity style) from the Rheinpfalz, or even something leaner, from the Saar. The wine's fruit will complement the papaya and the shrimp, while the slight sweetness will cool the heat.

HAWAIIAN LOBSTER WITH VANILLA-MINT-CURRY SAUCE

This recipe reflects Philippe's travels through Thailand. He devised a melting pot of flavors— including vanilla beans, mint and Maui onions—to create a curry which keeps the sweet, mild flavor of the lobster intact. Hawaiian lobster is usually spiny lobster, hand-caught off each island's coast. Occasionally, the flavorful slipper lobster is the prize catch.

4 servings

SAUCE
1 tablespoon peanut oil
1 teaspoon yellow curry paste
2 teaspoons curry powder
1 teaspoon turmeric
3 cups canned unsweetened coconut milk
1 vanilla bean, split lengthwise in half
2 kaffir lime leaves

LOBSTER AND VEGETABLES
4 live lobsters, 1 1/2 pounds each
2 tablespoons peanut oil
1 medium Maui onion or other sweet onion, cut into
  8 wedges
1 medium carrot, peeled and cut diagonally into thin
  slices
1 medium sweet potato, cut diagonally into thin slices
1 Japanese eggplant, cut diagonally into thin slices
1/2 cup Chicken Stock (see recipe, page 128) or canned
  low-salt broth
1/4 cup fresh mint leaves
4 fresh mint sprigs

For the sauce: Heat the oil in a heavy, medium saucepan over high heat. Add the curry paste and cook 2 minutes, stirring constantly. Mix in the curry powder and turmeric. Whisk in the coconut milk. Add the vanilla bean and kaffir leaves and bring to a boil. Season to taste with salt and pepper. Strain the sauce into a bowl. Return the vanilla bean to the sauce. **(Can be prepared 1 day ahead. Cover and refrigerate sauce.)**

For the lobster and vegetables: Bring a large pot of water to a boil. Add the lobsters head first and cook until the lobsters are cooked through, about 8 minutes. Using tongs, transfer the lobsters to a large bowl and cool. Cut off the lobster heads and discard. Cut off the claws. Crack the claws and remove the meat. Cut the underside of the tails and remove the tail meat in whole pieces. Cut each tail crosswise into 4 slices. **(Lobster can be prepared 1 day ahead. Cover and refrigerate.)**

Heat 2 tablespoons of oil in a heavy, large skillet over medium heat. Add the onion, carrot, sweet potato and eggplant and sauté 4 minutes. Add the stock and simmer until the liquid evaporates and the vegetables are tender, about 4 minutes.

Remove the vanilla bean from the sauce and cut into 4 pieces. Mix ¼ cup of the mint leaves into the sauce. Add the sauce and lobster to the vegetables in the skillet and bring to a simmer. Spoon the lobster curry onto 4 warm dinner plates. Garnish with mint sprigs and reserved vanilla bean and serve.

WINE NOTES
Hawaiian lobster is rich and sweet, so you need a wine with ample fruit levels and fairly high levels of acidity to keep the palate fresh. Bonny Doon made a wine in the 1991 and 1992 vintages called Pacific Rim Riesling, which would provide a great match. This Alsatian-style Riesling is dry, with moderate alcohol levels in the finish, which is important because of the dish's slight heat.

Other selections to try include a fresh, surprisingly rich, virtually dry Rynsky Riesling made by a co-op in Czechoslovakia, a simpler, refreshingly fruity style of Italian Pinot Grigio or a vibrant, lively New Zealand Muller Thurgau.

CHICKEN WITH OYSTERS
AND STRAW MUSHROOMS
IN SPICY SZECHWAN SAUCE

This inspired recipe combines the earthy flavors and sensual textures of the land and the sea. Serve with steamed rice or noodles, to balance the spice of the dish.

4 servings
SAUCE
3 tablespoons oriental sesame oil
2 tablespoons minced garlic
2 tablespoons finely chopped celery
2 tablespoons minced red jalapeño or serrano chilies, with seeds
2 tablespoons peeled, minced fresh ginger
1 cup diced tomatoes
1½ cups Chicken Stock (see recipe, page 128) or canned low-salt broth

2 tablespoons red wine vinegar
2 tablespoons dry white wine
2 tablespoons light soy sauce
2 tablespoons sugar
1 tablespoon cornstarch
2 tablespoons water
CHICKEN
2 tablespoons oriental sesame oil
4 boneless chicken breast halves, cut diagonally into strips
12 fresh oysters, shucked
2 cups straw mushrooms (enoki)
12 fresh cilantro sprigs
3 green onions, julienned

For the sauce: Heat the sesame oil in a heavy, medium saucepan over medium heat. Add the garlic, celery, chilies and ginger and sauté 2 minutes. Mix in the tomatoes, stock, vinegar, wine, soy sauce and sugar and simmer 5 minutes. Combine the cornstarch with water in a small bowl; stir to dissolve. Add the dissolved cornstarch to the sauce in the saucepan and bring to a boil, whisking occasionally. **(Can be prepared 2 hours ahead. Cover and let stand at room temperature.)**

For the chicken: Heat the sesame oil in a heavy, large skillet over high heat. Season the chicken with salt and pepper. Add to the skillet and sauté until cooked through, about 5 minutes. Transfer the chicken to 4 plates, dividing evenly. Add the oysters and mushrooms to the same skillet and sauté 2 minutes. Spoon the oysters and mushrooms around the chicken. Add sauce to the same skillet and bring to a boil. Spoon the sauce over the chicken, oysters and mushrooms. Sprinkle with cilantro and green onions and serve.

WINE NOTES
This dish has a lot of flavors and heat. Look to a Riesling Kabinett to handle it. Because of the chicken and mushrooms, go for a slightly richer and earthier style.

Red wine lovers should choose a wine that's fresh and profusely fruity with a very low key finish in terms of tannins and alcohol. Examples include Côtes de Sonoma Deux Cepages (a simple, straightforward, California Carignan-based wine) and some of the light and fruity Carignan/Grenache-based reds from southern France.

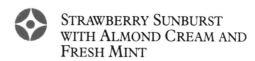

STRAWBERRY SUNBURST WITH ALMOND CREAM AND FRESH MINT

In this dramatic dessert, fresh strawberry slices are used to create a dazzling sunburst pattern. Since it's easy to assemble, it's a good choice for entertaining.

4 servings

STRAWBERRY SAUCE
1 pint strawberries, stemmed
2 tablespoons sugar
1 tablespoon fresh lemon juice
ALMOND CREAM
1 cup plus 2 tablespoons milk
2 extra-large egg yolks
1 tablespoon plus 1/4 cup sugar
2 tablespoons cornstarch
1/4 cup blanched slivered almonds
1/4 cup (1/2 stick) unsalted butter
1 tablespoon amaretto liqueur
3 pints strawberries, stemmed and sliced
8 fresh mint leaves, julienned

For the sauce: Purée the strawberries in a processor. Add the sugar and lemon juice and blend well. Strain the sauce through a sieve set over a bowl. Cover and refrigerate until cold. (**Can be prepared 2 days ahead.**)

For the almond cream: Bring 1 cup of milk to a boil in a heavy, medium saucepan. Whisk the yolks, 1 tablespoon sugar, cornstarch and remaining 2 tablespoons of milk in a medium bowl. Gradually whisk the hot milk mixture into the yolk mixture. Return the mixture to the same saucepan and whisk over medium heat until the custard thickens and boils, about 2 minutes. Transfer the custard to a bowl. Cover and refrigerate until cold.

Finely grind the almonds and remaining 1/4 cup of sugar in a food processor. Blend in the butter and amaretto. Add the custard and blend until smooth. (**Can be prepared 1 day ahead. Cover and refrigerate.**)

Preheat the broiler. Spread the almond cream over the base of 4 broilerproof plates. Arrange the sliced berries in a starburst pattern atop the almond cream. Broil until the almond cream is golden brown, about 5 minutes. Spoon the sauce around the berries. Garnish with mint and serve.

COCONUT-TAPIOCA PUDDING WITH MANGO AND PAPAYA

A cool, creamy finale for a spicy meal, this dessert blends Thai and French culinary principles and ingredients, crowned with Hawaii's premier tropical fruit.

4 servings

3/4 cup small pearl tapioca
2 cups canned unsweetened coconut milk
1/2 cup sugar
4 extra-large egg yolks
1 papaya, peeled, halved, seeded and sliced
1 mango, peeled, pitted and sliced
1 banana, peeled and sliced diagonally
1 cup strawberries, stemmed and halved
4 fresh mint sprigs

Rinse the tapioca in cold water and set aside. Bring 3 quarts of water to a boil in a heavy, large saucepan. Add the tapioca and bring to a boil, stirring occasionally. Reduce the heat and simmer until the tapioca is translucent, stirring occasionally, about 30 minutes. Strain the tapioca into a bowl.

Bring the coconut milk to a boil in a heavy, large saucepan. Whisk the sugar and yolks in a medium bowl to blend. Gradually whisk the hot coconut milk into the yolk mixture. Return the mixture to the saucepan and stir over low heat until the custard thickens and coats the back of a spoon, about 12 minutes; do not boil. Strain the custard into the bowl containing the tapioca; stir to combine. Cover and refrigerate until cold. (**Can be prepared 1 day ahead.**)

Chill 4 large plates. Spoon equal amounts of tapioca on each plate. Arrange the fruit decoratively atop tapioca. Garnish with mint and serve.

Coconut-Tapioca Pudding with Mango and Papaya

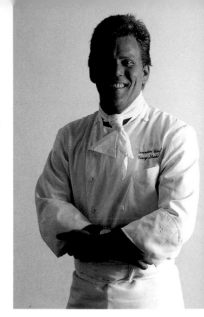

GARY STREHL

Elvis may be the king of rock and roll, but few would dispute that Gary Strehl is the prince of HRC chefs. After all, he's worked for Prince Hotels in Hawaii since 1986—three years as executive chef at the Maui Prince before becoming executive chef of Oahu's Hawaii Prince in 1989. Gary generated more than a few culinary waves for daring to create dishes like sesame grilled Kona crab hash at a time when many hotel chefs were sautéing filet mignon.

Like the singer from Graceland, Gary has never feared shocking his audience. And, while Gary's fans may not swoon at his sight (although they might if he ever came out of the kitchen), they certainly do at his food.

Gary was one of the first of the HRC chefs to land in Hawaii, arriving in 1978 to work in the kitchen of Kapalua Bay Hotel on Maui. With a curious and creative mind, he immediately began to think about what kind of stamp he could put on Hawaiian cuisine.

At the first Kapalua Wine Symposium in 1980, for example, he presented a dish of scallops and shrimp in a *lilikoi* (passion fruit) sauce. Most in attendance were used to tasting passion fruit in cakes or fruit salads, but never in a savory sauce. "At first they were surprised, but after a bite, they were convinced," says Gary. "No one was thinking beyond papaya and pineapple then. They just weren't utilizing the foods that were here."

Gary grew up in New Jersey, but he's quite at home living and cooking at the Pacific crossroads. After graduating with honors from the Culinary Institute of America in 1977 at the age of twenty-three, he worked in such New York restaurants as Tavern on the Green and Maxwell's Plum.

Kahuku Shrimp, Slipper Lobster and Scallops
with Citrus Luau Sauce (See recipe, page 97)

ASIAN DUCKLING CONFIT WITH WILD MUSHROOMS

Each bite of this HRC-style duck confit reveals layers of captivating flavors. Hoisin and Szechwan chili sauces, star anise, Chinese 5-spice powder and other Asian ingredients transform a classic concept into a cross-cultural wonder. Here's a dish with a taste that proves there's just cause for culinary corruption.

4 servings

> 2 ducks (5 pounds each), breasts removed with wings
>   attached, leg-thigh pieces removed
> 1 cup chopped green onions
> 2 teaspoons peeled, minced fresh ginger
> 2 teaspoons minced garlic
> 2 cups sliced shiitake mushrooms
> 2 cups sliced oyster mushrooms
> 8 cups duck stock or Chicken Stock (see recipe,
>   page 128)
> 1 cup Madeira wine
> 1 cup hoisin sauce
> ¼ cup Szechwan chili sauce
> 4 star anise
> ¾ teaspoon Chinese 5-spice powder
> ½ teaspoon chopped fresh thyme
> 1 tablespoon vegetable oil
> 4 cups sliced napa cabbage (wong bok)
> Steamed white rice

Season the duck breasts and leg-thigh pieces with salt and pepper. Heat a heavy, large Dutch oven over high heat. Add the duck pieces in batches and brown well, turning occasionally, about 8 minutes. Transfer the duck pieces to a plate. Pour off the fat from the Dutch oven. Add the green onions, ginger, garlic and mushrooms and sauté until the mushrooms soften, about 5 minutes. Return the duck to the Dutch oven. Add the stock, wine, hoisin, chili sauce, star anise, 5-spice powder and thyme and bring to a boil. Reduce the heat, cover and simmer covered until the breasts are medium-rare, about 12 minutes. Using tongs, transfer the breasts to a plate. Continue cooking uncovered until the leg meat begins to fall off the bones, about 1 hour. Return the breasts to the Dutch oven and heat through. Remove the duck from the Dutch oven. If the sauce is thin, simmer until reduced to a sauce consistency. Set aside.

Heat the oil in a wok over high heat. Add the cabbage and stir-fry 1 minute. Divide the cabbage and rice among 4 plates. Place the duck atop the cabbage and rice. Spoon the sauce over and serve.

WINE NOTES

A well-made California Pinot Noir with a lot of ripe fruit, good structure and moderate tannins is the first recommendation. This type of wine works well with duck, mushrooms and even hoisin sauce. Also, the tannins in the finish are able to counter the duck's innate fattiness.

Several other wines would also work well, such as true Cru-quality Beaujolais from a ripe year, Grenache-based reds from California or France, sturdy but not necessarily heavy California Merlot or fruity, elegant styles of California Zinfandel.

 ## KIAWE-FIRED HAWAIIAN SALMON WITH CHINESE MUSTARD AND TARO-COCONUT PESTO

This striking dish features the interplay of sweet and salty flavors, along with a myriad of textures and colors. Gary uses salmon farm-raised on the Big Island and grilled over *kiawe*, Hawaiian mesquite. If you're in a hurry, skip making the grilled eggplant and wilted greens; the salmon is outstanding on its own.

4 servings

TARO-COCONUT PESTO

> ½ cup raw macadamia nuts
> ¼ cup canned unsweetened coconut milk
> ¼ cup olive oil
> 3 tablespoons chopped fresh basil
> 2 tablespoons fresh cilantro
> 1 piece (¾ inch long) fresh ginger, peeled and minced
> 1 tablespoon cooked taro leaf or spinach
> 1 teaspoon oriental sesame oil
> 1 large garlic clove, minced

CHINESE MUSTARD

> 1 tablespoon dry mustard
> 1 tablespoon honey
> 2 teaspoons soy sauce
> ½ teaspoon peeled, minced, fresh ginger
> ½ teaspoon minced garlic

SALMON

> 1 large eggplant, sliced diagonally
> 4 tablespoons olive oil
> 1½ pounds center cut salmon fillets, cut into four
>   6-ounce (1-inch-thick) pieces
> 2 cups sliced mixed greens, such as mustard greens,
>   romaine and bok choy
> Fresh cilantro sprigs

Kiawe-fired Hawaiian Salmon with Chinese Mustard and Taro-Coconut Pesto

For the pesto: Blend all of the ingredients in a food processor until smooth. **(Can be prepared 1 week ahead. Cover and refrigerate.)**

For the mustard: Mix all of the ingredients in a bowl. **(Can be prepared 1 day ahead. Cover and refrigerate. Bring to room temperature before using.)**

For the salmon: Prepare the barbecue grill (medium heat) or preheat the broiler. Brush the eggplant with 2 tablespoons of oil and grill or broil until golden brown, turning occasionally, about 5 minutes. Transfer to a plate.

Preheat the broiler. Season the salmon with salt and pepper. Brush with 1 tablespoon of oil. Broil the fish until half-cooked, about 4 minutes. Spread 1 tablespoon of

pesto over each salmon piece. Top each piece with 1½ teaspoons Chinese mustard. Continue broiling until the fish is cooked through, about 4 minutes more.

Heat the remaining 1 tablespoon of oil in a heavy, large skillet over high heat. Add the greens and cook until just wilted, turning frequently with tongs, about 1 minute. Divide the eggplant between 4 plates. Top with the greens. Arrange the salmon atop the greens. Garnish with cilantro and serve.

WINE NOTES
This dish is great with a 1982 German Riesling Spatlese. Other wines to consider include elegant styles of Alsatian Pinot Blanc or Muscat with moderate alcohol levels and minimal oakiness.

GINGER ICE CREAM

Fresh ginger sneakily heats the palate up, while the sweet ice cream simultaneously cools it back down. Hawaiian ginger is particularly sweet and juicy.

Makes about 1 quart

2 cups milk
1 cup whipping cream
¼ vanilla bean
9 extra-large egg yolks
¾ cup sugar
½ cup water
¼ cup peeled, chopped fresh ginger
Pinch of freshly ground nutmeg

Bring the milk, cream and vanilla bean to a simmer in a heavy, medium saucepan. Whisk the yolks and ¼ cup of the sugar in a medium bowl to blend. Gradually whisk in the hot milk mixture. Return the mixture to the saucepan and stir over medium-low heat until the custard thickens and leaves a path on the back of the spoon when a finger is drawn across, about 6 minutes; do not boil. Strain the custard into a bowl; refrigerate.

Stir the remaining ½ cup of sugar, the water, ginger and nutmeg in a heavy, small saucepan over low heat until the sugar dissolves. Continue cooking until the mixture resembles syrup, about 4 minutes. Strain the mixture into the custard; refrigerate until cold.

Process the custard in an ice cream maker according to the manufacturer's instructions. Transfer to a container and freeze. **(Can be prepared 3 days ahead.)**

PUNA GOAT CHEESE AND POTATO BRÛLÉE

Bake potatoes with cream, butter, garlic and a potpourri of cheeses and you know you've got a winner. In particular, the Puna goat cheese, a mild, creamy cheese from the Big Island, ensures that these potatoes literally melt in your mouth. On the mainland, substitute a good mild goat cheese from California or France.

6 servings

2 pounds russet potatoes, peeled and quartered
6 garlic cloves, peeled
½ cup whipping cream
¼ cup milk
¼ cup (½ stick) unsalted butter
2 ounces soft, mild goat cheese
¼ cup grated sharp Cheddar cheese
¼ cup grated Swiss cheese
¼ cup minced green onions
3 tablespoons grated Parmesan cheese

Place the potatoes and garlic in a heavy, large saucepan. Add enough cold water to cover by 1 inch and bring to a boil. Cook until tender, about 20 minutes. Drain. Return the potatoes and garlic to the same saucepan and mash with a potato masher. Bring the cream, milk and butter to a boil in a heavy, medium saucepan, stirring frequently. Add the goat cheese, Cheddar cheese and Swiss cheese and whisk until the cheeses melt. Pour the mixture over the potatoes and stir to blend. Mix in the onions. Season with salt and pepper. Spoon the mixture into an 11-inch round ceramic baking dish with 1-inch-high sides. Sprinkle with Parmesan.

Preheat the broiler. Broil the potato mixture until the top is golden brown and the potatoes are heated through, about 5 minutes. Spoon onto plates and serve.

PUMPKIN SIU MAI WITH MAUI STRAWBERRY SALSA

Here's an HRC take on pumpkin pie. A rich pumpkin filling is encased in wontons, and the strawberry salsa is really a finely chopped berry and pineapple sauce. At the Hawaii Prince Hotel, Gary takes this dessert over the top by serving it with homemade Ginger Ice Cream (see recipe, this page).

6 servings
WONTON FILLING
7 ounces cream cheese, room temperature
6 tablespoons sugar
1 tablespoon cornstarch
½ teaspoon ground cinnamon
¼ teaspoon ground ginger
Pinch of ground cloves
¼ cup solid-pack pumpkin
2 extra-large eggs
1 tablespoon whipping cream

Pumpkin Siu Mai with Maui Strawberry Salsa

SALSA
12 medium strawberries, hulled and cut into ¼-inch
   dice
¼ pineapple, peeled and cut into ¼-inch dice
2 tablespoons chopped fresh mint leaves
2 tablespoons sugar
18 wonton wrappers
Vegetable oil (for deep frying)
Fresh mint sprigs

For the wonton filling: Preheat the oven to 350° F. Using an electric mixer, beat the first 6 ingredients in a large bowl to blend. Add the pumpkin, eggs and cream and blend until smooth. Transfer the mixture to a 9-inch round pie dish. Bake just until set, about 20 minutes. Cool. **(Can be prepared 1 day ahead. Cover and refrigerate.)**

For the salsa: Mix the strawberries, pineapple, chopped mint and sugar in a bowl. **(Can be prepared 4 hours ahead. Cover and refrigerate. Bring to room temperature before using.)**

Place ⅟₁₈ of the pumpkin filling in the center of a wonton wrapper. Brush the edge of the wonton with water. Fold the opposite corners of the wonton up and seal the edges firmly, forming a package. Place on a foil-lined baking sheet. Repeat with the remaining wontons and filling.

Heat the oil in a heavy, large deep skillet to 350°F. Add the wontons in batches and fry until golden brown, about 2 minutes. Using a slotted spoon, transfer the wontons to paper towels and drain. Divide the wontons among 6 plates. Surround with the salsa. Garnish with mint sprigs and serve.

ALAN WONG

Few chefs who grow up in pineapple fields wind up cooking on the *Today* show or get hailed as one of America's best chefs, but Alan Wong is no ordinary chef. His route is paved with more than good intentions; stints at West Virginia's Greenbriar and New York's tony Lutèce in the early eighties profoundly influenced the kind of dramatic food he creates at Mauna Lani Bay Hotel and Bungalows' CanoeHouse and Le Soleil restaurants on the Big Island today.

"What I really learned at Lutèce was passion," says Alan. "Witnessing the intense expression of delight on André Soltner's face when he came across quality ingredients was unforgettable."

Alan first learned about quality in those pineapple fields on Oahu in the little town of Waipio, where he grew up. To this day he talks about the flavor of the fresh-picked ripened fruit and remorsefully says that the pineapples most Hawaiian chefs get today are export quality and only one-quarter ripe when harvested.

When Alan first began working as a dishwasher in a Waikiki hotel, he couldn't even fry an egg. "My mom still can't believe what I do," he says with a smile. When he grew bored with one task, he moved on to another, working his way from dishwasher, busboy, waiter, host, cashier and front desk clerk to assistant manager. During this same period, he attended the University of Hawaii, but still couldn't decide what he wanted to do professionally.

Alan hit his stride when he enrolled in the two-year culinary program at Kapiolani Community College on Oahu. Upon graduating in 1979, he was honored with the "most outstanding student" award.

Wok-fried Tempura Ahi
with Shoyu Mustard–Butter Sauce
and Tomato-Ginger Relish
(See recipe, page 108)

Alan enrolled in a two-year apprenticeship program at Greenbriar in West Virginia. The impact of this experience was enormous. "Imagine a kid from the islands who transfers to the mainland, experiences four seasons for the first time, is suddenly a minority and is exposed to a new set of ingredients," says Alan. "It changed my life."

After completing his apprenticeship, Alan decided he wanted to work at New York's Lutèce. The head of the Greenbriar program laughed at Alan's slim chances, but lined up an appointment at the famed eaterie anyway. André Soltner promised that if a position opened, he would give it to Alan. So Alan remained in New York, waiting and working at a Central Park hotel, and finally his wish came true.

"I stayed at Lutèce three years, but it could have been longer," says Alan. "André, who was missing France at the time, warned me not to stay away from Hawaii too long or it might be too late to go back."

Alan returned to Waikiki to work in a hotel in 1986. After transferring to a hotel on Kauai, he went back to Kapiolani Community College in 1988, this time as a culinary instructor.

Word leaked out about this talented chef and in less than one year, he was approached to open CanoeHouse, the much-admired open-air restaurant at the tony Mauna Lani Bay Hotel and Bungalows on the Big Island of Hawaii. Alan's menu, utilizing Hawaiian foodstuffs with a melting pot of Pacific Rim ingredients and techniques, quickly brought him acclaim. Alan now also supervises Mauna Lani Bay's Le Soleil, where his Pacific Rim cuisine incorporates more Western influences.

"I like to describe my cooking as playful," says Alan. "Sometimes I feel like a kid putting things together and making them come out." However, dishes like wok-fried tempura *ahi* with *shoyu* mustard–butter sauce and tomato-ginger relish are a long way from child's play.

Although Alan clearly prefers Asian flavors, his French training is evident in the foundation of his dishes. Sometimes it pops up in presentations, when he prettily fans *ahi* slices across a plate. In other dishes, classic butter sauces, vinaigrettes and mayonnaises are infused with flavors like miso, lemongrass or Hawaiian chili peppers.

"My cooking is as much a fusion as I am," says Alan. "I'm Japanese, Chinese and Hawaiian. Most local ingredients are Asian and ingredients dictate the direction of the food."

Although some may view his cuisine as complicated, Alan sees it differently. "It's based on simple components," he says. "My flavors may be loud, but perhaps it's because I'm subdued."

What's most important to Alan is the absence of labels and parameters tagged to his cuisine. "I don't want to be part of a fad," he says. "I just want to produce good-tasting food. As I keep growing as a chef, my food grows, too." ∎

ASIAN GUACAMOLE

You've undoubtedly consumed dozens of guacamoles, but I'll bet you've never tried one like this before. Alan serves this sake-and-ginger-flavored dip with fresh taro chips; try substituting corn chips.

At Mauna Lani Bay Hotel and Bungalows' CanoeHouse restaurant, Alan often tops crispy chili-scallion chips with roasted duck, hoisin sauce and a spoonful of this guacamole. If you purchase store-bought chips and roast duck from Chinatown, your work for duplicating this appetizer is minimal.

4 servings

2 avocados, peeled, halved, pitted and cut into small cubes
1 tomato, cut into small cubes
½ small onion, minced
3 tablespoons fresh lime juice
3 tablespoons sake
3 tablespoons vegetable oil
1 tablespoon thinly sliced green onion
1 tablespoon minced fresh cilantro
1 tablespoon peeled, minced fresh ginger
½ teaspoon minced jalapeño chili

Combine all of the ingredients in a bowl and mash coarsely. Season with salt.

PUNA GOAT CHEESE SALAD WITH VINE-RIPENED LOKELANI TOMATOES, MAUI ONIONS AND KA'U ORANGES WITH LEMONGRASS DRESSING

This colorful salad is far more simple than its title suggests. Vine-ripened Lokelani tomatoes are grown up-country in Waimea on the Big Island. Ka'u Gold oranges are from Ka'u, on the southern shore of the Big Island. Ka'u oranges are rather ugly as a mold turns their skin brown. But their flesh is sweet and juicy, making them a prized fruit.

The sweet Ka'u oranges play well against the spicy Asian dressing, as does the crunch of the onion against the creamy cheese—another carefully conceived recipe that maintains appeal with each forkful.

4 servings

DRESSING
1 stalk lemongrass (12 inches long), cut into 1-inch
    pieces
1/4 cup sugar
1/4 cup fresh lime juice
1/4 cup soy sauce
1/4 cup water
1 piece fresh ginger (1 inch long), peeled and sliced
1 tablespoon fish sauce (nam pla)
1 1/2 teaspoons Szechwan chili sauce
3 garlic cloves

SALAD
8 ounces soft, mild goat cheese
1 garlic clove, minced
4 oranges
4 tomatoes, sliced
1 small Maui onion or other sweet onion, sliced

For the dressing: Combine all of the ingredients in a food processor and blend until minced. Transfer the dressing to a bowl. Let stand 2 hours at room temperature.

For the salad: Mix the goat cheese and garlic in a small bowl. Season with salt and pepper. Using a small, sharp knife, cut off the peel and white pith from the oranges. Cut between the membranes to release the segments. Arrange the tomatoes, onion and orange segments decoratively on plates. Place a spoonful of cheese in the center. Spoon the dressing over the salad and serve.

WINE NOTES
When you look at this recipe, the goat cheese stands out. But when you taste the salad, the key to the right pairing is in the salad dressing. This dressing has lemongrass, soy sauce, ginger, fish sauce and other exotic flavorings. Try a German Riesling Spatlese from a ripe year like 1989; perhaps from the Pfalz or Rheingau regions. The Riesling will also go well with the goat cheese.

SEARED MAHIMAHI ON SNOW PEAS AND SHIITAKE MUSHROOMS WITH MISO AND SESAME DRESSINGS

The appeal of this dish lies in its delicate flavors as well as its ease of preparation.

2 appetizer servings

MISO DRESSING
2 tablespoons rice vinegar
2 tablespoons Chicken Stock (see recipe, page 128) or
    canned low-salt broth
1 1/2 tablespoons miso
1 1/2 tablespoons sugar

SESAME DRESSING
2 tablespoons vegetable oil
1 tablespoon oriental sesame oil
1 tablespoon rice vinegar
1 teaspoon Dijon mustard
1 teaspoon white sesame seeds, toasted
1/2 teaspoon peeled, minced fresh ginger

MAHIMAHI
1/2 cup julienne of snow peas
1/2 cup julienne of shiitake mushrooms
1 7-ounce 3/4-inch-thick mahimahi steak, cut into
    4 medallions
1 tablespoon peanut oil
1/4 cup diced tomatoes
1 1/2 teaspoons black sesame seeds

For the miso dressing: Mix all of the ingredients in a bowl. Set aside.

For the sesame dressing: Mix all of the ingredients in a bowl. Set aside.

For the mahimahi: Blanch the snow peas in a saucepan of boiling water 10 seconds. Add the mushrooms and blanch 5 seconds. Drain. Transfer the vegetables to a bowl of ice water and cool. Drain.

Season the mahimahi with salt and pepper. Heat the oil in a heavy, medium skillet over high heat. Add the fish and cook until cooked through, about 2 minutes per side. Mound the snow peas, mushrooms and tomatoes in the centers of the plates. Top with the fish. Spoon both of the dressings over the fish. Sprinkle with sesame seeds and serve.

WINE NOTES
Sesame oil, miso and sugar contribute to this dish's apparent sweetness. There's also a little heat from the ginger and mustard. Consider a wine with tons of fresh fruit, good acidity and an even, smooth finish. Malvasia Bianca from California's Ca'del Solo or even some of the Sauvignon Blancs from California, New Zealand or the Loire Valley in France should be pleasing partners.

WOK-FRIED TEMPURA AHI
WITH SHOYU MUSTARD–BUTTER SAUCE
AND TOMATO-GINGER RELISH

Tempura *ahi* is served prettily fanned out in a European-style presentation, with an Asian-flavored *beurre blanc*. The tomato ginger relish balances the sauce's richness. *Shoyu* is the Japanese word for soy sauce.

4 servings

TOMATO-GINGER RELISH
1 cup diced tomato
¼ cup chopped green onion
¼ cup minced Maui onion or other sweet onion
2 tablespoons peeled, minced fresh ginger
1 tablespoon mirin (sweet rice wine)
1 tablespoon rice wine vinegar
1 tablespoon black sesame seeds
1 tablespoon white sesame seeds
1½ teaspoons crushed black peppercorns
1 teaspoon Hawaiian salt or kosher salt
1 teaspoon fish sauce (nam pla)

MUSTARD-BUTTER SAUCE
1 tablespoon dry mustard
1½ tablespoons warm water
1 tablespoon plus 1 teaspoon soy sauce
¼ cup dry white wine
1 tablespoon white wine vinegar
1 tablespoon minced shallot
Pinch of crushed white peppercorns
2 tablespoons whipping cream

AHI
1 cup all-purpose flour
¾ cup plus 2 tablespoons ice water
1 extra-large egg
4 sashimi-grade ahi steaks (approximately 3½ x 2½ inches, 3 ounces and ½ inch thick each)
4 tablespoons wasabi paste
2′ nori sheets (8¼ x 7½ inches), cut in half
Vegetable oil (for deep frying)
Soy sauce (for dipping)
All-purpose flour (for dredging)
½ cup (1 stick) chilled unsalted butter, cut into pieces

For the relish: Mix all of the ingredients in a bowl. (**Can be prepared 6 hours ahead. Cover and refrigerate.**)

For the butter sauce: Mix the mustard with 1½ tablespoons warm water in a small bowl until a paste forms. Gradually whisk in the soy sauce. Set aside. Boil the wine, vinegar, shallot and peppercorns in a heavy, small saucepan until almost no liquid remains in the pan, about 2 minutes. Add the cream and boil until slightly thickened, about 1 minute. Season to taste with salt. Set the reduction aside.

For the *ahi*: Whisk the flour, water and egg in a medium bowl. Set the batter aside. Season the *ahi* with salt. Spread the *wasabi* evenly over 4 *nori* half-sheets. Place 1 piece of the *ahi* on one end of each *nori* sheet. Fold the *nori* over the *ahi* to cover (ends will be exposed).

Heat the oil in a heavy, medium saucepan to 350° F. Dip 1 *ahi* roll in the soy sauce and then in the flour; shake off the excess flour. Dip in the tempura batter and fry in the oil until the outside is crisp and the tuna is rare inside, about 30 seconds. Using a slotted spoon, transfer to paper towels and drain. Repeat with the remaining rolls.

Bring the reduction sauce to a simmer. Gradually whisk in the butter 1 piece at a time. Add enough of the mustard mixture to the butter sauce to the desired taste. Spoon the sauce onto plates. Spoon the relish in the center of the plates. Slice the rolls and arrange them atop the sauce, spacing apart, and serve.

WINE NOTES
With a recipe containing ginger, mirin, black and white peppercorns, dry mustard and soy sauce, it's easy to understand that a slightly sweet wine goes well. Because of the tomatoes and soy sauce, and because the ahi is fried in oil, a slightly sweet Riesling from the Mosel or Saar regions is highly recommended. Finely made versions from the Pacific Northwest and from California can also be used.

MAHIMAHI CURRY WITH CILANTRO–MACADAMIA NUT PESTO AND PINEAPPLE-MANGO SALSA

Alan often prepares this dish with lobster at Mauna Lani Bay Hotel and Bungalows' CanoeHouse restaurant—and it's wonderful that way—but a less costly substitute like mahimahi proves equally satisfying. This curry possesses tremendous depth of flavor and the pesto adds a pleasing richness, yet its medium-strength heat is careful not to overwhelm the taste of the fish.

The Pineapple-Mango Salsa serves as a surprise; at first it's cooling, but then it blasts with its own heat.

When this curry's components are consumed simultaneously, their harmony spells victory on any discerning palate.

4 servings

PESTO
1½ cups loosely packed fresh cilantro with stems
½ cup raw macadamia nuts
2 small green onions, cut into pieces
2 small garlic cloves
1 piece fresh ginger (1 inch long), peeled and sliced
½ cup olive oil
MAHIMAHI CURRY
2 pounds mahimahi, cut into 2-inch pieces
Madras curry powder
¼ cup peanut oil
⅔ cup minced green onions
1 tablespoon cumin seeds
4 lemongrass stalks (12 inches long each), chopped
4 kaffir lime leaves
2 tablespoons peeled, minced fresh ginger
2 tablespoons Madras curry powder
1 tablespoon minced garlic
1 tablespoon red Thai curry paste
1 cup Chicken Stock (see recipe, page 128) or canned low-salt broth
2 cups canned unsweetened coconut milk
Pineapple-Mango Salsa (see recipe, this page)

For the pesto: Purée the first 5 ingredients in a food processor. With the machine running, gradually add the oil and blend until smooth. Transfer the pesto to a bowl. Season with salt and pepper. (**Can be prepared 1 week ahead. Cover and refrigerate.**)

For the curry: Lightly dust the mahimahi with curry powder. Season with salt and pepper. Heat the oil in a heavy, large skillet over high heat. Add the onions and cumin and sauté 2 minutes. Add the mahimahi and sauté just until cooked through, about 3 minutes. Using a slotted spoon, transfer the mahimahi to a bowl. Add the lemongrass, kaffir leaves, ginger, curry powder, garlic and curry paste and sauté 1 minute. Add the stock and bring it to a boil. Add the coconut milk and simmer until reduced to a sauce consistency, about 2 minutes. Mix in ¼ cup of the pesto. Add the mahimahi and stir to heat through. Season with salt and pepper. Spoon the mahimahi curry onto plates. Top with a spoonful of salsa and serve.

WINE NOTES
There is much complexity to this dish; you've got fish, curry, sweet-and-sour salsa and pesto to work with. Consider a French Chenin Blanc, such as semi-sweet Vouvray from a ripe year like 1989 or 1990. This wine has enough sweetness for the salsa, and enough acidity for the fish and pesto.

PINEAPPLE-MANGO SALSA

This sweet and spicy salsa does much to dress up plain grilled chicken or fish. The fish sauce, rice vinegar and honey impart unusual notes, allowing this salsa to also pair beautifully with chicken or fish marinated with Asian flavors.

6 servings

1 cup peeled, diced ripe pineapple
1 cup peeled, diced mango
1 cup diced tomatoes
¼ cup chopped green onions
2 tablespoons vegetable oil
1 tablespoon chopped fresh cilantro
1 tablespoon soy sauce
1 tablespoon fish sauce (nam pla)
2 teaspoons peeled, minced fresh ginger
1½ teaspoons minced jalapeño chilies
1½ teaspoons rice vinegar
1 teaspoon minced garlic
1 teaspoon kiawe honey or other honey

Mix all of the ingredients in a bowl. (**Can be prepared 4 hours ahead. Cover and refrigerate.**)

THAI CRAB-CRUSTED OPAH WITH FENNEL VINAIGRETTE

Opah, or moonfish, is a large-flaked, fatty fish. Alan recommends tuna or swordfish as mainland substitutes for this recipe. If raw eggs are a concern, you may substitute pasteurized liquid whole eggs sold in supermarkets for the vinaigrette.

6 servings

CRAB CRUST

½ cup canned unsweetened coconut milk
½ cup Chicken Stock (see recipe, page 128) or canned low-salt broth
6 kaffir lime leaves, minced
1 piece lemongrass (8 inches long), minced
¾ teaspoon minced garlic
1½ teaspoons peeled, minced fresh ginger
1 teaspoon red Thai curry paste
1½ teaspoons cornstarch dissolved in 2 teaspoons water
½ cup (1 stick) unsalted butter, cut into pieces, room temperature
10 Thai basil leaves, minced
1½ tablespoons fresh lemon juice
1½ tablespoons finely chopped red bell pepper
8 ounces crab meat
¼ cup minced fresh cilantro

FENNEL VINAIGRETTE

⅔ cup vegetable oil
2 tablespoons chopped fennel bulb
2 tablespoons white wine vinegar
1 extra-large egg yolk
2 pinches of sugar

FENNEL-CUCUMBER PURÉE

¼ cup olive oil
¼ cup chopped fennel bulb
1 piece Japanese cucumber or English hothouse cucumber (3 inches long), chopped
1 tablespoon chopped fresh cilantro
1 tablespoon fresh lime juice
¼ teaspoon hot pepper sauce (such as Tabasco)
2 tablespoons vegetable oil
6 opah fillets, 5 ounces each
3 bacon slices, cooked and crumbled
Peeled and diced tomatoes
Chopped fresh chives

For the crab crust: Bring the coconut milk and stock to a boil in a heavy, small saucepan. Add the lime leaves, lemongrass, garlic, ginger and curry paste. Add the cornstarch mixture and bring to a boil, stirring constantly. Reduce heat to very low. Add the butter and whisk until melted. Add the basil, lemon juice and bell pepper. Pour ¾ cup of the coconut sauce into a bowl and cool (reserve any remainder for another use). Add the crab and cilantro to ¾ cup of the sauce in the bowl and mix well. (**Can be prepared 4 hours ahead. Cover and refrigerate.**)

For the vinaigrette: Purée all of the ingredients in a blender until smooth. (**Can be prepared 4 hours ahead. Cover and refrigerate. Bring to room temperature before serving.**)

For the purée: Purée the first 6 ingredients in a blender until smooth. (**Can be prepared 4 hours ahead. Cover and refrigerate. Let stand 2 hours at room temperature before serving.**)

Preheat the oven to 450° F. Heat the vegetable oil in a heavy, large skillet over high heat. Add the fish and sear on both sides. Transfer to a baking sheet. Top the fish with the crab mixture. Bake until the fish is cooked through, about 10 minutes.

Spoon the vinaigrette on plates. Top with the fish. Spoon dots of the purée on the vinaigrette. Garnish with the bacon, tomatoes and chives and serve.

WINE NOTES

The crust has ginger, red Thai curry paste and lemongrass, while the fennel in the vinaigrette has real influence on the taste of the finished dish. A fruity-styled Riesling, Kabinett to Spatlese level, from the Mosel or Saar regions of Germany should go nicely. The slight sweetness of these wines could easily handle this dish's seasoning. Furthermore, the slatey, minerally character of these wines is an interesting match with the fennel and other exotic flavors.

Well-made French Vouvray Demi-Sec would make another good partner. Slightly sweet Vouvray and finer Demi-Sec examples of Montlouis work well with Thai seafood dishes. The faint sweetness can handle the heat and the crisp acidity cleanses the palate.

Thai Crab-crusted Opah with Fennel Vinaigrette

SHREDDED COCONUT-CHILI BEEF WITH TARO CRÊPES

This gutsy dish is Hawaii Regional Cuisine soul food at its best. The chorus of good flavors in the coconut-chili beef are as sublime as the crêpes made from taro. The accompanying tropical salsa brightens the plate and serves as a flavor counterpoint.

8 servings

COCONUT-CHILI SAUCE
4 shallots
3 garlic cloves
1 piece ginger (1½ inches long), peeled
5 dried red Japanese chilies
3 lemongrass stalks (8 inches long each), sliced
¼ cup plus 1 tablespoon peanut oil
½ cup freshly grated coconut meat
2 cups canned unsweetened coconut milk
¼ cup tomato paste
1 tablespoon tamarind juice
1½ teaspoons sugar
1½ cups Veal Stock (see recipe, page 128)
3 pounds beef shoulder, cut into 3-inch cubes

TARO CRÊPES
1 cup plus 2 tablespoons milk
½ cup all-purpose flour
½ cup cooked mashed taro
1 extra-large egg
¼ teaspoon salt
Butter
8 tablespoons Pineapple-Mango Salsa (see recipe, page 109)

For the sauce: Blend the first 5 ingredients in a food processor until the mixture resembles a paste. Heat ¼ cup of the oil in a heavy, large saucepan over medium-high heat. Add the paste mixture and fry until dry, stirring frequently, about 3 minutes. Add the grated coconut and sauté 3 minutes. Add the coconut milk, tomato paste, tamarind juice and sugar and simmer 3 minutes. Add the stock and simmer 5 minutes, skimming surface frequently. (**Sauce can be prepared 1 day ahead. Cover and refrigerate.**)

Heat the remaining 1 tablespoon of oil in a heavy, large Dutch oven over high heat. Add the beef in batches and brown well. Add 4 cups of coconut-chili sauce and bring to a boil. Reduce the heat, cover and simmer until the beef is tender, stirring occasionally, about 2½ hours. Cool slightly. Shred the beef with your fingertips and combine with the sauce in the Dutch oven. (**Can be prepared 1 day ahead. Cover and refrigerate.**)

For the crepes: Whisk the milk, flour, taro, egg and salt in a medium bowl to blend. Heat a 7-inch-diameter nonstick skillet over medium-high heat. Brush with butter. Add ¼ cup of the batter to the skillet and tilt so the batter coats the skillet. Pour the excess batter back into the bowl. Cook until the bottom is brown, about 2 minutes. Turn and cook the second side 1 minute. Turn the crêpe out onto a plate. Repeat with the remaining butter, forming 8 crêpes.

Bring the shredded chili beef to a simmer in the Dutch oven. Place ½ cup of the shredded chili beef at 1 end of 1 crêpe. Roll up into a cylinder and place seam side down on plate. Repeat with 7 more crêpes and chili and transfer to plates. Spoon 1 tablespoon of the chili sauce and 1 tablespoon of the salsa next to each crêpe and serve.

WINE NOTES
A cool, thirst-quenching beer is best for this dish; something snappy and refreshing, with enough flavor to handle the beef.

GRILLED LAMB CHOPS
WITH MACADAMIA-COCONUT CRUST,
CABERNET SAUVIGNON JUS
AND COCONUT-GINGER CREAM

These lamb chops are a marvel of tenderness edged with the intensity of the Cabernet Sauvignon sauce. The macadamia-coconut crust doesn't come across as too sweet, as it's balanced by this pungent sauce perfumed with star anise and fennel seeds.

4 servings

MACADAMIA-COCONUT CRUST

¾ cup honey
¾ cup grated coconut meat
¾ cup chopped macadamia nuts
3 tablespoons chopped fresh parsley
3 tablespoons chopped fresh thyme leaves
1 tablespoon minced garlic

COCONUT-GINGER CREAM

1 cup canned unsweetened coconut milk
1 piece fresh ginger (2 inches long), smashed
2 tablespoons sugar

CABERNET SAUVIGNON JUS

1 cup Cabernet Sauvignon
¼ cup mirin (sweet rice wine)
¼ cup mushroom soy sauce
1 cup Lamb Stock (see recipe, page 128)
8 star anise
2 teaspoons fennel seeds
2 cinnamon sticks
2 teaspoons coriander seeds

LAMB

¼ cup olive oil
3 racks of lamb (¼ pounds each), cut into double chops

For the crust: Mix all of the ingredients in a small bowl. **(Can be prepared 1 day ahead. Cover and refrigerate.)**

For the cream: Bring all of the ingredients to a boil in a heavy, medium saucepan. Boil until reduced by half, about 5 minutes. Transfer to a bowl; remove the ginger. **(Can be prepared 1 day ahead. Cover and refrigerate.)**

For the jus: Boil the Cabernet Sauvignon in a heavy, medium saucepan until reduced to ¼ cup, about 10 minutes. Add the mirin and soy sauce and boil until reduced by half, about 3 minutes. Add the remaining ingredients, reduce the heat to low, cover and simmer 15 minutes. Season with salt and pepper. Strain into another heavy, medium saucepan. **(Can be prepared 1 day ahead. Cover and refrigerate.)**

For the lamb: Prepare the barbecue grill (medium heat). Rub oil over the lamb chops. Let stand 30 minutes. Season the lamb with salt and pepper. Grill the lamb to the desired doneness, about 5 minutes per side for medium-rare.

Preheat the broiler. Place the lamb on a baking sheet. Press the crust mixture over the chops. Broil until golden brown, about 3 minutes.

Meanwhile, bring the jus and coconut cream to a simmer in separate saucepans. Ladle the jus onto plates. Spoon the cream decoratively in 4 to 5 nickel-size dots atop the sauce. Top with lamb and serve.

WINE NOTES

Cabernet Sauvignon seems to be the definitive partner and one with generous, ripe fruit and medium to medium-high tannin levels is the way to go. Many fine examples are produced in California.

You could also pair well with moderately aged, well-made Italian Barolo and Barbaresco. These wines are hard and unyielding in their youth, yet very perfumey and elegant with age. A well-stored 1978 would be right in between and still possess enough fruit and tannins needed for the lamb.

HOISIN-GLAZED PORK RIBS

Sometimes you look at a recipe and it only hints at the magic of when its components come together in the cooked dish. These mouth-watering, glistening, finger-licking-good ribs happen to fall in that category.

They also happen to be one of the most popular dishes ever served at Mauna Lani Bay Hotel and Bungalows' CanoeHouse restaurant. Although they're listed on the menu as a *pupu,* or appetizer, they're often ordered as a mountainous entrée and gnawed down to a hill of bones.

6 servings

1 cup ketchup
¾ cup hoisin sauce
½ cup honey
5 tablespoons soy sauce
5 tablespoons dry sherry
¼ cup plus 2 teaspoons white wine vinegar
¼ cup sesame seeds
2 tablespoons plus 2 teaspoons curry powder
2 tablespoons plus 2 teaspoons oriental sesame oil
2 tablespoons grated orange peel
2 tablespoons fermented black beans
2 tablespoons minced gärlic
1 tablespoon chili paste with garlic
3 pounds pork baby back ribs

Whisk all of the ingredients except the ribs in a large bowl to blend. Divide the ribs between 2 large baking dishes. Brush with half of the sauce. Cover the ribs and remaining sauce separately and refrigerate overnight.

Preheat the oven to 375° F. Transfer the ribs to heavy, large baking sheets. Roast the ribs until tender, basting frequently with some of remaining sauce, about 1 hour.

Place the remaining sauce in a heavy, small saucepan and bring to a simmer. Transfer the ribs to a platter. Cut into individual ribs. Serve, passing the remaining sauce separately.

WINE NOTES
These ribs are a natural with Grenache-based reds from a ripe vintage. Choose a wine with very ripe, delicious—almost sweet—fruit and medium tannins. Make sure the alcohol content is moderate to ensure a smooth, even finish.

California Zinfandel is another easy option. Select a wine packed with fruit, yet elegant in style and with moderate alcohol levels.

 LYCHEE-GINGER SORBET

Alan created this recipe after tasting a dessert wine with the nuances of lychee. He usually serves it with Waimea strawberries, sweet and juicy berries which grow up-country on the Big Island.

If using fresh lychees, you may need to increase the amount of sugar. Taste the sorbet mixture before churning and sweeten with additional sugar as needed.

Makes about 1 quart

2 cups water
¾ cup sugar
2 tablespoons peeled, minced fresh ginger
2 cups puréed fresh lychees or puréed, drained canned lychees in syrup

Bring the first 3 ingredients to a boil in a heavy, medium saucepan, stirring until the sugar dissolves. Strain into a large bowl. Add the lychee purée and refrigerate until cold. Process the purée in an ice cream maker according to the manufacturer's instructions. **(Can be prepared 3 days ahead. Freeze in covered container.)** Scoop the sorbet onto chilled plates and serve.

Hoisin-glazed Pork Ribs

ROY YAMAGUCHI

oy Yamaguchi is opening so many restaurants throughout the Pacific Rim, that travel agents can soon set up foodie tours for Roy's fans, designed exclusively around his eateries. These epicurean odysseys can begin on Oahu, with a visit to Roy's first and signature establishment, Roy's Restaurant in Hawaii Kai. Then it's a short hop by jet to Maui, for a vibrant meal at Roy's Kahana Bar & Grill and the adjacent, family-style RJ's Ranch House.

Board an international flight to Tokyo for dinner at Roy's Tokyo Restaurant, before jetting to the Guam Hilton and a meal at Roy's Guam. And by the time you've digested all of the above, there'll probably be another five or six of Roy's restaurants open in the Orient. Talk about one peripatetic chef!

Roy may be peripatetic, but his cuisine isn't. This chef sticks to one course when it comes to culinary style. Roy's focus is what he calls Euro-Asian food, no matter where the restaurant's geographic locale. Roy's dishes are highly inventive, but firmly based on classic European culinary techniques. His effortless ability to seamlessly infuse Oriental ingredients into Western-principled dishes is viewed with awe by most, with envy by many.

Roy is one chef who truly earned his success; it didn't come easy. Born and raised in Japan, he took the advice of a guidance counselor who suggested he attend cooking school. He arrived at New York's Culinary Institute of America in 1974 with big dreams and a tiny budget. It took months for his belongings to arrive from Japan, and since he couldn't afford to purchase anything new, he slept on a pillowcase stuffed with underwear and socks.

Roy graduated from the CIA in 1976 and flew to Los Angeles seeking employment. To save money, he often walked miles for job interviews. He actually turned down an offer from the legendary L'Ermitage restaurant and worked in other kitchens around town for two years until he decided he was good enough for the city's foremost dining establishment of the time.

Roy moved on to the kitchen of tony Michael's in Santa Monica, California, before becoming chef of the Le Gourmet restaurant at the former Sheraton Plaza La Reina by the Los Angeles International Airport in 1981. It was in this unlikely setting that Roy dared to experiment with the blend of Oriental and French culinary styles. And the buzz over Roy's cooking began.

In 1984, Roy became executive chef and partner of 385 North in West Hollywood, and the buzz turned into a roar. The clear, distinct flavors of his cross-cultural dishes were the talk of newspaper food sections and culinary magazines nationwide.

"I never wanted to open French or Japanese restaurants, because they already existed," explains Roy. "I was classically trained in French cooking and I still love French food, but I like to balance it with Italian, Thai, Japanese and Chinese factors. Basically," says this succinct chef, "I cook what I like to eat."

While Roy was receiving accolades at 385 North, Hawaii kept popping into mind. His grandfather had lived in Maui since 1918 and his dad was born on Maui; the islands were the idyllic site of many of Roy's summer vacations. How nice it would be, he mused, to open a restaurant at the crossroads of the Pacific.

Just before Christmas in 1988, he moved to Hawaii and opened Roy's Restaurant in a Honolulu suburb. His sun-drenched flavors enthralled his Oahu audience. This eaterie was quickly dubbed the "Spago of Hawaii," luring many mainland as well as local celebrities to call it their favorite kitchen away from home.

Despite such enormous success, Roy remains low-key. He's reluctant to tell people he meets that he's a famous chef and restaurateur. "I usually say I'm in between jobs," shrugs Roy. "I just don't like to talk about myself."

In his minimal spare time, Roy is taping a PBS Hawaii television program called *Hawaii Cooks with Roy Yamaguchi.* Among his almost countless honors, he was recently named one of the best American regional chefs by the James Beard Foundation at the annual James Beard Awards.

Yet Roy makes it clear that what he truly loves most is standing in front of a stove. "I like to cook more than anything else in the world," says Roy. "For me, that's where it's at." ■

Rustic Opakapaka with White Beans,
Thyme and Olive Oil (See recipe, page 119)

116

CRISP VEGETABLE SUSHI WITH THAI PEANUT DIPPING SAUCE

The fennel and yams give this HRC-style sushi a surprising flavor twist. The sweet/hot Thai dipping sauce has more complexity than most; it can also be served with satays or crudités.

8 servings

DIPPING SAUCE

1 cup canned unsweetened coconut milk
¼ cup chopped onion
¼ cup smooth natural-style peanut butter
¼ cup chopped fresh cilantro
2 tablespoons brown sugar
2 tablespoons rice wine vinegar
2 tablespoons sliced fresh basil leaves
1½ tablespoons soy sauce
1½ kaffir lime leaves
1 tablespoon yellow curry paste
2 garlic cloves, minced
½ shallot, minced

SUSHI

1½ cups julienne of carrot
1½ cups julienne of celery
1½ cups julienne of fennel bulb
1½ cups julienne of daikon radish
2 cups julienne of peeled purple sweet potatoes or orange-fleshed sweet potatoes
8 sheets roasted seaweed sushi nori (about 8 x 7-inch rectangles)
¼ cup soy sauce
Peanut oil (for deep frying)

For the sauce: Combine all of the ingredients in a saucepan. Bring to a simmer, stirring frequently. **(Can be prepared 1 day ahead. Cover and refrigerate.)**

For the sushi: Bring a large pot of water to a boil. Add the carrots and cook until crisp-tender, about 1 minute. Transfer to a bowl of ice water using a slotted spoon and cool. Return the water in the pot to a boil. Add the celery, fennel and daikon and cook until crisp-tender, about 15 seconds. Using a slotted spoon, transfer the vegetables to the same bowl of ice water and cool. Return the water in the pot to a boil. Add the sweet potatoes and cook until crisp tender, about 1 minute. Using a slotted spoon, transfer the potatoes to a bowl of ice water and cool. Drain the vegetables.

Place 1 *nori* sheet on a bamboo sushi roller. Starting 1 inch in from 1 short side, sprinkle ⅛ of the vegetables in a 1-inch-high, 1½-inch-wide strip across the *nori*. Sprinkle the *nori* with some of the soy sauce. Using the sushi roller as an aid, roll the *nori* into a cylinder, covering the vegetables completely; seal the edges. Repeat with the remaining *nori*, vegetables and soy sauce.

Heat the oil in a deep fryer or a heavy large deep skillet to 350° F. Fry the sushi in batches until crisp, about 3 minutes. Using a slotted spoon, transfer to paper towels and drain. Cut each sushi roll crosswise into thirds. Bring the sauce to a simmer; pour into a bowl and set on the platter. Surround the sauce bowl with sushi and serve.

WINE NOTES

At Roy's Restaurant, wine maven/manager Randy Caparoso recommends Babcock Riesling from California. Its sweetness cools and soothes the palate, while the acidity clears it.

Alternatively, a cool, snappy Pilsner-style beer will cool the palate.

HIBACHI-STYLE TUNA WITH MAUI ONIONS AND PONZU SAUCE

Hibachi cooking is big in Hawaii, and this recipe could bolster its mainland popularity—although you can use a standard barbecue grill. The tuna takes on a rich, mahogany hue from the sweet/salty marinade. After it's grilled, it's lightly bathed in a citrusy vinaigrette and served on a bed of crunchy vegetables.

4 servings

PONZU SAUCE

1 cup mirin
¾ cup low-sodium soy sauce
3 tablespoons fresh lemon juice
1 teaspoon dried red pepper flakes

TUNA

½ cup soy sauce
½ cup sugar
4 green onions, sliced
1½ teaspoons chopped garlic
1 tablespoon peeled, minced fresh ginger
4 sashimi-grade ahi steaks, 5 ounces and 1 inch thick each
1 small Maui onion or other sweet onion, julienned
½ Japanese cucumber or English hothouse cucumber, julienned
1 package (2 ounces) radish sprouts

For the sauce: Boil the mirin in a heavy, small saucepan until reduced to ⅓ cup, about 5 minutes. Pour into a small bowl. Whisk in the remaining ingredients. **(Can be prepared 1 day ahead. Cover and set aside at room temperature.)**

For the tuna and vegetables: Mix the first 5 ingredients in a large baking dish. Add the fish; turn to coat. Cover and let stand 1 hour at room temperature.

Prepare the hibachi-style grill or barbecue grill (high heat). Remove the fish from the marinade and grill the fish about 1 minute per side. Toss the onion, cucumber and sprouts together in a bowl. Divide the vegetables among 4 plates. Top with the fish. Spoon the Ponzu Sauce over the fish and serve.

 RUSTIC OPAKAPAKA WITH WHITE BEANS, THYME AND OLIVE OIL

While some HRC chefs look only to the East for inspiration, Roy often straddles both sides of the crossroads. The earthy Italian overtones lent to this Hawaiian pink snapper preparation create the kind of dish that you can't stop eating until the plate is empty. Sea bass or orange roughy will also work in the recipe.

4 servings

1 yellow bell pepper
1 red bell pepper
2 fresh thyme sprigs
2 fresh rosemary sprigs
7 tablespoons extra-virgin olive oil
3/4 cup dried small white beans
3 ounces pancetta or bacon, diced
1/2 small white onion, diced
1/2 tablespoon chopped garlic
3 cups Chicken Stock (see recipe, page 128) or canned low-salt broth
1/2 cup peeled, seeded and chopped tomato
1 tablespoon minced fresh thyme
1/4 teaspoon minced fresh rosemary
4 opakapaka fillets, 6 ounces and 1 1/2 inches thick each
4 ounces paper-thin prosciutto slices, julienned
1 teaspoon balsamic vinegar

Char the peppers over a gas flame or in a broiler until blackened on all sides. Seal the peppers in a paper bag and let them steam 10 minutes. Peel, seed and cut the peppers into julienne strips. (**Can be prepared 1 day ahead. Cover and refrigerate.**)

Rub the herbs between your fingertips and combine with the oil in a bowl. Cover and set aside at room temperature. Place the beans in a large saucepan. Add enough cold water to cover by 3 inches and soak overnight.

Drain the beans. Remove the herbs sprigs from the oil and discard. Heat 1 tablespoon of oil in a heavy, large saucepan over medium-high heat. Add the pancetta and cook until brown, stirring frequently, about 4 minutes. Add the onion and garlic and sauté until tender, about 6 minutes. Add the stock, 1 1/2 cups water, beans, tomato, minced thyme and minced rosemary. Season with pepper and bring to a boil. Reduce heat and simmer until the beans are tender, stirring occasionally and adding more water if necessary, about 1 1/2 hours. Drain the beans if necessary. (**Can be prepared 4 hours ahead. Cover and let stand at room temperature.**)

Heat 2 tablespoons of oil in a heavy, large skillet over high heat. Add the fish and cook until cooked through, turning once, about 3 minutes per side. Transfer the fish to a platter. Tent with foil to keep warm. Add the bell peppers and prosciutto to the fish cooking skillet and stir to heat through. Mix in the vinegar. Bring the bean mixture to a simmer. Spoon the bean mixture onto plates. Top with the fish. Spoon the remaining 4 tablespoons of oil around the beans and serve.

WINE NOTES

As this dish is very Mediterranean in style, well-made wines from the coastal region of southern France and Italy work well. Try Clos Nicrosi from the island of Corsica or Carretta's Bianco del Poggio (Nebbiolo vinified wine) from the Piedmont region of Italy. Other considerations include some of the dry rosés from Provence, France, and the better producers of Italy.

Randy Caparoso, the venerable mastermind behind Roy's progressive wine list and programs, notes that at the restaurant, this dish is often paired with red wine. Sometimes it's a lighter style of California Merlot, a Loire Valley Cabernet Franc or a light-to-medium southern French red (like Domaine de la Gautière or Tempier's Bandol "Cuvée Speciale"). However, the most enthusiastic response goes to a pairing with a Burgundian Pinot Noir with lots of enjoyable fruit, firm acidity and softer tannins.

CURRY-BLACKENED HAWAIIAN SWORDFISH WITH CUCUMBER, TOMATO AND GINGER RELISH

Blacken Hawaiian swordfish (*shutome*) with ingredients like lemongrass, ginger and garlic, and you're guaranteed one flavor-infused fish. The accompanying cucumber, tomato and ginger relish first cools the palate and then heats it back up, thanks to the spicy sesame oil and ginger. This recipe doubles or triples easily.

2 servings

MARINADE
¼ cup olive oil
3 tablespoons hot oriental sesame oil
2 tablespoons soy sauce
2 tablespoons minced lemongrass
2 tablespoons curry powder
1 teaspoon grated fresh ginger
1 teaspoon minced garlic
½ teaspoon cumin powder
2 swordfish steaks, 7 ounces and 1-inch thick

RELISH
1 tablespoon olive oil
½ teaspoon hot oriental sesame oil
1 piece fresh ginger (1 inch long), grated
¼ teaspoon minced garlic
½ cucumber, halved lengthwise, peeled and seeded, sliced
1 small tomato, diced
¼ teaspoon soy sauce
⅛ teaspoon salt
⅛ teaspoon white pepper

For the marinade: Mix all of the ingredients except the fish in a bowl. Place the fish in a large glass baking dish. Pour the marinade over the fish and turn to coat. Cover and let stand 1 hour at room temperature.

For the relish: Heat both of the oils in a heavy, large skillet over high heat. Add the ginger and garlic and sauté 1 minute. Mix in the cucumber and tomato. Remove the skillet from heat. Mix in the soy sauce, salt and white pepper.

Meanwhile, heat a heavy, large skillet over high heat. Remove the swordfish from the marinade and place in the hot skillet. Sauté until cooked through, turning once, about 5 minutes. Divide the fish between plates. Spoon the relish over the fish and serve.

WINE NOTES
Try a red wine with this dish. You need a youthful, fresh, ripe wine with firm acidity and moderate tannins and alcohol. Consider a ripe and juicy Pinot Noir, Tempier's Bandol ''La Tourtine'' or a 1990 Chinon.

Randy Caparoso, Roy's sommelier, likes to recommend red wines with a rustic character such as Talosa's Rosso di Montepulciano from Italy, light, fruity, traditional-style Spanish reds or even a well-made Bourgueil from the Loire Valley of France.

MONGOLIAN-STYLE CHICKEN PIZZA

At Roy's Restaurant on Oahu, crusty pizzas fly out of the oven faster than you can count them. It seems that all Roy's guests crave his exotic pies, and this one—evocatively garnished with pickled red ginger and radish sprouts—is one of the most requested.

Makes four 7-inch pizzas

DOUGH
¼ cup warm water (105° F to 115° F)
2¼ teaspoons sugar
1½ teaspoons dry yeast
2 cups (or more) all-purpose flour or bread flour
⅔ cup warm water (105° F to 115° F)
½ cup semolina
2 tablespoons extra-virgin olive oil
1½ tablespoons honey
½ teaspoon salt
TOPPING
½ cup hoisin sauce
1 teaspoon Szechwan chili sauce
1 teaspoon teriyaki sauce
½ teaspoon peeled, grated fresh ginger
½ teaspoon minced garlic
2 boneless chicken breast halves (6 ounces each) with skin
1½ cups grated mozzarella cheese
½ cup grated fontina cheese
1 tablespoon grated fresh Parmesan cheese
2 tablespoons yellow cornmeal
¼ cup each julienne of red, green and yellow bell peppers
1 large shiitake mushroom (about 1½ ounces), stemmed and julienned
2 ounces pickled red ginger
1 package (2 ounces) radish sprouts

For the dough: Whisk the first 3 ingredients in a small, metal bowl to dissolve the yeast. Let stand 10 minutes. Mix 2 cups of flour, ⅔ cup of water, semolina, oil, honey and salt in the bowl of a heavy duty mixer fitted with a dough hook. Add the yeast mixture and mix until the dough is soft and no longer sticky, adding more flour if necessary, about 1 minute. Lightly oil a large bowl. Add the dough; turn to coat. Cover the bowl with plastic wrap and let the dough rise in a warm, draft-free area until doubled in volume, about 1 hour. While the dough rises, prepare the toppings.

For the toppings: Prepare the barbecue grill (medium-high heat) or preheat the broiler. Mix the first 5 ingredients in a small bowl. Brush the chicken with some of the hoisin mixture (reserve the remaining hoisin mixture for pizzas) and grill or broil until almost cooked through, about 3 minutes per side. Transfer the chicken to a plate and cool. Cut the chicken into strips. Mix all of cheeses in a medium bowl. Cover and set aside.

Preheat the oven to 400°F. Sprinkle 2 large baking sheets with cornmeal. Turn the dough out onto a lightly floured surface. Cut the dough into 4 pieces. Roll out each dough piece to a 7-inch round. Place 2 pizzas on each baking sheet. Brush with some of the reserved hoisin mixture. Sprinkle half of the cheese mixture all over the pizzas, dividing evenly. Sprinkle with the bell peppers, mushroom and chicken. Sprinkle the remaining cheese evenly over the pizzas. Bake the pizzas until golden brown and the topping bubbles, about 20 minutes. Cut the pizzas into 4 wedges and reassemble on plates. Garnish the center with pickled ginger and sprouts and serve.

WINE NOTES
This pizza needs a red wine with ripe fruit, firm acidity and medium tannins. Consider an upbeat version of Italian Barbera such as Moccagatta's with its delicious, fresh fruit, Qupe's fresh, peppery and slightly smoky Syrah from California or a tempered Australian Shiraz like Rosemount's.

*Lemongrass Island Chicken with
Crispy Pan-sautéed Thai Noodles
in Ginger-Lime Sauce
(See recipe, page 124)*

LEMONGRASS ISLAND CHICKEN WITH CRISPY PAN-SAUTÉED THAI NOODLES IN GINGER-LIME SAUCE

The HRC touches to this recipe ward off any possibility of consuming a dry or bland chicken breast. The lemongrass marinade infuses all its good flavor into the poultry and then makes an appearance in an accompanying sauce. Crispy noodles are formed into crunchy pancakes and used as a bed for the chicken.

6 servings

CHICKEN AND SAUCE
1 small bunch fresh cilantro
2 garlic cloves
1 lemongrass stalk (12 inches long), cut into ½-inch pieces
1 shallot, quartered
¾ cup canned unsweetened coconut milk
¼ cup peanut oil
2 teaspoons fresh lemon juice
½ teaspoon pepper
6 boneless chicken breast halves
3 cups Chicken Stock (see recipe, page 128) or canned low-salt broth
2 tablespoons peeled, minced fresh ginger

NOODLES AND VEGETABLES
6 ounces fresh chow mein noodles
8 tablespoons olive oil
7½ teaspoons oriental sesame oil
4 ounces fresh shiitake mushrooms, stemmed and sliced
¾ cup snow peas, stringed and julienned
½ red or yellow bell pepper, julienned
2 celery stalks, julienned
1 large carrot, peeled and julienned
¾ cup mung bean sprouts
2 teaspoons peeled, minced fresh ginger
1 garlic clove, minced
1 tomato, peeled, halved, seeded and julienned
1 small fresh cilantro bunch, chopped
1 tablespoon soy sauce
¼ cup (½ stick) unsalted butter, cut into pieces, room temperature
2 tablespoons fresh lime juice

For the chicken and sauce: Mince the first 4 ingredients in a food processor. Transfer to a large bowl. Mix in the coconut milk, oil, lemon juice and pepper. Season with salt. Add the chicken and marinate 1 hour.

Remove the chicken from the marinade. Place the marinade, chicken stock and minced ginger in a heavy, large saucepan. Boil until the marinade mixture is reduced to 1 cup, skimming any fat from the surface, about 25 minutes. Strain. **(Can be prepared 1 day ahead. Cover and refrigerate the chicken and sauce separately.)**

For the noodles and vegetables: Add the noodles to a large pot of boiling water. Return the water to a boil and cook 1½ minutes, stirring occasionally. Drain. Rinse the noodles with cold water. Drain well. Mix with 1 tablespoon of olive oil.

Preheat the oven to warm. Divide the noodles into 6 portions. Heat 1 tablespoon of olive oil and 1½ teaspoons of sesame oil in a heavy, large skillet over medium heat. Add 2 noodle portions and flatten slightly into 6-inch rounds. Cook until golden brown, about 6 minutes per side. Transfer to paper towels. Repeat with the remaining oil and noodles in 2 more batches using 1 tablespoon of olive oil and 1½ teaspoons of sesame oil for each batch. Transfer the pancakes to a baking sheet and keep warm in the oven while preparing vegetables.

Heat 2 tablespoons of olive oil in a heavy, large skillet over medium heat. Pat the chicken dry. Add to the skillet and sauté until cooked through, about 4 minutes per side. Transfer to a plate; tent with foil to keep warm.

Heat the remaining 2 tablespoons of olive oil and 3 teaspoons of sesame oil in the same skillet over high heat. Add the mushrooms, snow peas, bell pepper, celery, carrot and bean sprouts and stir-fry 1 minute. Add the ginger and garlic and cook 30 seconds. Add the tomato and cilantro and stir-fry 1 minute. Mix in the soy sauce.

Bring the sauce to a simmer in a heavy, small saucepan. Add the butter and whisk just until melted. Whisk in the lime juice.

Place 1 pancake on each of 6 plates. Top with the vegetables and chicken. Spoon the sauce around the pancakes and serve.

WINE NOTES
Consider a rosé like Babcock Fathom Rosé, which is dry and fruity at the same time. Since it's made from Pinot Noir, Sauvignon Blanc, Semillon and Gewurztraminer, you can understand why. The fruity quality soothes the mouth and the crisp acidity cleans it up afterward. White wines with similar characteristics, such as the Italian Arioso under the Il Podere dell'Olivos label and the California Conundrum from Caymus, also work well. Demi-Sec Vouvray is another option.

You can also select a red wine that is fresh, vibrant and lively. Wines that come to mind include Azelia's Dolcetto D'Alba, a light Spanish red like Montesierra, Bonny Doon's Clos de Gilroy from California or a light California Pinot Noir.

GRILLED SZECHWAN-STYLE BABY BACK RIBS

The first sign that these ribs are out of the ordinary is that they're simmered in chicken stock redolent with ginger, garlic and cilantro. Then they're brushed twice with a hoisin-based sauce—after simmering and before grilling—which ensures they're permeated with flavor to the bone.

4 servings

RIBS
1 small bunch fresh cilantro
½ bunch fresh parsley
2 garlic cloves
1 piece fresh ginger (1 inch long), peeled
12 cups Chicken Stock (see recipe, page 128) or canned low-salt broth
3¼ pounds baby back ribs (2 racks)
SAUCE
⅔ cup hoisin sauce
2 tablespoons miso (soybean paste)
4 teaspoons minced fresh ginger
4 teaspoons minced garlic
4 teaspoons sake or dry sherry
4 teaspoons soy sauce
2 teaspoons sugar
2 teaspoons chili paste with garlic

For the ribs: Mince the first 4 ingredients in a processor. Transfer to a large Dutch oven. Add the stock and ribs and bring to a boil. Reduce the heat, cover and simmer over medium heat until the ribs are tender, about 30 minutes.

For the sauce: Mix all of the ingredients in a medium bowl.

Drain the ribs and transfer to a baking sheet. Brush with some of the sauce. Let the ribs cool about 1 hour. **(Can be prepared 1 day ahead. Cover the ribs and remaining sauce separately and refrigerate.)**

Prepare the barbecue grill (medium-low heat). Brush the ribs with some of the sauce again. Grill until deep brown, about 4 minutes per side. Cut the racks into individual ribs and serve with the remaining sauce.

WINE NOTES
As this tasty dish possesses some real heat at the finish, the natural choice would be a California Zinfandel. Select a lighter, toned-down version with tons of fresh, berrylike fruit, moderate alcohol and just enough tannin to counteract the dish's oiliness. Make sure to serve the wine at about 60 degrees.

 ## COCONUT-CRUSTED BIG ISLE GOAT CHEESE TARTLETS WITH MACADAMIA NUT PRALINE

A tropical twist on cheesecake, these coconut-crusted tartlets are lined with chiffon cake and topped with a sweetened goat cheese mixture and macadamia nut praline.

4 servings

PRALINE
½ cup sugar
1 cup toasted macadamia nuts
CAKE
½ cup cake flour
6 tablespoons sugar
¾ teaspoon baking powder
⅛ teaspoon salt
2 tablespoons vegetable oil
1 extra-large egg yolk
¼ teaspoon vanilla extract
2 extra-large egg whites
⅛ teaspoon cream of tartar
TOPPING
2¼ ounces fresh mild goat cheese
2¼ ounces cream cheese
¼ cup sugar
1 tablespoon fresh lemon juice
½ teaspoon grated lemon peel
COCONUT CRUST
3 tablespoons unsalted butter
1½ cups sweetened, shredded coconut
1 papaya or mango, peeled, seeded and sliced
Sweetened whipped cream (optional)

(continued on next page)

For the praline: Lightly oil a large cookie sheet. Stir the sugar and 2 tablespoons of water in a heavy, medium saucepan over low heat until the sugar dissolves. Increase the heat and boil without stirring until the syrup turns deep golden brown. Add the nuts and toss to coat. Spread out on prepared sheet and cool. Coarsely chop the praline. **(Can be prepared 1 day ahead. Cover and refrigerate.)**

For the cake: Preheat the oven to 325° F. Sift the first 4 ingredients into a large bowl. Sift again. Whisk 3 tablespoons water, oil, yolk and vanilla in a medium bowl to blend. Whisk in the dry ingredients. Using an electric mixer, beat the whites and cream of tartar in a small bowl to form very stiff peaks. Fold the whites into the batter. Pour the batter into an ungreased 8-inch-diameter springform pan with 3-inch-high sides. Bake until a toothpick inserted in the center comes out clean, about 30 minutes. Transfer the cake to a rack and cool. Turn the cake out. Cut two 1/8-inch-thick horizontal slices from cake. Cut out two 3-inch rounds from each cake slice (for a total of 4 rounds), reserving the remaining cake for another use. **(Can be prepared 1 day ahead. Cover and let stand at room temperature.)**

For the topping: Using an electric mixer, beat the goat cheese and the cream cheese in a small bowl until combined. Add the sugar and beat 3 minutes. Add the lemon juice and the lemon peel and beat 3 minutes. Set aside.

For the coconut crust: Preheat the oven to 300° F. Melt the butter in a heavy, medium skillet over medium heat. Add the coconut and stir until well combined. Place four 3-inch-diameter tartlet pans with 1 1/8-inch-high sides on a baking sheet. Press the coconut mixture onto the bottom and sides of the pans. Bake until golden brown, about 15 minutes. Maintain the oven temperature.

Place 1 cake round in the bottom of each coconut crust. Overlap enough sliced fruit atop the cake to just cover. Spread the goat cheese mixture over fruit. Sprinkle some of the praline over the top. Bake until the topping is almost set, about 25 minutes. Cool completely. Refrigerate until chilled, about 2 hours.

Using a small sharp knife, cut around the tart pan sides to loosen the crusts. Remove pan sides from the tartlets. Transfer the tartlets to plates. Serve with whipped cream.

 ## TROPICAL ISLAND TART

Roy created this recipe as a means to showcase Hawaii's premier fruits, but they're in for some competition from the browned butter filling and flaky tart shell. Softly whipped cream infused with macadamia nut liqueur adds the crowning touch.

8 servings

CRUST
1 1/4 cups all-purpose flour
10 tablespoons (1 1/4 sticks) chilled unsalted butter, cut into pieces
1/3 cup sugar
1 extra-large egg yolk

FILLING
3 extra-large eggs
1 1/4 cups sugar
1/3 cup all-purpose flour
3/4 cup (1 1/2 sticks) unsalted butter
1 teaspoon vanilla extract
1/2 cup fresh raspberries
1/2 cup peeled, cubed mango
1/2 cup diced, drained fresh pineapple
1/2 cup fresh blueberries
1/2 cup toasted macadamia nuts
1 cup chilled whipping cream
2 tablespoons macadamia nut liqueur

For the crust: Blend all of the ingredients in a food processor until the mixture begins to clump together. Gather the dough into a ball. Flatten into a disk. Wrap in plastic and refrigerate 30 minutes.

Preheat the oven to 350° F. Roll the dough out on a lightly floured work surface to a 1/8-inch-thick round. Transfer the dough to an 11-inch-diameter tart pan with a removable bottom; trim the edges. Freeze 15 minutes. Line the crust with foil. Fill with dried beans or pie weights. Bake until set, about 20 minutes. Remove the foil and beans and bake until pale golden brown, about 10 minutes. Transfer the crust to a rack and cool. **(Can be prepared 1 day ahead. Cover and let stand at room temperature.)**

For the filling: Preheat the oven to 350° F. Using an electric mixer, beat the eggs, sugar and flour in a large bowl until well blended. Set aside. Melt the butter in a heavy, medium saucepan over medium-high heat until the mixture begins to brown, about 3 minutes; do not burn. Pour the browned butter into the egg mixture and beat well. Mix in the vanilla. Fold in all of the fruit and nuts. Pour the mixture into the prepared crust. Bake until the filling is puffed and set, about 30 minutes. Transfer to a rack and cool.

Beat the cream and liqueur in a medium bowl to form soft peaks. Remove the tart from the pan. Cut into wedges and serve with whipped cream.

Tropical Island Tart

BASICS

VEAL, BEEF OR LAMB STOCK

Makes 6 cups

6 pounds veal, beef or lamb bones
4 carrots, chopped
3 celery stalks with leafy tops, chopped
1 large onion, chopped
1 large leek, chopped
1 large tomato, chopped
1½ cups dry white wine
12 cups water
12 whole black peppercorns
4 fresh parsley sprigs
3 fresh thyme sprigs
1 large bay leaf

Preheat the oven to 400° F. Arrange the bones and the vegetables in a roasting pan. Roast until brown, stirring frequently, about 40 minutes. Transfer the bones and vegetables to a heavy, large pot. Add the wine to the roasting pan. Set the roasting pan over medium-high heat and bring to a boil, scraping up the browned bits. Pour the wine mixture into the pot. Add the water, peppercorns, parsley, thyme and bay leaf and bring to a boil. Reduce the heat and simmer until the liquid is reduced to 6 cups, about 4 hours. Strain the stock. Cool, then degrease. **(Can be prepared ahead and refrigerated up to 2 days or frozen up to 6 months.)**

CHICKEN STOCK

Makes 6 cups

12 cups water
5 pounds chicken wings and backs
2 carrots, sliced
2 celery stalks, quartered
1 large onion, quartered
2 garlic cloves
4 fresh parsley sprigs
2 fresh thyme sprigs
1 bay leaf
½ teaspoon whole black peppercorns

Combine all of the ingredients in a heavy, large pot. Reduce the heat and simmer until the liquid is reduced to 6 cups, about 4 hours. Strain. Cool and degrease. **(Can be prepared ahead and refrigerated up to 2 days or frozen up to 6 months.)**

FISH STOCK

Makes about 5 cups

1½ pounds bones, tails and heads from halibut or
*   other nonoily white fish*
6 cups (about) water
1 cup dry white wine
2 small leeks, sliced
2 large celery stalks, chopped
2 small onions, quartered
2 small carrots, sliced
6 fresh parsley sprigs
1 bay leaf
10 whole peppercorns
Pinch of salt

Rinse the fish bones under cold water. Place the bones in large pot. Add the remaining ingredients and bring to a boil, skimming the surface occasionally. Reduce the heat and simmer 30 minutes. Strain through a sieve; do not press on the solids. **(Can be prepared ahead and refrigerated up to 2 days or frozen up to 6 months.)**

CRAB STOCK

This intensely flavored stock is used in two of Jean-Marie Josselin's recipes: Crab and Wild Mushroom Risotto and Spiced Hawaiian Fish and Prawn Soup. You can also use it in almost any recipe calling for fish stock when you wish to give a dish an Asian flair.

Makes about 5½ cups

1 large cooked crab
¼ cup olive oil
2 large tomatoes, cut into quarters
1 medium carrot, sliced
½ medium onion, sliced
4 large garlic cloves
1 tablespoon paprika
Pinch of cayenne pepper
¼ cup tomato paste
1 cup dry white wine
6 cups (about) water
4 kaffir lime leaves
2 lemongrass stalks (12 inches long), chopped

Crack the crab and remove the meat. Cover and refrigerate the meat and reserve for another use. Cut the crab shells into pieces. Heat the oil in a heavy, large saucepan over high heat. Add the crab shells and sauté until golden brown, about 2 minutes. Add the tomatoes, carrot, onion, garlic, paprika and cayenne and sauté 2 minutes. Stir in the tomato paste. Add the wine and bring to a boil, stirring occasionally. Add enough water to cover the crab and vegetables and bring to a boil. Add the kaffir leaves and lemongrass, reduce the heat and simmer for 10 minutes. Strain the mixture into a saucepan. Transfer the contents of the strainer to a processor and purée. Add the purée to the stock and bring to a simmer. Simmer 5 minutes. Strain the stock into a bowl. Cover and refrigerate until ready to use. **(Can be prepared ahead and refrigerated up to 2 days or frozen up to 1 month.)**

CHILI PEPPER WATER

Many Hawaii residents keep a bottle of chili pepper water in their refrigerators, as it's used frequently as a condiment, like Tabasco sauce. Here's the much-requested recipe for the chili pepper water served at CanoeHouse restaurant at Mauna Lani Bay Hotel and Bungalows. It was created by Charles Park, a culinary connoisseur who is also general manager of this luxury hotel.

It's spicy, so use it sparingly. The chilies tend to settle on the bottom; you can shake it before using for a hotter sauce.

Makes about 1½ cups

⅓ cup cold water
½ small garlic clove
2 red jalapeño or serrano chilies, stemmed and halved
1 tablespoon distilled white vinegar
2 teaspoons peeled, minced fresh ginger
⅛ teaspoon Hawaiian salt or kosher salt
1¼ cups water

Purée the first 6 ingredients in a blender. Bring 1¼ cups of water to a boil in a medium saucepan. Add the purée and return the mixture to a boil. Cool. **(Transfer to a glass jar and refrigerate. Keeps indefinitely.)**

PASTRY CRUST

Makes enough for one 9-inch tart

1¼ cups unbleached all-purpose flour
½ teaspoon salt
5 tablespoons chilled unsalted butter, cut into pieces
2 tablespoons chilled solid vegetable shortening
3 tablespoons (about) ice water

Combine the flour and the salt in a food processor. Add the butter and the shortening and cut in using on/off turns until the mixture resembles coarse meal. Blend in enough water by tablespoons until the dough forms moist clumps. Gather the dough into a ball; flatten into a disk. Refrigerate 30 minutes. **(Can be prepared 1 week ahead. Keep refrigerated. Let the dough soften slightly before rolling.)**

GLOSSARY OF HAWAII REGIONAL CUISINE INGREDIENTS

AHI *Ahi* is the Hawaiian name for two popular tunas: yellowfin and bigeye. The bigeye is plumper, possesses a higher fat content and is harvested primarily during winter months (October to April). Yellowfin is most abundant in the summer (May to September). *Ahi* can reach up to 250 pounds. Often consumed as sashimi, its red flesh turns beige when cooked and tastes much like steak. Sashimi-grade *ahi* has a higher fat content and deeper red color and must be used for raw preparations. If not eaten raw, *ahi* tastes best quickly cooked and served rare.

AKU This Hawaiian tuna is also called skipjack, striped tuna or *katsuo*. A near-surface schooling tuna, it's caught year-round and ranges in weight from 4 to 30 pounds. High-quality *aku* has firm flesh with a deep red color. When cooked, it turns a lighter hue. It's often eaten raw as sashimi or in the Hawaiian *poke* (raw marinated fish), and is bolder tasting than *ahi*. When cooked, it's usually broiled or grilled. *Ahi* is a good substitute.

AZUKI BEANS Squarish, reddish beans grown and eaten in China and Japan, azuki beans possess a mild, nutty flavor and are sold in Asian markets. They can be stored indefinitely in an airtight container.

BANANAS Bananas were brought to Hawaii by migrating Polynesians. It is believed they brought three varieties with many mutants. Today there may be some twenty varieties that grow in the Islands. Bananas are grown on all the islands and the biggest harvest season is the fall months.

Common varieties include the Valery and Williams. More unusual types include: apple banana, a small, delicate variety that is slightly more tart than sweet and offers an applelike aftertaste; Cuban Red, which possesses reddish skin and sweet, rich-tasting, creamy yellow flesh with a black cherry aftertaste; and ice cream banana, with bluish-silvery skin that turns pale yellow when ripe—some say it tastes like vanilla ice cream.

Cooking bananas, or plantains, are also popular in Hawaii. *Maia maoli*, a large, yellow banana that freckles when ripened, was brought over to Hawaii by migrating Polynesians and is still a kitchen staple today.

BEAN THREAD VERMICELLI See cellophane noodles.

BREADFRUIT (Ulu) Steamed and served buttered or made into poi in traditional Hawaiian cooking, breadfruit (*ulu*) grows on broad-leafed trees. It was brought to Hawaii by migrating Polynesians. Used almost exclusively as a vegetable, breadfruit is usually consumed when whole or partly green and is bland, starchy, slightly musky and fruity in taste. Fully ripened, it turns sweet and creamy. In Hawaii, it's often roasted whole on the hibachi. Usually, it's cooked like potatoes, which are a good substitute; breadfruit is difficult to obtain on the mainland.

CALAMANSI *Calamansi* is the Filipino name commonly used for calamondin, a small, orange citrus fruit which resembles a kumquat. It's highly acidic and its juice is used much like lemon juice.

CARAMBOLA (Star Fruit) Called star fruit, *carambola* possesses an elongated shape and five deep ridges. Its yellow-orange skin is waxy and its flesh is juicy tart. It's served raw without seeding or peeling. In Hawaii, it's primarily commercially grown in the Puna district on the Big Island. It's sold in exotic produce sections of some supermarkets.

CELLOPHANE NOODLES These clear noodles are made from a paste of mung bean flour and water. Also called bean thread vermicelli, they turn slippery-soft when cooked. They're sold in Asian markets.

CHERIMOYA *Cherimoya* possesses smooth, sweet, juicy flesh, a tropical taste and a creamy texture. Sometimes called sweet sop in Hawaii, this fruit is mostly grown commercially on the Big Island. *Cherimoya* is sold in Asian and specialty food markets as well as some supermarkets.

CHINESE BLACK BEANS Fermented, salted black soybeans, Chinese black beans are rinsed lightly and often chopped slightly to release their flavor before using. They're sold in Asian markets and keep indefinitely.

CHINESE MUSTARD CABBAGE A spicy cabbage sometimes called *gai choy*, mustard cabbage is sold in Asian markets. Substitute mustard greens if necessary.

CILANTRO Also known as Chinese parsley and coriander, cilantro is a member of the carrot/parsley family and a Middle Eastern native herb—although it's a staple of Chinese and Southeast Asian cooking. Its distinctive, earthy taste often heightens other flavors in a dish and also balances richness. Cilantro is sold in Asian and Latin markets and many supermarkets.

COCONUT MILK The two original coconuts introduced to Hawaii by migrating Polynesians are still thriving today, along with perhaps six other varieties introduced by Westerners.

A coconut is mature when its husk begins to turn brown and the meat reaches maximum thickness. The nut must be pierced through its "eyes" and the liquid drained. Fortunately, considering the time and labor involved in preparing fresh coconut milk (the liquid squeezed from grated and soaked coconut meat), excellent canned, unsweetened varieties—in particular, Thai products—can be purchased in Asian markets. Open cans will stay fresh in the refrigerator for a few days.

DAIKON An Oriental radish, a daikon is a large white root vegetable with a fairly mild taste and crisp texture. It's sold in Asian markets.

DURIAN A green, globe-shaped fruit about the size of a coconut and completely covered with sharp prickles, the durian is renowned for its highly unpleasant aroma, its sweet, delicious flesh and vanilla-custard-like texture. Exotic fruit growers on the Big Island are working on developing a crop.

FIDDLEHEAD FERNS See *pohole* and *warabi*.

FISH SAUCE Called *nam pla* in Thailand and *nuoc mam* in Vietnam, fish sauce is a pungent, salty, brownish liquid drained off from fish (usually anchovies, sometimes shrimp or other small fish) fermented in brine. It keeps indefinitely unrefrigerated and is sold in Asian markets and some supermarkets.

FIVE-SPICE POWDER An aromatic Chinese spice powder most commonly made from star anise, Szechwan peppercorns, fennel, cinnamon and cloves. It's sold in Asian markets and some supermarkets.

GINGER A spicy tropical rhizome (underground stem) rather than a root, ginger is not native to Hawaii but grows profusely in the islands. Hawaiian ginger is sweet and juicy; its quality is attributed to the rich volcanic soil it grows in. Much Hawaiian ginger is grown in the Hilo area of the Big Island. Purchase hard, heavy rhizomes; soft, wrinkled ginger denotes a lack of freshness.

Young Hawaiian ginger, available from August to December, has pink and purplish bud tips and possesses the texture and heat of the daikon, with a delicate ginger flavor.

GUAVA Hawaiian guavas are roundish in shape, usually possessing a yellowish skin and pinkish flesh. This nonnative fruit possesses a distinct tropical taste and a pronounced aroma. Several varieties grow in Hawaii, such as the strawberry guava—which has a berrylike flavor—and the pineapple guava, which has pineapple notes to its taste. The Beaumont pink variety is the most common. Guava grows commercially on the Big Island and Kauai, but it grows wild on all the islands. HRC chefs often use guava in vinaigrettes, meat marinades and dipping sauces.

HAPU'UPU'U Called Hawaiian sea bass but really a grouper, this fish possesses sweet white meat under its dark spotted skin. A bottom fish, it ranges from 5 to 30 pounds and is most abundant in late fall and spring. Its flesh is medium-dense, lean and mild and is best cooked by steaming or slow-baking. Good substitutes are sea bass, catfish, cod, grouper, haddock, halibut and monkfish.

HAWAIIAN CHILI PEPPER About 1 inch long and red or yellow in color, this extremely hot Hawaiian pepper can be substituted with a jalapeño or serrano chili, but it's most similar to the fiery Thai "bird's-eye" chili pepper.

HAWAIIAN SALT A coarse-crystal salt similar to kosher salt—a good substitute—this mild sea salt, also called *alae* salt, is naturally colored red from the iron in the soil.

HEBI A shortbill spearfish, the deep-water *hebi* weighs between 20 to 40 pounds. It's available year-round, but is most abundant from June through October. Its amber-colored flesh is similar to *nairagi* or *kajiki*. Its flavor is mild but bolder than *ahi*. It's usually cut into steaks and broiled or grilled. It also works well in soups, chowders and stews. Swordfish and shark are good substitutes.

HIRAME A Japanese flat flounder with white, flaky meat and a mild flavor, *hirame* can be substituted by whole sole. *Hirame* is farm-raised on the Big Island and usually weighs about 2 pounds.

HOISIN SAUCE Sweet, garlicky and spicy, hoisin sauce is primarily made from fermented soybean paste, sugar, garlic and spices. This reddish-brown, thick sauce is sold in Chinese markets and most supermarkets.

HOT BEAN SAUCE Oriental bean sauce made spicy with either dried chili peppers or chili paste, this condiment is sold in Asian markets.

INAMONA These roasted *kukui* nuts are pounded and salted and used in traditional Hawaiian cooking. Toasted, crushed macadamia nuts can be substituted for the native Hawaiian *kukui* nuts.

KAFFIR LIME LEAVES These aromatic, citrus-flavored leaves of the Southeast Asian kaffir lime tree are often sold fresh in Asian markets. Dried leaves are easier to find, but are less aromatic and flavorful. If purchasing dried leaves, soak in warm water about 20 minutes before using. Kaffir lime trees grow profusely in Hawaii.

KAHUKU PRAWNS AND SHRIMP Both Kahuku prawns and shrimp are farm-raised on Oahu. Prawns are freshwater-raised and are sweeter and slightly softer than the saltwater-raised Kahuku shrimp. Substitute the highest-quality shrimp or prawns available in your area.

KAJIKI Pacific blue marlin, *kajiki* is also called *a'u*, the Hawaiian term for all marlin species. This billfish is more abundant during the summer and fall and can be identified by its larger bill and rough gray skin. Its weight runs from 80 to 300 pounds. The amber meat turns white when cooked, is very lean, and should not be overcooked. It's often broiled, poached or stir-fried. Good substitutes are shark and swordfish.

KA'U ORANGE *Ka'u* oranges (and limes) are grown on the southern shore of the Big Island, an optimal growing locale. The Ka'u orange is an ugly fruit as a mold turns the skin brown, but the flesh is sweet and juicy.

KECAP MANIS A dark, thick, Indonesian soy sauce sweetened with palm sugar, garlic, star anise and other flavorings, *kecap manis* is sold in Asian markets.

KIAWE Commonly referred to as Hawaiian mesquite and used in a similar fashion when grilling, this mild-flavored, aromatic plant grows wild in Hawaii and is especially abundant in dry, low-lying areas. *Kiawe* honey is a sweet, perfumed honey from bees that feed on the short-blooming *kiawe* blossoms.

KIM CHEE Also referred to as *kimchi*, this Korean pickled cabbage (usually napa cabbage) seasoned with salt, garlic, chili peppers, green onions, ginger and other spices possesses a powerful aroma and is often extremely hot.

KONA COFFEE The first coffee plants arrived in Kona, Hawaii, in 1825 on a British warship. They had been acquired in Brazil during the ship's voyage.

Acclaimed for its legendary aroma and mellow flavor, Kona coffee is made from beans grown on the Big Island in the Kona district. Nurtured by the rich, volcanic soil, protective cloud cover and rainfall, Kona coffee is the only coffee commercially grown in the United States. (Some coffee is grown on Kauai, Molokai and Maui, but it goes by a Hawaiian grade versus the Kona grade.)

Many boutique Kona coffee growers sun-dry their beans and some are organically grown. The slightly smoother Peaberry coffee possesses a little different taste characteristic and is quite prized.

KUKUI NUTS This native Hawaiian nut, cream to grayish in color, is difficult to obtain and is often substituted with macadamia nuts. Extremely high in oil, *kukui* nuts can create a laxativelike effect, so they're consumed sparingly.

KUMU A member of the goatfish family, this reef fish is prized by Hawaii's residents for its delicate, flaky, white meat. *Kumu* is not commercially caught—it's usually speared or incidentally caught. To protect its delicate flavor, *kumu* is often cooked by steaming or in papillote with minimal sauce.

LANAI AXIS VENISON The wild Lanai axis venison possesses remarkably tender meat with a much admired delicate flavor. Although available year-round, it is often difficult and pricey to obtain.

LAU LAU In traditional Hawaiian cooking, *lau lau* combines salted butterfish and pork steamed in taro (*luau*) leaves and tied with *ti* leaves. HRC chefs often use fresh fish such as *opakapaka*, omit the pork and add vegetables and seasoning.

LEMONGRASS A member of the grass family, lemongrass grows as long, greenish stalks with serrated-edged leaves from a creamy narrow base. Its pale, inner stalks are most edible and are usually finely slivered for cooking. Lemongrass possesses a pungent lemonlike flavor and highly aromatic, almost perfumy, scent. It's also available dried, but its flavor is greatly diminished. It's sold in Asian markets.

LILIKOI (Passion Fruit) The Hawaiian name for passion fruit, *lilikoi* can be yellowish, brownish or purplish in color with yellow-orange, teardrop-shaped pulp and dark seeds. It's highly aromatic—almost perfumelike in scent—and its flavor is delicate and tropical. There are many varieties of *lilikoi* in Hawaii, including the banana *lilikoi*, which possesses a subtle bananalike flavor. The first passion fruit were planted on Maui in the nineteenth century.

HRC chefs use it in vinaigrettes, marinades, dipping and seafood sauces besides the more traditional dessert recipes. *Lilikoi* grows wild on vines in forests and is sold primarily through cottage operations.

LIMU (Seaweed) Hawaiian seaweed (also called sea vegetables), *limu* comes in some twenty-five varieties today, although forty types were once eaten by Hawaiians. Some popular types include *limu kohu*, which is fine and reddish in color with a strong flavor. It's primarily found on the Big Island and Kauai, and is the most prized and expensive seaweed.

The light-brown, flat *limu lipoa* has a strong perfumelike aroma and is a favorite of the *limu* connoisseur. It was used much like a spice in the native Hawaiian diet, taking the place of sage and pepper.

The dark-green, flat *limu ele'ele* is found in island streams (where freshwater meets the sea) and adds a nutlike flavor. It's commonly sold in Hawaii's supermarkets.

Ogo is the Japanese name for certain types of limu, primarily the *limu manauea*. It ranges in color from deep yellow to deep rose. It has a clean sea flavor and crunchy texture. Today, all *ogo* is farm-raised.

LUMPIA WRAPPER Often labeled "eggroll skins," the Philippine thin *lumpia* wrappers are sold either in a round or square shape. The square wrappers are most suitable for frying. They're usually made with cornstarch and/or flour, egg and water. Store *lumpia* wrappers tightly wrapped in the refrigerator for up to one week.

LYCHEE Fresh lychees are aromatic, juicy, soft and sweet and their taste has been compared to that of grapes and roses. Their shells are reddish and their flesh is opalescent white. They must be peeled before eaten. Fresh, unpeeled lychees can be stored in the refrigerator for a few weeks. Lychees grow on all the islands and are harvested during the summer months. Canned lychees are an acceptable substitute and are sold in Asian markets and some supermarkets.

MACADAMIA NUTS A native of Australia, the macadamia nut was introduced to Hawaii in the 1880s. Commercial growers in Hawaii developed new strains and the industry flourished. This bland-tasting, rich nut is creamy in color and is primarily grown on the Big Island, but it's also found on Maui.

MAHIMAHI Also called dolphinfish (it's not related to the marine mammal), mahimahi possesses tender, flaky, lean meat. Its mild pink flesh turns off-white when cooked. An open ocean fish mostly caught in the spring or fall, mahimahi usually ranges from 8 to 25 pounds, but larger fish are often caught. It adapts well to all cooking methods, but since it's lean, be careful not to overcook it. Good substitutes are snapper, black cod, catfish, flounder, halibut and pompano.

MANGO Native to the base of the Himalayas, the mango is often called "the king of fruits." The fragrant Hawaiian mango possesses a yellow-red skin and moist, sweet, reddish-yellow flesh. Many varieties grow from sea level to 1,000 feet elevation on both the dry and rainy sides of the Islands. The most popular variety is the Hayden. Their growing season in Hawaii is from June through September.

MAUI ONION A sweet, moist, mild-tasting onion with a high sugar content, the Maui onion is grown in Kula, the up-country growing area on Maui. It's more than just the seed stock which makes this onion so sweet; the volcanic soil, mild temperature and amount of rainfall create ideal growing conditions. Vidalia and Walla Walla onions are good mainland substitutes. Maui onions are often sold in West Coast supermarkets.

MIRIN Sweetened rice wine that's also called sweet sake, mirin is sold in Asian markets and some supermarkets.

MISO Thick soybean paste, miso ranges in color and textures and is made by salting and fermenting soybeans and rice or barley. Generally, the lighter the miso, the sweeter its taste. It's sold in Asian markets and can be stored in the refrigerator for a few months.

MOANO A member of the goatfish family, this reef fish averages from 8 ounces to 2 pounds. Its meat is delicate, sweet and mild. Substitute any white-meat fish with a high fat content. Although its name is *moano*, it's often called *moana* in Hawaii.

MONCHONG Also called bigscale or sickle pomfret, this deep-water fish is gaining popularity in Hawaii. It has firm, white flesh with pinkish overtones and ranges from 4 to 25 pounds. Catches are small and erratic. Its high fat content makes it suitable for broiling, grilling, baking or sautéeing. It's often used in Hawaiian seafood stews. Sea bass and John Dory are good substitutes.

MOUNTAIN APPLE Although it's called an apple and looks and tastes like one, the mountain apple really isn't one. A member of the myrtle family, mountain apples were dried by early Hawaiians before they were consumed —the wood of the tree was considered sacred. Mountain apples possess a single seed, can vary in skin color from light pink to red and have a white- to pink-toned flesh. They taste like perfumed apples.

NABETA *Nabeta* is a small, gray fish with moist white meat and a mild flavor. A local Japanese delicacy, it's often the subject of tournaments on Maui. It's also known as sheepshead fish in mainland Asian markets. It's cooked whole, usually pan-fried. Substitute pompano or rock cod.

NAIRAGI A striped marlin, *nairagi* is a migratory species that passes through the Hawaiian Islands twice each year, in the winter and the spring. Its size ranges from 40 to 130 pounds. Often considered the best eating of all marlin species, its flesh varies from orange-red to clear pink. The darker-fleshed fish is often used as sashimi. Broiling or grilling is a good cooking method, but it should be cooked only until rare. Swordfish and *ahi* are good substitutes.

NOHU Similar to the French *rascasse* (scorpion fish), *nohu* is Hawaiian rock cod. Its average size is 2 to 3 pounds and its flesh is white, lean and large-flaked. It's best cooked by steaming or slow-baking. Monkfish is a good substitute.

NORI When dried and compressed, this seaweed is most often used for wrapping sushi rolls. *Nori* is also called purple laver. Japanese markets carry the largest selection. It's most often toasted before it's used by quickly passing one side over a gas flame a few times or by briefly placing it in a very hot oven until crisp.

OGO (Seaweed) See *limu*.

OHELO BERRY A Hawaiian fruit which primarily grows on the volcanic slopes of the Big Island, the tart *ohelo* berry is rarely used for cooking purposes any longer, as it's the primary diet of the *nene*, an endangered native goose.

ONAGA A bottom fish also called a red snapper, *onaga* is better known by its Japanese name than its Hawaiian (*'ula'ula*). Caught in the deep waters along rocky bottoms, *onaga* is leaner during the summer and fattier in the winter. Its weight ranges from 1 to 18 pounds. Peak availability is in the winter, when it's often consumed as sashimi. Its moist, exceptionally delicate pink flesh turns white when cooked and takes well to all cooking methods, but is most often steamed, baked or sautéed. Good substitutes are snapper, monkfish and orange roughy.

ONO Also called *wahoo*, *ono* is in the mackerel family and possesses white, flaky, firm, mild meat that turns white when cooked. An open ocean fish, it's most plentiful from summer to fall and ranges from 8 to 30 pounds. It's often used for sashimi. Since it is a lean fish, it should not be overcooked. Quick cooking methods such as steaming, sautéeing or broiling work best. *Ono* takes well to marinades and basting. Good substitutes are mackerel, tuna, swordfish and shark.

OPAH Also called moonfish, its pinkish flesh is large-flaked and fatty. A nonschooling, open ocean fish, the rich *opah* takes well to sauces and is often poached, steamed or baked. This fish ranges from 60 to 200 pounds. For many years, *opah* was regarded as a good luck fish and was never sold. Instead, it was given away as a gesture of good will. Swordfish, bluefish and other fish with high oil contents are good substitutes.

OPAKAPAKA A Hawaiian pink snapper, its highly delicate, moist flesh is a clear light pink which turns white when cooked. Caught year-round, this bottom fish ranges from 1 to 12 pounds. It takes well to all cooking methods, and is often poached, baked or sautéed. Its fat content is higher in the winter and it's often consumed raw at that time. Good substitutes include snapper, monkfish, orange roughy and sea bass.

OPIHI A small, black limpet or mollusk often eaten raw (sometimes it's grilled), *opihi* taste similar to oysters, with a snaillike texture. *Opihi* are gathered from rocks in wave-wash areas, which make it dangerous to collect. *Opihi* are expensive and prized.

ORIENTAL SESAME OIL The fragrant, nutty-tasting oil made from roasted sesame seeds, sesame oil is used primarily as a flavoring agent as it burns easily if used for cooking. It's sold in Asian markets and some supermarkets.

OYSTER SAUCE Primarily made from oysters, water and salt, the thick, brownish oyster sauce lends a rich and salty oyster flavor to dishes. It keeps indefinitely in the refrigerator and is sold in Asian markets and some supermarkets.

PANDANUS LEAF The thin, pointed, young leaves of the bushlike pandanus plant are used as a natural green food coloring or as a pungent flavoring. They're also called screw pine leaves and are sold in Asian markets.

PANKO These unseasoned, large-flaked Japanese breadcrumbs are often used by HRC chefs as they don't absorb much oil in the cooking process and they impart an excellent texture. They're sold in Asian markets and some supermarkets.

PAPAYA Shaped like pears, papayas possess a sweet, subtle-flavored pulp and slightly peppery seeds. Some say its flavor is a cross between a Crenshaw melon and a peach. When consumed green or unripe, its flesh is firm and crunchy and its texture and flavor is similar to that of squash. Papaya was introduced to the Islands in the 1880s by Europeans.

Many varieties of papayas flourish in Hawaii, such as the bright-yellow-fleshed Solo papaya—which is widely grown, mostly on the Big Island in the Puna district—and the smaller, sweet, reddish-orange Sunrise, which is found on Kauai and the Big Island.

PAPIO See *white ulua*.

PERILLA A cousin of mint and basil, perilla grows in green or red hues. This aromatic leafy plant is also called by its Japanese name, *shiso*.

PICKLED GINGER Preserved in rice vinegar, brine or rice wine, pickled ginger turns pinkish from the chemical reaction with the liquid. Slightly spicy and slightly sweet, it's sold in Asian markets and some supermarkets.

PINEAPPLE It is surmised that the juicy, sweet pineapple was brought to the islands by Spaniards from South America in the early 1800s.

Unlike many other fruits, pineapple does not increase in sweetness after it's picked. To select a good pineapple, look for a bright, fresh crown and avoid ones with soft or brown spots and bruises. Smell the nonstem end. It should smell sweet, not sour. If it possesses no aroma, it will not taste sweet.

HRC chefs use pineapple in almost every dish, from curries, salsas and sandwiches to seafood dishes and desserts.

POHA Also called a Cape gooseberry, the Hawaiian *poha* berry is encased in a parchment-like husk and twisted at the tip. Inside is a golden, marble-size berry, tart and slightly acidic. It's usually eaten raw, but sometimes quickly poached. HRC chefs often use the *poha* to glaze game and other meat, in salad dressings and in jams and marmalades.

The *poha* probably originated in South America, and now grows perennially in the tropics. In Hawaii, it usually grows on open mountain slopes.

POHOLE (Fiddlehead Ferns) *Pohole* is the Maui name for fiddlehead ferns. These curled young fern tips are delicate in flavor and are often consumed raw or blanched.

POKE A traditional Hawaiian dish, *poke* is made with raw fish such as *ahi* mixed with seaweed, Hawaiian salt, Hawaiian chili peppers, roasted, salted and ground *kukui* nuts and sesame oil. HRC chefs often add such ingredients as soy sauce, coconut milk, tomatoes and green onions to a standard *poke*.

POMELO Also called Chinese grapefruit and considered to be the ancestor of the grapefruit, pomelo (or pummelo) is the largest citrus fruit. It has a thick pith and rind and the fruit ranges in color from yellow to pink. Its taste is semisweet. It grows on all the islands at low elevations near the ocean.

PUNA GOAT CHEESE Puna goat cheese is the common name for Orchid Island Chevre, which is produced in the Puna district of the Big Island. This superior, mild, creamy goat cheese is made in the traditional French style. Orchid Island Chevre is produced at Kuokoa Farm, the only licensed goat dairy and goat cheese producer in the state.

All the milk (primarily nubian milk, which is high in butterfat) used to make this cheese is produced on this family farm. Puna goat cheese can be substituted by a high-quality, mild, California or French goat cheese.

RADISH SPROUTS These peppery sprouts from the daikon radish are slender, silky and white with green tops. Sometimes called *kaiware*, they add a spicy kick to HRC dishes and are best eaten raw. Sold in Asian markets, radish sprouts should be stored in the refrigerator.

RICE NOODLES Also known as rice vermicelli, these noodles are made from finely ground rice and water. They cook almost instantly. When deep-fried, they expand four or five times their dry size and become very crisp. They can also be soaked and stir-fried and served as soft noodles.

RICE PAPER Made from rice flour, water and salt, rice paper should be soaked or brushed with water to soften it before use. It's sold in Asian markets and some supermarkets.

SAKE Also known as Japanese rice wine, sake is made from fermented rice. Clear in color and mild in flavor, sake has a low alcoholic content. In cooking it adds depth of flavor and also acts as a tenderizer.

SAMBAL OLEK A condiment from Malaysia or Indonesia, the spicy *sambal olek* is a ground red chili paste. It's sold in Asian markets.

SESAME SEEDS The oval, edible sesame seeds of the sesame plant possess a subtle, nutty flavor and high oil content. Black sesame seeds are slightly more pungent and bitter than white ones. Sesame seeds are sold in Asian markets and some supermarkets.

SHIITAKE MUSHROOMS Related to Chinese black mushrooms, fresh shiitakes can be purchased in Asian markets and most supermarkets. They're cooked like any fresh mushroom. Dried shiitakes must be reconstituted in water before use; avoid using the stems.

SHUTOME The popular name for broadbill swordfish caught in Hawaiian waters, the shutome is also called *a'u ku* in Hawaiian. This migratory fish—which can vary in weight from 10 to 600 pounds—is abundant from April through July. Its taste is mild but distinct. It possesses a high fat content, which tastes more rich than oily. The pinkish meat is usually broiled, poached, stir-fried or baked. Substitute any swordfish.

SLIPPER LOBSTER A small, earth-colored, flat lobster with a shovel-nose and without pinchers, the Hawaiian slipper lobster lives in the sand and has more flavorful meat and a wider tail than the spiny lobster. It averages about 1 to 2 pounds.

SOBA NOODLES Made from buckwheat and wheat flours, soba noodles are thin and brown in color. Cooked quickly and until soft, these noodles can be served hot or cold. They're sold in Asian markets and some supermarkets.

SOY SAUCE Called by its Japanese name, *shoyu*, in Hawaii, the variety of soy sauce used in Hawaii is usually Japanese, which is a little sweeter and less salty than Chinese varieties. A naturally fermented flavoring agent that is often aged, it's made with roasted soybean meal and usually wheat. It's sold in most supermarkets.

SPINY LOBSTER A small, round and colorful lobster without pinchers, the Hawaiian spiny lobster averages 1 to 2 pounds and possesses sweeter meat than the slipper lobster.

STAR ANISE The brownish eight-pointed seeds of a Southeast Asian evergreen, star anise looks like stars and taste like licorice.

SZECHWAN CHILI SAUCE Also called chili paste or chili paste with garlic, this spicy sauce/paste is primarily made with chili peppers, oil, salt and garlic. It's sold in Asian markets and some supermarkets.

TAKO *Tako*, or octopus, is caught in the Hawaiian waters. It needs to be tenderized before cooking. It's eaten in a variety of fashions, including smoked and dried. In Hawaii, it's a popular *pupu* (appetizer).

TAMARIND A sour flavoring agent, tamarind is the edible, refined pulp from the pods of tamarind trees. It's sold in Asian and Latin markets.

TARO The staple crop of the Hawaiian culture, taro is highly nutritious. Traditionally made into *poi* (cooked taro root, pounded and kneaded into a paste, mixed with water, strained and sometimes fermented) in Hawaiian cooking, taro plants come in many varieties. There are some 45 in the Islands. Taro is sometimes called *dasheen*.

Taro possesses an artichoke/chestnut flavor and a chestnut texture. It can often be used in dishes calling for artichokes and chestnuts, but it needs to be served immediately after cooking or it turns waxy. It's often made into chips, as taro reacts particularly well when cooked with fat.

Brown and barrel-shaped, its flesh is usually white or gray and sometimes speckled. Sold in Latin-American and Asian markets, taro turns gray or purplish when cooked.

To cook taro, cut a little off of both ends and place in a large pot of boiling water. Cook until it can be pierced through the center with a wooden skewer. Let it cool and then scrape off the skin.

A note of caution: Do not eat taro or its leaves raw, as they contain calcium oxalate crystals, which irritate the throat. Also, you might wish to wear gloves when handling to avoid skin irritation.

TARO LEAVES Also called *luau* leaves, taro leaves are the delicious, delicate leaves of the taro plant. Do not eat the leaves raw, as they contain calcium oxalate crystals, which irritate the throat. Using gloves, remove as many of the thick ribs on the leaves as possible and then place the leaves in boiling water until tender, about 45 minutes to 1 hour. Spinach is a good substitute.

THAI CURRY PASTE The flavor foundation of Southeast Asian (and some HRC) curries, Thai curry paste combines aromatic herbs, spices and vegetables that are ground into a paste. Yellow pastes tend to be mildest, red pastes can vary in heat and green pastes are generally the hottest. Prepared curry pastes are sold in Asian markets.

THAI SAI A bitter Chinese cabbage with oval, dark green leaves and white stems, it's sold in Asian markets.

TI LEAF The smooth leaves of the *ti* plant are used as a wrapper for steamed or baked foods. Hawaiians also consider the *ti* leaf a symbol of good luck. Banana leaf, often sold in Latin or Asian markets, is a good substitute for cooking purposes.

TOBIKO The orange-red roe of flying fish, *tobiko* possesses a mild flavor and slight crunch. It's sold in Asian markets and can sometimes be purchased from sushi bars.

TOFU Also known as soybean curd, tofu has a light, creamy texture and fresh, mild taste. It's sold in Asian markets and most supermarkets.

TOMBO Called albacore tuna elsewhere, *tombo* is softer than *ahi* or *aku,* so it's more difficult to prepare as sashimi. Its weight usually runs between 40 to 80 pounds and it's most abundant from May through September. It's often marinated and broiled or grilled and basted. As its meat is lean and dense, it's best to undercook it. *Ahi* or swordfish are good substitutes.

UKU Known as gray snapper or jobfish, this bottom fish is mostly harvested from April through July. Its pink, pale flesh is delicate, moist and firm and its taste is slightly more pronounced than *onaga* or *opakapaka.* Its weight ranges from 4 to 18 pounds and it's often sautéed or broiled. Substitute snapper or sea bass.

WAIMEA STRAWBERRIES Grown up-country in the Waimea area of the Big Island, these picked-only-when-ripe strawberries are remarkably juicy and sweet and can grow as big as golf balls.

WARABI (Fiddlehead Ferns) The Hawaiian term (a Japanese word) for fiddlehead ferns, *warabi* are the coiled new fronds of ferns rather than a specific species. They keep for three to four days refrigerated. They are often blanched before consumed in salads. *Haricots verts* can be substituted.

WASABI The *wasabi* root looks like horseradish, but it's smaller in size. It's rarely seen fresh in the United States; it's sold powdered in cans or in paste form in Asian markets.

It's best to purchase it powdered, as the paste form is inferior in quality. *Wasabi* is traditionally mixed in a small cup with a little water until it turns pastelike in consistency. It is a traditional custom in Hawaii, as in Japan, that the cup is then turned upside down, which is supposed to increase its heat. Store powdered *wasabi* in the refrigerator for up to a few months.

WHITE ULUA White *ulua,* called jack or jackfish, can average from 10 to 40 pounds. Smaller ones (under 10 pounds) are called *papio.* A deep-water, bottomfish caught year-round, white *ulua* has dense, clear white meat similar to a snapper or pompano (good substitutes), but more pronounced in flavor. It is often baked, poached or sautéed.

WILD BOAR Also called feral pigs, wild boar can only be hunted for personal purposes in the islands. Thus, restaurants must purchase wild boar from out of state. The meat is usually marinated and smoked. Migrating Polynesians brought the original pigs which have since crossed with the European pig.

NOTES ON HAWAIIAN WORD PRONUNCIATION

Although this book is about Hawaii's *new* cuisine, some of the terms used are native Hawaiian and may be difficult to pronounce. Here is a brief summary of how best to pronounce them.

A is pronounced "ah" as in "father."
    For example: Ka'u oranges; Onaga; opakapaka

E is pronounced "e" as in "bet."
    For example: Tempura, nebeta

I is pronounced "ee" as in "gasoline."
    For example: Hilo ginger; sashimi; ti leaf

O is pronounced "oh" as in "sole."
    For example: Shutome; opah; taro

U is pronounced "oo" as in "crude."
    For example: Kula corn bread; Limu poke salad; Puna goat cheese

AI is pronounced "eye" as in "aisle."
    For example: Molokai sweet potato; Lanai

AU is pronounced "ow" as in "cow."
    For example: luau; Maui onions; lau lau

EI is pronounced "ay" as in "pay."
    For example: chow mein noodles

OI is pronounced "oy" as in "joy."
    For example: poi; Lilikoi vinaigrette

When a "W" follows an "i" or an "e," it is usually pronounced like a "v."
    For example: Kiawe

Following a "u" or an "o," "w" is usually pronounced like a "w."

As a rule, each vowel is pronounced separately.

MAIL-ORDER SOURCES

These high-quality companies are just a sampling of the many which provide Hawaii Regional Cuisine ingredients on a mail-order basis.

FRESH ISLAND FISH CO., INC.
RRI Box 373-B
Wailuku, Hawaii 96793
808-244-9633
(Ocean-caught and aquacultured Hawaiian fish and seafood)

HANA HERBS
P.O. Box 323
Hana, Hawaii 96713
808-248-7407
(Fresh Hawaiian herbs and pohole *[fernshoots])*

HAWAIIAN VINTAGE CHOCOLATE COMPANY
4614 Kilauea Avenue, Suite 435
Honolulu, Hawaii 96816
808-735-8494
(Couverture-quality white, semisweet and bittersweet chocolate, produced from cocoa beans harvested on the Big Island)

LANGENSTEIN FARM
84-4956 Mamalahoa Highway
Captain Cook, Hawaii 96704
800-621-5365 or 808-328-9486
(100 percent pure Kona estate coffee, sun-dried and air-roasted; available in various roasts)

MACFARMS OF HAWAII
3615 Harding Avenue #207
Honolulu, Hawaii 96816
808-737-0645
(Dry-roasted, unsalted macadamia nuts)

OILS OF ALOHA
Macadamia Nut Oil Company
P.O. Box 685
Waialua, Hawaii 96791
800-367-6010 or 808-637-5620
(Macadamia nut cooking oil)

ORCHID ISLAND CHEVRE
Kuokoa Farm
P.O. Box 452
Kurtistown, Hawaii 96760
808-966-7792
(Big Island [Puna] goat cheese)

PAPAYA ORCHARDS OF HAWAII, INC.
800 Leilani Street
Hilo, Hawaii 96720
800-678-6248 or 808-969-6747
(Fresh papaya and frozen passion fruit, papaya and guava purée)

ROOSTER FARMS COFFEE CO.
P.O. Box 471
Honaunau, Hawaii 96726
808-328-9173
(100 percent pure Kona coffee, hand-picked and sun-dried; available in various roasts, both organic and regular)

ROYAL HAWAIIAN SEA FARMS
P.O. Box 3167
Kailua-Kona, Hawaii 96745
808-329-5468
(Hawaiian sea vegetables; limu *and* ogo)

TAKE HOME MAUI, INC.
121 Dickenson Street
Lahaina, Hawaii 96761
1-800-545-MAUI or 808-661-8067
(Maui onions, pineapple and papaya; assorted macadamia nut products)

SCHOOL OF FISH

Hawaii Regional Cuisine is primarily about seafood, but the ability to fish for tonight's dinner in Hawaiian waters is out of most of our reach. Thus, the next best is knowing how to purchase premium-quality fish. Here are a few simple rules to guide you at the supermarket or seafood store.

• The fish counter should be odorless and spotless.
• Smell the fish before purchasing. Extremely fresh fish may have a faint, seaweed/ocean odor, but most fish should be odor-free. If you smell anything, you're smelling bacteria.
• Fillets and steaks should appear translucent, almost shiny, and the flesh should be firm and elastic to the touch.
• White fish fillets and steaks should have white flesh; pink is indicative of bruising.
• Ice should not be resting on fillets and steaks; if it melts into the fish, it dilutes the flavor.
• Whole fish should be displayed with ice on top as well as around it; the ice discourages bacteria.
• Whole fish should possess pink or bright-red gills and reflect light. If it's headless, avoid fish with browning at the neck as that denotes age.
• Whole fish should retain most of its scales; more scales remaining on a scaly fish indicates careful handling.
• The popular perception that clear eyes mean a fresh fish isn't true. Some eyes go cloudy quickly; other fish's eyes stay bright long after the fish is old.
• Tuna should be red in color and on display wrapped airtight in plastic wrap; otherwise it oxidizes and turns brown.
• Never purchase packaged fish if there's water in the wrapping.
• Scallops should be translucent, never opaque.
• Mollusk shells should be closed. When tapped, mussel and clam shells should close.
• Always check oysters' origin; do not purchase open oysters even if they're alive.
• Shrimp, if dead, should be headless. Otherwise, they might be mushy.

FARM TOURS

The following are some of the premier farms, cooperatives and agencies in the state that are supporters of the Hawaii Regional Cuisine. Most are not tourist destinations, but have agreed to provide tours or information if their schedule permits. It's a necessity to call for an appointment.

AQUACULTURE DEVELOPMENT PROGRAM
335 Merchant Street, Suite 348
Honolulu, Hawaii 96813
808-587-0030
(Under the guise of the State of Hawaii in the Department of Land and Natural Resources, this agency provides information and tours on aquaculture in Hawaii.)

KEAAU BANANA PLANTATION, INC.
P.O. Box 787
Keaau, Hawaii 96749
808-966-7408
(Variety of Hawaiian bananas on the Big Island)

KUOKOA FARM
(Goat cheese producer; see Orchid Isle Chevre under Mail-Order Sources)

LOKELANI GARDENS
P.O. Box 2612
Kamuela, Hawaii 96743
808-885-3495
(Vine-ripened tomatoes, Hawaiian rhubarb, seasonal specialty vegetables, herbs, poha berries and edible flowers on the Big Island)

PLANT IT HAWAII
P.O. Box 388
Kurtistown, Hawaii 96760
808-966-6633
(Fruit tree nursery on the Big Island; also Hula Brothers, Inc., a fruit orchard, at the same address)

ROYAL HAWAIIAN SEA FARMS
P.O. Box 3167
Kailua-Kona, Hawaii 96745
808-329-5468
(Aquacultured sea vegetables on the Big Island)

HAWAII REGIONAL CUISINE CHEFS

SAM CHOY
SAM CHOY'S RESTAURANT AND CATERING
73-4328 Malu Place
Kuilua Kona, HI 96740
(808) 325-7641
Fax (808) 329-7080

ROGER DIKON
PRINCE COURT
Maui Prince Hotel
5400 Makena Alanui Road
Kihei, HI 96753
(808) 874-1111
Fax (808) 879-8763

MARK ELLMAN
AVALON
844 Front Street
Lahaina, HI 96761
(808) 667-5559
Fax (808) 661-4492

BEVERLY GANNON
HALIIMAILE GENERAL STORE
900 Haliimaile Road
Haliimaile, HI 96768
(808) 572-2666
Fax (808) 572-7128

JEAN-MARIE JOSSELIN
A PACIFIC CAFE
Kauai Village
Kapaa, HI 96746
(808) 822-0013
Fax (808) 882-0054

GEORGE MAVROTHALASSITIS
LA MER
Halekulani Hotel
2199 Kalia Road
Honolulu, HI 96815
(808) 923-2311
Fax (808) 922-5111

PETER MERRIMAN
MERRIMAN'S
Highway 19 and Opelo Road
Waimea, HI 96743
(808) 885-6822
Fax (808) 885-8756

AMY FERGUSON OTA
THE RITZ-CARLTON, MAUNA LANI
1 North Kaniku Drive
Kohala Coast, HI 96743
(808) 885-2000
Fax (808) 885-8886

PHILIPPE PADOVANI
IHILANI
Manele Bay Hotel
P.O. Box 774
Lanai City
Lanai, HI 96763
(808) 565-7700
Fax (808) 565-2433

GARY STREHL
PRINCE COURT
Hawaii Prince Hotel
100 Holoman Street
Honolulu, HI 96815

ALAN WONG
THE CANOEHOUSE AND LE SOLEIL
Mauna Lani Bay Hotel and Bungalows
1 Mauna Lani Drive
Kohala Coast, HI 96743
(808) 885-6622
Fax (808) 885-4556

ROY YAMAGUCHI
ROY'S RESTAURANT
6600 Kalanianaole Highway
Honolulu, HI 96825
(808) 396-7697
Fax (808) 396-8706

INDEX

Page numbers in **bold** indicate illustrations

ABOUT THE AUTHOR

JANICE WALD HENDERSON is a Los Angeles-based food and travel journalist who has been reporting on the development of Hawaii Regional Cuisine for the past decade. She is a food reporter on KCAL's *Live in L.A.*, a television talk show; the senior editor of *Chocolatier* magazine; a regular contributor to *Bon Appétit;* and her articles have appeared in *Vogue, Food & Wine* and numerous other publications. She is also the program coordinator of Cuisines of the Sun, an international culinary event that takes place annually in Hawaii at Mauna Lani Bay Hotel and Bungalows.